T0186676

The
**International
Simulation** *and* **Gaming
Yearbook
Volume 5**

The International Simulation and Gaming Yearbook Volume 5

Research into Simulations in Education

Edited by Peter Saunders and Benita Cox

SAGSET – The Society for Interactive Learning

KOGAN PAGE

London • Stirling (USA)

First published in 1997

Kogan Page Limited
120 Pentonville Road
London N1 9JN
and
22883 Quicksilver Drive
Stirling, VA 20166, USA

© SAGSET and named contributors, 1997

British Library Cataloguing in Publication Data

A CIP record for this book is available from the British Library.

ISBN 0 7494 2174 6
ISSN 1351-4644

Typeset by Kogan Page
Printed and bound in Great Britain by Biddles Ltd, Guildford and King's Lynn

Contents

Preface

In January 1995 I hesitantly volunteered Imperial College as organizing institution for SAGSET's July 1996 conference – a full 18 months ahead and thus nothing to worry about. I hesitated not because Imperial might have doubts about running conferences, such matters are grist to the college's mill, but because I did not feel sufficiently confident of my owns skills and capabilities.

The first high was when Benita (Baggy) agreed to help – without her expertise both on the technological aspects and the educational validity of the contributions the conference could not have been hosted by Imperial. Having such a strong colleague was a tremendous confidence booster, if only as someone to blame if it all went wrong!

The second lift was when Mervyn Jones and Betty Yue of Imperial's Continuing Education Centre lent their whole-hearted support. Betty and Mervyn took on all the administration – sending out the call for papers, advertising, fielding abstracts and papers, and booking accommodation. This left us with nothing but the conference design and quality to worry about.

One small pleasure was when we realized that the number of full contributions was going to exceed our photocopier's capabilities (and we pay £60,000 a year for it!) and hence we would need two volumes of conference materials.

The main drawback to organizing the conference was that there were not enough abstracts, not enough papers and not enough people. In fact, the conference ran well and it was difficult to fit in all the material that we had. Several participants claimed that they had not had enough time even with the twin-track sessions. But as conference organizers, we say again that there was not enough... no matter how many came, there would not have been enough!

Because Betty and Mervyn's administrative skills were so strong, the only glitch in the operation of the conference was the fact that the air-conditioning in the Mech Eng building failed.

At SAGSET's Annual General Meeting, which is always held on the first day of the conference, Baggy was voted on to the Council and I was elected Chair for three years. I have not yet worked out whether this should be classified as a high or a low!

The main pleasure for me was meeting lots of new friends whose ideas on areas related to SAGSET were fascinating and very helpful – there were 48 people there (including Baggy and me). They came from all over the world, from Australia, France, Germany, Holland, Japan, Sweden, Poland and the USA and even Lithuania. I now have a very pleasant addition to my coffee table – a hardback, full-colour guide to the pleasures of Lithuania!

ACKNOWLEDGEMENTS

Finally, I need to give a profound vote of thanks to a number of people without whom this Yearbook would not exist: staff at Kogan Page for their continued strong backing, Siew Tin Lim who prepared the manuscript so efficiently, Baggy Cox who has provided expert academic rigour, Imperial College and its Centre for Continuing Education who organized the 1996 conference from which most of the Yearbook's material is taken. The loudest shout of thanks must be to my family – Jackie, Tabitha, Abigail, Miranda and Cat – who bore, by far, the largest burden.

Peter Saunders, 1997

Foreword

SAGSET, the Society for the Advancement of Games and Simulations in Education and Training, was formed in 1970 to encourage and support the development of gaming, simulations and other forms of active learning in all aspects of education and training – from primary school to university, and from trade union to senior management.

Since then simulation has broadened its concern to include all aspects of interactive learning, especially when training workshops are involved. Simulations and games are teaching and learning techniques in which participants are directly involved in making decisions and learning from the results of those decisions. They are highly motivating and enable the exploration of complex interdisciplinary subjects as well as more traditional ones.

SAGSET membership gives access to publications and conferences. The publications include this Yearbook, which is free to members, *InterAct* and a backlist. As will be seen, the Yearbook is an authoritative publication that looks at aspects of the development and use of simulations, games, role play, case studies and other active learning experiences. It was first published in 1993 to replace the quarterly journal and the sixth volume will be published early in 1998. Its contents will be the current research into simulations and games which will be presented at the 1997 conference along with contributions received directly from prospective contributors.

InterAct is a newsletter for the exchange of views, information on conferences worldwide, and suggestions for the development of interactive learning. The backlist consists of back copies of editions of the SAGSET journal pre-1993 that are available.

SAGSET's home page nest on the web can be found at:

http://graph.ms.ic.ac.uk/sagset/home.htm

In addition to abstracts of recent conferences, there is a member's meeting room to allow members to get to know one another and to offer details of their gaming activities.

The Society also has an open (but moderated) e-mail discussion group. To join send the following text message to majordomo@ic.ac.uk subscribe sagset-list   (not forgetting to hit the enter/carriage return key)

You should be rewarded with a welcome message and a second message to majordomo@ic.ac.uk with the following text

help   (not forgetting to hit the enter/carriage return key)

will get the list of available commands.

Membership, which brings a free copy of the Yearbook and a £30 conference discount, costs only £26 for individuals in the UK (£29 Non-UK) and £37 (£40) for institutions. Details from: Peter Walsh, SAGSET, 45 Cushy Cow Lane, Ryton, Tyne and Wear NE40 3NL; Tel and Fax: 0191 413 2262.

SECTION 1: Theoretical and methodological perspectives

Chapter 1

Towards creating a global educational technology culture

Benita Cox and Peter Saunders

ABSTRACT

Designers of software for educational games have recently turned their attention to designing games for use over the Internet. This chapter explores the need for these designers to be aware of a new set of requirements which emanate from the diversity of cultural and gender backgrounds of the participants involved in playing games over wide area networks. No longer can it be assumed, as was the case when a game was played at a central point, that all participants are from similar cultural backgrounds or, indeed, that they will be of the same gender.

This uncertainty as to the profile of the target participants gives rise to a need for designers to consider what the potential impact of these differences might be on game playing and whether these should be reflected in the design of the game. For example, consideration needs to be given as to whether cultural or gender differences impact on the ways in which participants formulate their game-playing strategy or whether different styles exist in communication and decision-making processes and the degree to which these may influence the outcome of the game.

INTRODUCTION

New challenges exist for designers of educational software in their design of games for use over the Internet. In particular designers are faced with the difficulties of accommodating cultural and gender differences which may influence the learning process. In the following discussion, the effect of cultural and gender differences on learning behaviours which are relevant to playing educational games and more specifically business game simulations are discussed. Previous discussions on cultural differences in the processes of communication, decision making, intelligence gathering and problem solving are extended to include an awareness of gender differences (Cox and Saunders, 1996). Finally, the effect of these differences on the design of individual modules typically found in business game simulations, such as those of marketing, human resource management and accounting are discussed.

CULTURAL DIFFERENCES IN EDUCATIONAL GAME PLAY

Cultural differences are frequently intuitively felt rather than being objectively measurable (Usunier, 1993). Despite the lack of hard evidence for the existence of cultural differences it is our belief that any educational game that is intended for intercultural participation must address the question of 'cultural and gender neutrality'. This is not to say that achieving 'cultural neutrality' is necessarily a desirable state in software design; however, care should be taken to ensure that no group participating in a game is disadvantaged as a result of cultural or gender differences. Designers of educational Internet games should therefore strive, as far as possible, to create an 'operational culture' for all participants. By operational culture is meant a culture in which the individual may interact at a given point in time or in a given situation according to a set of standards, shared by the group, which determine what is important, what is feasible, what to do and how to go about doing it (Goodenough, 1971).

Clearly, the definition and provision of a fully operational culture within a business game is not currently feasible and the extent to which this will be achievable in the future is debatable. As such, this chapter does not purport to define exhaustively the full range of potential impacts that cultural or gender differences may have on cyber-based educational games, nor does it attempt to provide full solutions to those areas of impact which are easily identified. It does, however, highlight the need for designers to take cultural and gender factors into account when designing a game aimed at multicultural participants, to compare the way in which the functions typically represented in business games are conducted in various cultures and to be aware of the interactions between business and cultural context as well as factors influencing intercultural interaction.

EFFECTS OF CULTURAL DIFFERENCES ON CORE SKILLS REQUIRED TO PARTICIPATE IN BUSINESS GAME SIMULATIONS

In this chapter we will look specifically at the design of business game simulations. There are a number of core learning skills that are required to participate in these games, the most pertinent of which are those of strategy formulation, decision making, communication and problem solving. In the following discussion we consider the potential impact of each of these on simulation design. The importance and relevance of the following discussion will obviously be dependent on the type of business game being played, for example, whether it is competitive or non-competitive and the extent to which the decisions of players influence the results of one another. However, regardless of the ultimate objectives of the game, it is considered important that the following be given due consideration.

Differences in strategy formulation

The objectives of business games vary widely. However, in many instances the objective is to find a winning team. The attitudes of different cultures vary in their view of 'winning'. There will be many factors affecting strategies for winning, one of which is likely to be the participants' perception of displays of power and the degree of acceptance of aggressive behaviour. Graham (1981) states that power relations will determine who adopts and who adapts behaviour in a cross-cultural setting. Nearly all accounts, including those secured in different cultures indicate a higher degree of aggressive behaviour among males than among females (Fincher, 1975; Hogan, 1973; Maccoby, 1966). Care must be taken, therefore, to provide a setting which affords equal opportunities for establishing power for all teams. This begs the question and requires the definition of what this setting is, taking into account the objectives, practices, motivations and beliefs of multicultural participants as well as gender differences.

A major determinant of power relations is the language used. Individuals speaking in their home language have an advantage in manipulating concepts and linguistically taking command of the situation. A high percentage of business game simulations are written in English and there is a tendency among English speakers to view English as sufficiently international to render all communicators equal. This results in insufficient attention being given to the effect of language differences on power relations. For this reason, let us consider some of the more pertinent effects of cultural differences on communication.

Differences in communication

Different cultures use the same words to express different meanings. Sapir points out that no two languages are ever sufficiently similar to be considered as representing the same social reality. The worlds in which different societies live are different worlds, not the same world with different labels attached (Sapir, 1929). Thus the simulation designer needs to be aware that words used in the design of a game may not convey the same reality for all participants. In England, when somebody says 'No' to a question, it means that they have not agreed. In Japan, on the other hand people are reluctant to reply negatively. They reply to questions either positively or non-commitally. Therefore, in order to get an accurate answer one must word the question so that the reply can be given without the respondent having to say 'No'. Clear definition of words is particularly important in Internet applications where participants usually cannot see each other and hence cannot enhance the message with non-verbal communication such as gesticulation, body movement and eye contact. Systems designers should therefore pay strict attention to the choice of words which they use and select interpreters who will be aware of cultural differences in meaning. One way of addressing this problem may be to make use of the back-translation technique (Campbell and Werner, 1970). This involves the translator translating from the source language into a target language, then another translator who is not familiar with the source-language text, translating the first translation back into the source language and a comparison being made between the two versions of the source language.

Differences in decision-making processes

A number of research studies have highlighted the existence of cultural differences in decision-making processes. Differences exist, for example, between the Japanese and the Western styles of decision making. The Japanese reach decisions by group consensus while Western cultures tend to have hierarchical structures where decisions are made at the apex (Laser *et al.*, 1985). The typical sequence of decision making in Western culture may be depicted as a stepwise process involving:

- intelligence gathering;
- design of possible solutions;
- choice from the list of possible solutions;
- review of the implementation of the choice. (Simon, 1970)

This type of action/decision process is, however, viewed mainly as an implementation issue by the Japanese. They view the first step in decision making as that of consulting a broad range of individuals at various levels in the organization, who will provide input on how to do something and not necessarily on why to do it (Usunier, 1993).

In order to eliminate some of the decisional bias that may arise in designing international simulations consideration may be given to the following (Lee, 1966).

- Define the problem or the objectives according to the customs, behavioural standards and ways of thinking of the various participants' culture.
- Define the problem or the objectives according to the behavioural standards and ways of thinking of the culture where the decision will be implemented.
- Isolate the influence of the culture on the problem and identify the extent to which it complicates the decision-making process.
- Redefine the problem and the objectives without the bias related to the culture and then find the solutions and make decisions which fit within the cultural context.

Differences in problem solving

Culture and gender affect the way in which problems are solved. Galtung (1981) distinguishes between actual reality and potential reality in problem solving and contrasts the intellectual styles of four different cultural groups: the 'Gallic', the 'Teutonic', the 'Saxonic' and the 'Nipponic'. He found that Saxons prefer to look for facts for evidence in problem solving, which results in factual accuracy but weaknesses in both theory formation and paradigm awareness. Teutonic and Gallic styles place emphasis on theoretical arguments, using facts principally to illustrate what is said. The Nippon style is heavily influenced by Hinduism, Taoism and Buddhism and views knowledge as being a temporary state; they dislike clear statements which have a ring of immodesty about them.

Differences in approaches to problem solving are well illustrated in a study by Hofstede (1980). Students of various nationalities were given a case study to analyse and solve. The case outlined a conflict situation between the sales department and product development. The French suggested that the situation should be solved in a hierarchical setting, a solution being sought from the chairperson. The Germans felt that the lack of formal rules and written procedures was to blame whereas the English felt that the problem was the result of a lack of communication.

Across a wide range of cultures, men have consistently emerged as more field independent than women (Witkin and Berry, 1975). Explanations for this vary from those based on cultural reasons, such as women being more conditioned to find social approval, to the genetic, for instance men have innately high spatial ability (Maccoby, 1966). Whatever the reason, the design of the game should challenge the abilities of both sexes.

EFFECT OF CULTURAL DIFFERENCES ON BUSINESS GAME MODULE DESIGN

Below, consideration is given to the potential effect of cultural differences on the different modules typically represented in business games. Games can be classified as those which are total enterprise games and cover all the major business functions or are functional business games dedicated to a single business function. Either way these games will most likely cover the major business functions of:

■ marketing;
■ human resource management;
■ accounting. (Keys and Biggs, 1990)

Marketing

'Consumers buy meanings and marketers communicate meanings through products and advertisements'. Many of these meanings are culture-based and are intersubjectively shared by a social group (D'Andrade, 1987). In designing a cyber-based business game this consideration becomes crucial as the outcome of the game will frequently be influenced by the players' marketing strategy. In particular, three areas of the marketing process require attention: product selection, pricing strategy and advertising spend.

Product selection
One of the most distinguishing factors of a game is the type of product which the game portrays (Keys and Biggs, 1990). There is no evidence that common tastes for standardized, low-priced, quality goods exist across cultures (Wind, 1986). It is therefore of great importance that in selecting a representative product or products for a game, consideration is given to the extent to which the product is 'culture-free'. For example, food stuffs are highly culture bound and previous research suggests that high-technology products such as computer hardware and heavy equipment are

appropriate for global strategies, whereas clothing or household cleaners are less so (Peterson *et al.*, 1985).

In selecting the product for the cyber-game, questions need to be asked as to how the product selected meets the cultural life-style of the participants. For example, a bicycle may be viewed as a vital means of transport in one culture and as a leisure item in another. Consideration should also be given as to whether there are any cultural customs associated with the product – in Britain, blue is seen as the colour for boys and pink as the colour for girls.

Where the product selected for the game is of a technical nature, such as computer equipment, it is important to consider whether international standards exist for its use. For example, the use of Electronic Data Interchange is widespread in the West with clearly predefined communication standards; this is not necessarily the case in many of the developing countries. Service requirements for the product may also differ between various cultures depending on the level of expertise and labour costs. It is also important to take care that the product selected for the game is in a similar phase of the adoption process in all the participating cultures. Innovative products may be more widespread in one culture than another.

Pricing strategy selection

Pricing plays a crucial role in business simulations. It is frequently the mechanism used to achieve maximum company profit, gain market share, increase cash flows or increase the unit volume of sales. However, once again, pricing strategies are influenced by cultural factors.

Usunier (1993) draws attention to variations in pricing between Northern and Southern European countries. Prices tend to be high in Northern Europe where high price is correlated with product durability. He suggests that a possible explanation for this is that these countries are Lutheran by religion and thus favour austerity to limit consumption. In contrast, Southern European countries tend to be Catholic where the Church has never been concerned with the price and quality of material possessions and does not consider spending as shameful. Durability of products is less important as a result of climatic conditions which allow for more of an outdoor life.

Determining advertising spend

Very broad cultural differences exist in advertising spend, regardless of whether countries have comparable levels of economic development. Switzerland and the United States tend to be the highest spenders per capita on advertising among the developed nations, while spending in the under-developed countries is significantly less. Advertising spend will be influenced by the medium available for the delivery of the marketing material. Western cultures are more likely to select satellite television as the communication channel for their product where target audiences are high, while in less advanced economies the selection may be newspapers or posters. Some countries will have restrictions on the amount of advertising time that is permitted on a channel.

Personnel and human resource management

While there are few business games dedicated exclusively to personnel/HRM issues, many games require some decisions to be made related to them. Reporting on a game dedicated to HRM, Keys noted the following decision categories included within the game:

- acquisition of human resources;
- development of human resources;
- rewarding of human resources;
- maintenance of human resources. (Keys and Biggs, 1990)

In acquiring human resources players are likely to be required to hire different categories of workers. They must deal with issues of affirmative action, in particular with respect to females and minority groups. Once again, we consider cultural factors to be highly influential in determining strategy. Labour legislation and practices as well as systems of reward and conditions of employment will differ markedly from country to country. Wage rates will vary with minimum wage rates likely to be far higher in developed countries. In some cultures anti-discrimination policies associated with employment conditions, such as those based on age or sex, may be highly pervasive whereas in others they may not exist at all. Health and safety issues also vary widely. In developing countries such legislation is far less rigid than in developed countries.

Further, relationships with trade unions vary between cultures. For example, in Japan the single-union deal is popular while this is less the case in Western countries. It is also interesting to note that productivity outputs may vary according to the culture of the labour force. An interesting case is that of Volkswagen, the German car manufacturer, when it took over Spain's SEAT automobile manufacturer. It was assumed by many that this move was driven by a low-cost production strategy based on the fact that the Spanish labour force attracted lower wages than their German counterparts. However, what this view failed to take into account was that productivity was higher at the German plants than at the Spanish plants, with the net result that the car could be produced cheaper in the home market.

Accounting

It seems clear that accounting systems are societal constructs (Tinker *et al.*, 1982). Roberts (1995) believes that we should be aware that there is a danger of ethnocentrism in taking the object 'accounting' at its face value. He suggests that classification is a process, because it describes, imposes its own world view and sets up patterns of thinking, characterization and influence which may mislead or veil the nature of accounting in different countries. Nobes (1989) puts forward the proposition that the increasing globalization of the securities market will mean that accounting differences will become accounting obstacles.

One of the main problems for business games designers is that business performance is predominantly judged by financial criteria: increased profitability, larger net assets, greater cash flows, more dividends and higher share price, to mention but a few. Modelling this kind of complexity is certainly beyond the current games available. The problem is exacerbated because financial reporting on a global basis is fraught with difficulties – even two economies as similar as the USA and the UK have regulatory and legal differences which cause comparability to be eroded.

Financial reports have differences throughout the world. Some of the main areas of international difference include the following:

- fairness,
- taxation,
- conservatism and accruals,
- provisions and reserves,
- valuation bases,
- consolidation,
- uniformity and accounting plans, and
- shareholder orientation of financial statements. (Nobes and Parker, 1994)

It can be seen from the above that the interrelationship between these elements must create wide divergence in accounting practice between countries. At a global level, which accounting system drives any particular report is likely to be a consequence of the legal environment, religion or of colonization. Those countries which were once colonies of the UK almost all have 'tradition and practice' corporate financial reporting. This includes the USA and Canada. Where these countries have influenced other countries (eg, South America), their accounting systems predominate too. The Indian sub-continent, Malaysia, Singapore and the whole of Australasia have corporate financial reporting heavily rooted in that of the UK.

The game AIV NETWORK$ (1995) is an interesting example of how potential problems may arise from differences in reporting financial information. In this game the gross receipts and payments for subsidiaries are written off to the profit and loss account in the period when the transaction occurs. This may well be standard accounting practice in France or Japan but in the UK is prohibited. The UK/USA approach shows the acquisition of a subsidiary by increasing assets in the balance sheet. When disposed of, the balance sheet reduces, with net gains or losses being written off to the profit and loss in the period of sale. The net effect of this is that an $8 million purchase under a UK/USA system would have no profit and loss effects until the point of sale, but in AIV NETWORK$ it reduces that period's profit by $8 million.

In addition to the differences in reporting practices outlined above, trading internationally in itself presents further problems. An example of this is seen in the complexities encountered in multi-currency trading. The moment traders buy or sell anything outside their domestic environment they become involved in multi-currency financial reporting problems. Those games which report only one currency for global activity (GAZILLIONNAIRE, AIV NETWORK$) ignore the fact that multinational trading is, perforce, multi-currency trading. At present there are no easy solutions to this problem; however, some pertinent questions are being raised in international financial debates including:

- should the reports be all in one currency,
- in which currency should the reports be stated,
- what method of 'translating' between currencies should be chosen, and
- whether the conflict between economic and translation exposure should be managed. (Choi and Mueller, 1978; Pearcy, 1984)

One suggestion to overcome the first problem is to have a 'decision oriented unit' (an index of currencies) or have multinationals report in Special Drawing Rights (Jacobi, 1984).

CONCLUSION

The advent of wide area communications has changed the challenges to software designers. On the one hand user-friendly software and easy-access networking facilities have diminished many technological difficulties while on the other, the extended reach of systems has changed the profile of target users. This chapter has attempted to highlight the need for awareness among software designers for increased attention to be given to the potential effects of cultural and gender differences among target users, in particular in the design of business game simulations. If truly global cultures are to be achieved then there is a need for awareness of the existence and impact of cultural and gender differences.

REFERENCES

AIV NETWORKS (1995) Infogrames Multimedia Ltd, London.

Adler, N (1991) *International Dimensions of Organizational Behavior*, PWS-Kent, Boston, MA.

Campbell, T and Werner, O (1970) 'Translating, working through interpreters and the problem of decentering', in Naroll, R and Cohen, R (eds) *A Handbook of Method in Cultural Anthropology*, The Nature History Press, New York, pp.398–420.

Choi, F D S and Mueller, G G (1978) *An Introduction to Multinational Accounting*, Prentice Hall, Hemel Hempstead.

Cox, B and Saunders, P (1996) 'Designing for cyber-based simulations', *The Journal of Computing and Higher Education*, **8**,1, 4/1996, 29–47.

D'Andrade, R (1987) 'A folk model of the mind', in Quinn, D and Holland, N (eds) *Cultural Models in Language and Thought*, Cambridge University Press, Cambridge, pp.112–48.

Fincher, J (1975) *Human Intelligence*, Dutton, New York.

Galtung, J (1981) 'Structure, culture and intellectual style, An essay comparing Saxonic, Teutonic, Gallic and Nipponic approaches', *Social Science Information*, **20**, 6, 817–56.

Goodenough, W H (1971) *Culture, Language and Society*, Modular Publications, 7, Addison-Wesley, Reading, MA.

Graham, J L (1981) 'A hidden cause of America's trade deficit with Japan', *Columbia Journal of World Business*, Fall, 5–15.

Hofstede, G (1980) *Culture's Consequences: International differences in work-related values*, Sage, Beverly Hill, CA, p.60.

Hogan, R M (1973) 'Conduct and moral character: A psychological perspective', *Psychological Bulletin*, **79**, 217–32.

Jacobi, M H (1984) 'The unit of account in consolidated financial statements of multinational enterprises', in Holzer, H P (ed.) *International Accounting*, Harper & Row, London.

Keys, J B and Biggs, W D (1990) 'A review of business games', in Gentry, J W (ed.) *Guide to Business Gaming and Experiential Learning*, Kogan Page, London.

Laser, W, Shoji, M and Hiroshi K (1985) 'Japanese marketing: towards a better understanding', *Journal of Marketing*, **49**, Spring, 69–81.

Lee, J A (1966) 'Cultural analysis in overseas operations', *Harvard Business Review*, March–April, 106–11.

Maccoby, E (ed.) (1966) *The Development of Sex Differences*, Stanford University Press, Stanford, CA.

Nobes, C (1989) *Interpreting European Financial Statements*, Butterworths, Oxford.

Nobes, C and Parker, R (1994) *Comparative International Accounting*, 4th edn, Prentice Hall, Hemel Hempstead.

Pearcy, J (1984) *How to Account for Foreign Currencies*, Macmillan, Basingstoke.

Peterson, B, Cato Associates Inc. and Cheskin, M (1985) *Survey on Global Brands and Global Marketing*, Empirical Report, New York.

Porter, M E (1990) *The Competitive Advantage of Nations*, Free Press, New York.

Roberts, A (1995) 'Classification in international accounting', *Accounting Organisations and Society*, **20**, 7/8, 639–64.

Sapir, E (1929) 'The status of linguistics as a science', *Language*, **5**, 207–14.

Simon, H (1970) *The New Science of Management Decision*, Harper & Row, New York.

Tinker, A M, Merino, B D and Neimark, M D (1982) 'The normative origins of positive theories: ideology and accounting thought', *Accounting, Organisations and Society*, **7**, 2, 167–200.

Usunier, J C (1993) *International Marketing; A Cultural Approach*, Prentice Hall, Hemel Hempstead.

Wind, Y (1986) 'The myth of globalization', *Journal of Consumer Marketing*, **3**, Spring, 23–6.

Witkin, H A and Berry, J W (1975) 'Psychological differentiation in cross-cultural perspective', *Journal of Cross-cultural Psychology*, **6**, 84–7.

ABOUT THE AUTHORS

Benita Cox is a senior lecturer in Information Management at Imperial College of Science, Technology and Medicine. She holds an MSc in Management Science and a PhD in Artificial Intelligence from Imperial College. She has published widely in the areas of Intelligent Tutoring Systems and computer-based learning. She won the prize for the best research paper at the ABSEL Conference in 1994 (authored jointly with Jeremy Hall).

Peter Saunders has ten years of commercial experience of financial management, including periods with Shell and Stanley Tools prior to taking a prize-winning Masters degree in Business Administration specializing in International Business. At Imperial, his responsibilities include programmes for postgraduate and post-experience participants. At Cranfield School of Management, his previous post, Peter was responsible for management development courses for those running their own firms. In addition to finance and accounting, his specializations include entrepreneurship and business simulations on computers. He has written three books including *Debtor Control, Budgeting*, and *The Cranfield New Entrepreneur*.

Address for correspondence: The Management School, Imperial College of Science, Technology and Medicine, 53 Prince's Gate, London SW7 2PG.

Chapter 2

Damage caused by simulation/games

Ken Jones

ABSTRACT

Games and simulations are powerful learning tools when used separately. When mixed together into a simulation/game they become powerful agents of personal damage – damaging personal relationships and reputations and causing emotional hurt and distress. Friendships can be broken, professional reputations ruined and such antagonisms can develop that some people never speak to each other again. Facilitators are not only victims but are usually bewildered victims, almost inevitably unaware of what hit them and sometimes not realizing that they have been hit. One consequence is that genuine games and genuine simulations get a bad name because of the utter confusion of terminology and methodology.

The conclusion is that simulation/games should not be used. What should be done is to (a) clarify the concepts of games and simulations to reveal their incompatibility; (b) explain this to the participants; and (c) make whatever design changes are necessary to the materials to remove inconsistencies.

INCOMPATIBILITY

Games and simulations are incompatible because the motives (duties, responsibilities and ethics) are incompatible. In games (of skill) the players have a duty to try to win. In simulations the participants have a duty to fulfil their roles (functions, jobs) to the best of their ability, having regard to circumstances and the ethics of the real world. These two motives – gaming on the one hand and 'professional' behaviour (including real-world ethics) on the other – are incompatible.

Most facilitators and most authors are unaware of the incompatibility. This is partly due to using the terms interchangeably and indiscriminately. Participants are likely to be in the same state of ignorance and to accept the same floating and dangerous terminology.

A simulation/game, as defined by SAGSET and ISAGA, is a combination of the two methodologies. It is neither a game nor a simulation but a third and separate category of event. This is quite true. It is a separate category, although not in the way envisaged by those who drew up the definition and who assumed compatibility. It is important to note that the issue is the behaviour (actions, motives, thoughts) of the participants. It is not about the label on the box or the terminology of the briefing. If everyone (author, facilitator, participants) called an event a game and everyone behaved with the motives and duties of a simulation, the event would be a simulation. If everyone called an event a simulation/game but everyone behaved with the motives and duties required in a game then the event would be a game, not a simulation/game.

The question is simple and practical: is the behaviour consistent with a single methodology? The answer depends on the motives (duties, responsibilities and ethics) of individual participants. If some participants are in the gaming mode while others are in the simulation mode the event, by definition, is a simulation/game. The issue is behaviour, not semantics.

DAMAGE

Simulations and games are powerful learning tools. Simulation/games are even more powerful because of the additional element of methodological conflict of which the participants and the facilitator are unaware.

Consequently, the damage of a simulation/game is extremely potent. Had the facilitator been aware of the conflict the event would either not have been run in the first place or the debriefing would have taken some of the heat out of the situation by revealing that the conflict was one of methodology, not about the personalities or ethics of the participants. It is a characteristic of simulation/games that some of the participants get the blame. The scope for damage is considerable:

1. *Immediate personal damage to participants.* This occurs in behaviour during the event – incompatible behaviour with emotional consequences. It ranges from mild emotional hurt to severe traumas and even physical violence.
2. *Subsequent personal damage to participants.* This is damage to reputations and friendships and also damage to self-esteem. Participants often blame themselves for what went wrong. But whether it is self-criticism or indignation about unjust accusations, the thoughts and feelings are reinforced by powerful and often indelible memories of the event. Participants vividly remember the emotional unpleasantness – whether the behaviour was their own or other people's – the accusations, the sneers, the smugness, the bewilderment and the guilt.
3. *Immediate and subsequent damage to the careers of participants.* In the majority of cases a simulation/game is run for the purpose of education and training. Here the career damage relates mainly to the assessment by the facilitator of the personalities and characters of the participants. The facilitator almost invariably blames the participants – 'After all, there was nothing in the materials to make those participants so aggressive or so greedy and I certainly did not tell them to behave like that'. The criticisms might be written in reports or merely remembered. In either case the judgements can influence subsequent opinions and decisions. If the simulation/game is run not for the purpose of education but for assessment (including appointments or promotions) there is an immediate effect on careers in the reports of the assessors. 'Applicant W

appeared greedy', 'Applicant X worked for his own interests and not for the good of the team', 'Applicant Y became over-emotional and appeared to lack the ability of calm judgement'. 'Applicant Z was over-serious and seemed to lack a sense of humour', etc.

4. *Immediate and subsequent damage to the careers of facilitators.* Some immediate damage is likely to occur in the debriefing. In simulation/games, facilitators usually criticize the behaviour and ethics of some of the participants and/or encourage participants to criticize themselves and each other. Unfounded and misconceived criticisms add to the hurt and fester in the memory. The feelings of injustice can grow and mutate into forms of apathy, aggression, non-cooperation, coldness, hostility and sabotage. Such consequences damage teacher–student relationships and can damage the career of the teacher. If the event was sufficiently dramatic, accounts of the incident would spread around the establishment and probably reach the ears of colleagues and of those in authority – to the detriment of the facilitator.

5. *Immediate and subsequent damage to interactive events.* Simulation/games give games and simulations a bad name. The fact that they are undiagnosed makes it all too easy to suggest that all interactive events are suspect and dangerous. It is virtually certain that a major reason why simulations and games do not receive the appreciation they deserve is that they have been sabotaged by confusion with simulation/games.

EXAMPLES

Articles or lectures which describe what are obviously simulation/games do not discuss the methodology. If the methodology had been understood the simulation/game would not have been run. One of the indications that a reported event might have been a simulation/game is that the labels are used interchangeably – the floating terminology not only of games, simulations, simulation/games, role plays and exercises but also of player, actor, student, participant – all being used interchangeably.

Usually, the outcomes of such simulation/games are presented as success stories. Noble objectives have been achieved, insights gained and awareness of the subject matter heightened. Almost certainly it is the facilitator's concentration on the noble objectives, plus the lack of appropriate diagnostic tools, that produces such lack of perception. They are not looking for what goes wrong and they have no concepts which can detect methodological clashes. Also, in the field of games and simulations, there is a desire to produce rose-coloured results in order to convince colleagues that simulations and games are a good thing. Adverse and negative findings tend to be swept under the carpet.

To understand the essential and inevitable incompatibility of a simulation/game it is useful to look at examples rather than definitions. The first two events are hypothetical, and illustrate the point that motives (ethics, duties and responsibilities) are the key to differentiating between methodologies.

You let me win

Towards the end of a game of skill a 5-year-old girl says to her father, 'Oh Daddy! You let me win!'

Why should the girl be upset and hurt? After all, the object of a game is to win and she had achieved that object. In any case, the girl probably knows that the father had not acted out of malice but out of love. It was because he loved her that he let her win. So why was she so upset?

At the age of 5 the girl realizes that in games of skill each player has a duty to try to win, not just one player. It is not an optional item, it is an obligation – otherwise the person is not a player. Trying to win is an essential but unwritten part of the rules. She remembers that last week she won a game of chess against a boy at school and afterwards the boy said, 'I was just playing for fun. I let you win', which made her angry and she told him she would never speak to him again.

The girl knows, of course, that one can follow the surface rules of a game (particularly a game of chance rather than skill) and have fun without trying to win, but this is a fun session or pastime, not a game.

In the present case her father was not only in breach of contract with the magic kingdom of games, he had abandoned the role of player and taken on the role of benefactor. Not only of benefactor but of deceiver as well. He had pretended to play to win, yet had made moves which he knew would bring defeat. It was duplicity and deception. She had been excited about a victory, yet suddenly it was snatched away with the realization that her father had let her win. She was upset, annoyed, disappointed. The duplicity damaged the girl's trust in her father. If he could be so deceitful in a game he might be deceitful in other matters. Moreover, the girl realized that the father's attitude to her was not what she wanted – he was not treating her with the respect due to a player and he was patronizing; he was treating her as a child.

The father was also damaged. He was upset because his daughter was upset. His reputation had suffered. He probably felt guilty, even though his motive for throwing the game had been kindness. He knew he had mimed the action of trying to make good moves to conceal the making of bad moves. He also knew, what his daughter might not know, that in the adult world the throwing of a game can have extremely damaging consequences.

From this example it becomes clear that any game of skill (unless treated by mutual agreement as a pastime or training session) necessities a person having a duty, obligation and responsibility to try to win. It is an essential part of the player's contract and involves honour and integrity. Like the idea of fair play it involves ethics. The ethics of a game are implicit in the rules and the rules are designed to be fair. It is a magic kingdom in which the rules contain their own justification simply because they are rules, and honour, integrity and fairness are part and parcel of a player's contract. Otherwise, the player loses that status to become something else – a real-life cheat, a benefactor, a saboteur, and the event is no longer a game.

What about the real world?

Standing before a class of 14-year-old students the facilitator, Amanda, says, 'Today we are going to play a game. It is called The Charity Game. Each of you has ten votes which you have to cast in favour of business enterprise or charity. You can award all your ten points to business enterprise, or all ten points to charity, or any mixture you choose. You award your points individually, without telling your neighbours what you have done. Write your name on the top of your piece of paper and then go to the voting booth and write the number of points in the two boxes. The winner of the game is the person who gives most points to business enterprise. However, there is no winner if less than 20 per cent of the marks are awarded to charity. That it to say, on average each person must award at least two points to charity. I have here a coffee shop voucher for the winner which will buy a couple of cups of coffee'.

Two of the students, Betty and Carol, are best friends and sit together. Betty likes games because they are specially designed to be fair to all the players; this is so different from real life which is often very unfair.

In this game everyone stands the same chance of winning. Betty's first thought is that she should give nine points to business enterprise and one point to charity. Then she realizes that if she does this she would be beaten by a player who awards all ten points to business enterprise. She knows that if she gives ten points to business enterprise this makes it marginally less likely that the prize would be awarded. However, Betty decides it is the only play she can make to avoid being beaten. She awards ten points to business enterprise.

Carol, meanwhile, is thinking about charity – about poor people, people who are sick, people who are the victims of society. Also there are charities for music and the arts and the good things of life. At first Carol thinks it would be fair to split the marks down the middle – five for business enterprise and five for charity. But she still feels this is not enough. Too many people are greedy and don't care. Finally she casts all ten of her points for charity.

Amanda counts the votes and says, 'There is one prize winner and that is Betty. Well done Betty, come and collect your voucher.' There is some applause as Betty proudly collects her prize, waves the coupon to the class and walks back to her seat next to Carol. 'Congratulations,' says Carol, 'that was smart of you.' 'Let's share the prize. Come for a coffee after class,' says Betty. 'Sorry,' says Carol, 'I have something else on.'

Amanda starts the debriefing. She does not reveal the individual scores. She says, 'That was The Charity Game, but what about the real world? Is there any connection between the game and the real world? How do you feel about that?'

Carol is ashamed of Betty's behaviour but tries not to show it. She was appalled at Betty's expression of triumph when holding up the wretched coffee shop voucher – as if she had won it by her own skill rather than by the self-sacrifice of Carol and others. She says nothing to criticize Betty and when the teacher asks her what she thinks about greedy and selfish people she says that she thought they might have been born that way and could not help it.

Betty, meanwhile, is bewildered. Something has gone wrong. The coffee shop voucher which she proudly won through her skill at gaming is turning to ashes in her fingers. The class are talking about selfish people. Surely they cannot think that she is selfish. Some classmates are smiling at her condescendingly. She is feeling bitter and resentful. She is beginning to dislike Carol and she feels she no longer trusts Amanda. Previously she liked Amanda, but now Amanda appears to be a sanctimonious prig. Without quite knowing why, Betty feels she is being victimized and demonized.

The debriefing continues after class, but not when Betty is present. They tell each other how many marks they awarded to business enterprise and charity. Some tell lies, adding a few surreptitious points to the charity box but they feel guilty about this. They feel resentful that they are invisibly being pressured into deceit. Misled by Amanda's use of the word 'game' they too call it a game and many feel that Amanda should not run games which cause so much unpleasantness.

Some parents hear of the incident and cannot see why some children should be so upset but they decide to be more cautious when dealing with Amanda in future. Betty asks her parents to move her to another school, saying that she does not like the other students in her class and that she hates Amanda and no longer likes Carol. The parents become worried and unhappy and find it difficult to decide what to do.

Amanda, meanwhile, was delighted with the session and writes a description for an educational journal. The aim of The Charity Game, she writes, was to reveal the conflicts which can occur in society between a desire to pursue one's own selfish interests and the good of society as a whole. She reports that the debriefing revealed that almost all the class appreciated the lesson. She was surprised, she wrote, that some members of the class seemed to treat the game very seriously and there appeared to be a clash of personalities. Subsequently, one or two readers of the journal write to her and congratulate her on on her article and say that they too intend to use the game. Amanda notices that some members of the class seem less open and friendly with her than previously and assumes that they have personal problems. One or two parents and colleagues also seem rather more distant than before and her career does not appear to be making much progress.

Taking over

This example is not hypothetical. It comes from a recent personal letter from an American friend who is aware of my distinction between games and simulations. The event took place in the USA about 30 years ago, in an academic institute. About 40 members of the staff participated in a large socio-political event. The writer of the letter was a member of one of four sub-groups – the Green Group. The person I have named 'X' was a director of the institute and the Greens elected him as their leader. Early in the event the Greens decided to refrain from spending any money units on social welfare until they had stock-piled enough money to buy the police department and get control of the entire society. The letter says:

> 'For the first several rounds we were clearly treating the experience as a game. We had such great fun planning our coup and anticipating the reaction of the other three sub-groups. When it became clear that we had a very good chance of actually taking over the society,

we began to get suspicious of each other. So we devised a plan for ensuring that no one person in our group could seize power.'

The plan was for a declaration stating that no decision by the Greens was valid without the signatures of all the Greens. X succeeded in subverting this plan by deftly removing some carbon paper and became dictator, requesting the facilitator to place the other Greens under house arrest. The letter goes on:

> 'In the debriefing it was clear that this was more than a game. The debriefing continued for several intense hours and informally for months after the simulation was over. If the Greens as a group had bought the police force as we had planned instead of X, the other groups would have been irritated by us but they wouldn't have made judgments about our character. X's actions were considered particularly heinous because he acted alone and he betrayed his own group. It took him quite a while before he regained the trust of his staff.'

It is obvious that X suffered considerable real-life damage. Not only was it quite a while before he regained the trust of his staff, but probably his staff never forgot what he did. After all, the event took place 30 years ago and is still vividly remembered. Yet was X to blame? Was he, in real life, a devious person who would betray his colleagues? A more plausible explanation is that most participants, including X, began by being in the game mode, believing they had to try to win and probably took it for granted that the event was partly a fun session which would not be treated seriously. As the event progressed, people gradually abandoned the role of players and became citizens in a simulation, probably unaware of their changed motives, ethics and duties. Probably X failed to make the transition because of his concentration on completing the manoeuvre he had devised and initiated. He, and one or two others, may have been the only ones still in the game mode at the end of the event.

The debriefing appears to have been the usual tragic horror of both the accusers and the accused lacking the concepts which would have enabled them to consider the possibility of entrapment by methodology.

The name of the game

The next example comes from the SAGSET journal. It concerns STARPOWER, a well-known event in which there are three groups – Squares, Circles and Triangles – and begins with a trading session. It is almost always referred to as a game. After several rounds the facilitator stops the event and gives the Squares (the wealthiest group) the power to change the trading rules. Usually the event deteriorates fairly rapidly after that point.

> 'On one occasion a group of leftish liberal studies lecturers announced, "The name of the game is GRAB", and very shortly afterwards I was knocked to the floor and a pack of bonus cards torn from my hand. This was a pity – a meeting intended to show the hidden violence of our established society showed instead only the boorishness of some of its opponents.'

In this example the 'name of the game' is a phrase relating to 'real life', not the name of the actual game. The 'leftish liberal studies lecturers' did not say, 'The name of the game is STARPOWER'. They meant something on the lines of, 'This is a simulation about power in the real world and if you are deprived of it then grab a piece of it'. As usual with a simulation/game the facilitator is bewildered and cannot give a plausible explanation for the robbery with violence. The conclusion that it was because the lecturers were 'boorish' is par for the course.

Probably the event began with most or all of the participants in the game mode taking seriously their duty to win by means of increasing their wealth by trading. Gradually some participants moved out of the gaming mode and, abandoning the role of players, appointed themselves to the roles of law-abiding citizens or muggers.

The paragraph quoted is the full description. There is no mention of what happened next. Yet probably the facilitator never forgot the look on the faces of those who knocked him to the ground. The assailants and witnesses of the assault would also probably remember the episode vividly for years. News of the event must have spread like wildfire. What was the reaction of other members of the staff? Did the heads of department, governors and parents hear of it? How did it affect relationships with students? Were there snide questions at liberal studies lectures – 'Sir, what do you think personally about violence, sir?' Did the incident affect the career prospects or reputations of those concerned? How much harm was done?

Reaching for the lollipop

This account is from the journal of ISAGA and also refers to STARPOWER.

'A good example happened 15 years ago; the students still remember it. We were playing STARPOWER, and a woman brought lollipop treats for the Circles on the second day of play. The powerful Squares levied a tax and tried to take a lollipop away. The taxman was almost decked when he reached for the lollipop; but I stepped in the middle. We discussed this emotional incident in class, and they wrote about it in their journals, which helped them cool down.'

Again, this paragraph is the full account of what occurred. Again, there is no discussion of methodology and, again, the participants get the blame. Why did the facilitator allow lollipops into this self-contained event and permit so unfair a distribution? It was rather as if foreign aid food parcels were sent into a country without the permission of its government and handed out to the middle classes only. The victim, of course, was the taxman who will probably remember the event for the rest of his life – including the names and faces of the students who attacked him. As the author says, the students still remember it despite the fact that it was an incident 15 years earlier. Probably the attackers remember it with guilt. Presumably the mini-debriefing was designed to elicit self-criticism: 'We were too emotional during the game', 'I should not have lost my temper', 'It was only a game and I should not have tried to hit him', and so forth. As usual the victims probably smiled bravely and subsequently told the facilitator that the event was valuable. If some of the ex-participants blamed the facilitator for setting up the situation there is no evidence that the facilitator was aware of this.

Sons of bitches

The following quotation comes from an article in the journal of ISAGA about PRISONER'S DILEMMA, an event in which the scenario is that two prisoners are jointly accused of an unspecified crime and have to plead guilty or not guilty, separately and without consultation. If both plead not guilty they jointly receive a lesser sentence than if they both pleaded guilty. However, if they plead differently the person who pleaded guilty will receive a light sentence (because the person informed on his or her colleague) while the person pleading not guilty receives a heavy sentence.

> 'One of the most significant aspects of this study, however, did not show up in the data analysis. It is the extreme seriousness with which the subjects take the problems. Comments such as, "If you defect on the rest of us, you're going to live with it for the rest of your life" were not uncommon. Nor was it unusual for people to wish to leave the experimental building by the back door, to claim that they did not wish to see the "sons of bitches" who double-crossed them, to become extremely angry at other subjects, or to become tearful.'

Again, there is serious personal damage, perhaps 'for the rest of your life'. The cause of the damage was said to be 'the extreme seriousness with which the subjects take the problems'. No mention of methodology, of course. News of this event must have spread quickly. Students, staff, parents, governors and even reporters might have heard of it and taken whatever action (or inaction) they thought appropriate. It is not simply that people were being hurt inside the event, but outside as well. Walking into a coffee shop one does not wish to sit next to the son of a bitch who betrayed one. Appointments boards are not usually over-enthusiastic about promoting disloyal sons of bitches nor, probably, facilitators who run events which have such harmful consequences.

Within the event the basic question is, 'What is my relationship to my co-prisoner?' Participants in a simulation mode would see the co-prisoner as a friend, or at least a comrade in crime – after all, they are jointly accused of the same crime. The obvious duty is not to betray one's friend and observe honour among thieves. This means always pleading not guilty. If, on the other hand, the person is in the game mode, the co-prisoner would be seen as an opponent, as someone who could win – after all, the facilitator is likely to have used the word 'game'. The duty is to try to win, certainly to try to avoid losing. The only way to win and avoid losing is to plead guilty. For those who did not know whether to try to win or try to stay loyal the uncertainty itself could produce anxiety, quite apart from the results of the choice. It would be a Kafka-like situation without the conceptual tools to explain the behaviour afterwards. The 'sons of bitches' would be those in the game-mode, including those who were in tears. Those who uttered the threats and who did not wish to see their betrayers were obviously in the simulation mode and would probably seek revenge, if only ostracizing their betrayers. The possibility that all the participants were doing the duty required by their particular mode apparently never occurred to anyone.

Elsewhere in the article, PRISONER'S DILEMMA and similar events are called 'social dilemma games'. Yet there is no social dilemma. The players in the game mode had a clear duty to try to win (or at least avoid losing) while the participants in the simulation mode had a clear duty not to betray their co-defendant. The explanation that the emotional upsets (to put it mildly) were caused by 'the extreme seriousness with which the subjects take the problems' is typical of a facilitator's misconceptions about a simulation/game. Facilitators focus on their aims and objectives and are surprised and bewildered by explosions. As usual, of course, the participants are blamed.

Only playing the game

The next example concerns THE COMMONS GAME, an event in which participants can vote privately – basically for their own self-interests or for the community. The quotation comes from the ISAGA journal:

> 'Players were directed to accumulate the maximum number of points. The player with the highest number of points received $5. The words "win" or "winner" were never used by the game directors… Greed and curiosity to get the commons up or down played significant roles in determining the teams' results. No goals were set at the beginning of the game; however, they tended to evolve during the game. Occasionally, players forgot about the commons and only "played the game".'

It does not take much imagination to visualize the sort of damage suffered by the winner of the $5 – the person most likely to be labelled greedy and uncaring. Others were obviously 'greedy' as well: 'Greed and curiosity to get the commons up or down played significant roles.'

In the debriefing students might have used such words as 'selfish', 'disloyal', 'untrustworthy'. Private thoughts might have included, 'In the negotiating sessions you were the one who argued most persuasively that we should all vote for the commons, yet we now discover that you didn't do that. You voted for yourself. I didn't know you could be so deceitful. I shall never trust you again.' As usual with simulation/games, the finger of shame is pointed at those who were in the game mode. Probably there would be counter-accusations – 'Why are you so serious, can't you take a joke? It was just a game and we were having a bit of fun. Anyway, I (we) won.' If such accusations and counter-accusations take place publicly in the debriefing the facilitators tend to ignore the friction and concentrate on the official aims and objectives. As personal damage is not an objective it tends to be overlooked. In any case, perhaps the worst scenario is that the accusations and counter-accusations are unstated and damage reputations without the opportunity for rebuttal.

The facilitators' criticism of those who 'only played the game' is not only manifestly unjust, it confirms that the facilitators were unaware of their own (and the built-in) trickery. They seemed to go out of their way to create ambiguity, bewilderment and unease. However, this is a rare example of a simulation/game in which the facilitators seemed aware that methodology might just have some influence on the event. Although the words 'win' and 'winner' were not mentioned in the briefing, the word 'game' is in the title of the event and the facilitators underlined the concept by offering $5 to 'the player with the highest number of points.' Those in the game mode who 'only played the game' were later criticized for 'forgetting about the commons'. To run a so-called game and then criticize players for playing it reinforces the conclusion that the facilitators were in a state of bewilderment.

CONCLUSIONS

Distress and hurt in simulation/games are inevitable to a greater or lesser degree. The damage is usually reinforced in the debriefing. It is possible, even probable, that participants may strive to conceal their wounds, but hurt is still hurt. The participants and the facilitator are in no position to analyse the situation correctly. This is largely because of unawareness of the methodology. The concepts are awash in a sea of floating labels. In simulation/games, the eyes of facilitators tend to be fixed on noble objectives in a bizarre tunnel vision. Facilitators are often completely unaware of the damage – not only to participants but to their own personal and professional standing – of deterioration in teacher-student relationships, of whispers by colleagues and reappraisals by those in authority.

The methodology of interactive events is also damaged by simulation/games. Genuine and consistent games and simulations get a bad name by association.

Simulation/games should not be used; they should be prevented. They are an unnecessary evil. They can be prevented by understanding the methodology and by explaining it. Before any game or simulation the participants should be told what sort of ethical behaviour is required – a duty to win a game and ignore the ethics of the real world or a duty to be 'professional' in a situation (simulation) with functional roles and responsibilities.

What should be done is to clarify the concepts of games and simulations to reveal their incompatibility, to explain this to the participants and make whatever design changes are necessary to the materials to remove any inconsistencies.

ABOUT THE AUTHOR

Ken Jones has been designing and writing about games, simulations, exercises and role-plays for many years. His recent books include: *Icebreakers – A sourcebook of games, exercises and simulations*, 1995 (2nd edn), Kogan Page, London and Gulf, Houston; *Simulations – A handbook for teachers and trainers*, 1995 (3rd edn), Kogan Page, London; *Imaginative Events – A sourcebook of innovative simulations, exercises, puzzles and games*, 1993, McGraw-Hill, Maidenhead; and *Creative Events for Trainers*, 1997, McGraw-Hill, Maidenhead.

Address for correspondence: Ken Jones, 4 Ashdown Lodge, 1c Chepstow Villas, London W11 3EE. Tel: 0171 229 7669.

Chapter 3

Group exercises – collaboration or competition?

Bob Matthew and Pete Sayers

ABSTRACT

Over the years we have become increasingly exasperated by group exercises where the groups end up being highly competitive with one another. This usually results in a 'must do better than them' mentality, rather than a 'what can we learn from this exercise' mentality. This led us to reflect on how we designed, managed and ran group exercises. In particular we ended up with some clear ideas about how to design and manage group exercises which implicitly and explicitly require group collaboration for successful completion. One interesting and unexpected result of this design process has been a significant increase in the enthusiasm of the participants and the energy level shown by the groups in carrying out such exercises.

This chapter is an attempt on our part to share our observations on group process, the design process we have adopted and some observations on the effects of running exercises in this way.

OUR EXPERIENCE

In our work both as staff developers (both Bob and Pete) and as a teacher in civil engineering (Bob) we have been collaborating on the design and use of group-based exercises for some nine years. These exercises have been developed as group- and team-building exercises for staff and students within the University of Bradford, as well as problem-based exercises used on course modules within the department of Civil Engineering.

We have gone on to develop a series of exercises for group/team-building exercises where the objective of the process was for one participant group to devise and run a team exercise for another group of participants. This idea is inspired by the much-quoted statement that the best way to learn something is to teach it. We have modified this to read, 'the best way to learn something or develop a skill is to devise, run and debrief a learning experience to help another group learn that skill.'

Over the years of running such exercises with academic staff, undergraduates and occasionally outside clients we have reflected on what we have been doing and how we do it, both in terms of how we facilitate the groups (Sayers and Matthew, 1996) and how we devise and run such learning events. The latter is the subject of this chapter.

OUR AIM

In the early days of running group exercises for both undergraduates and academic staff, rather naively perhaps, we never gave much thought to group competition or collaboration. Many incidents occurred over a period of three years that made us stop and reflect on what we were doing, ask what the outcomes were, and consider whether these outcomes were what we had intended or whether they were, indeed, desirable.

This period of reflection led us to a number of conclusions which are worth explicitly stating here. We are happy to accept that they may appear obvious, but then hindsight is so much easier than foresight!

Conclusion one: in devising group exercises there needs to be built in a balance between competition and collaboration.
Conclusion two: if inter-group collaboration is not designed in to an exercise, it becomes a competition by default – hence too many group exercises are heavily orientated towards competitiveness.

Without wishing to become embroiled in an argument over the political correctness of whether competition or collaboration is more socially desirable, we would maintain that in order to maximize the learning opportunities in group exercises, participant groups need to learn to collaborate. This means introducing group exercises where groups have to collaborate with each other to complete a group task. We acknowledge, however, that some competition (inter-group rivalry) is necessary, primarily in our experience to give a group a sense of identity ('We know we're in *this* group, because we're not in *that* group'). This sense of identity is important for the initial development of the group and its process (Mulligan, 1988).

We have learnt much about the benefit of fostering and encouraging inter-group collaboration and detail the key points of this learning below. Collaboration allows groups to identify resources in a more creative way, to use them more effectively and indeed tackle successfully problems beyond the possibilities of any one group. It also enables one group to assist another group, the net result of which is that both groups improve their skills and performance.

To explain how we arrived at these ideas it is necessary to take you, the reader, through some of our reflective process. Let's start with the observations on group process we have made over the years.

OBSERVATIONS ON THE GROUP PROCESS

These observations are based on working with three separate client groups: undergraduate civil engineers, course representatives (students who sit on university staff–student liaison committees), and academic staff on staff development courses.

With all three client groups we have used group-based learning activities exten-sively. (For further detail, see Matthew and Hughes, 1991a, 1991b; Matthew *et al.*, 1996.) We have developed a style of facilitation which derives from Blanchard *et al.* (1986). In these events we start with a prescriptive, directive style, move to coaching, then supporting and, finally, delegating to our learners. We have explained the theory behind this method of facilitating in more detail in Sayers and Matthew (1996). In that chapter we explain that the most difficult of these four styles is 'supporting'. Our first attempts to move into supportive mode were frustrated by a number of interesting phenomena we observed in the groups we were facilitating.

Because competition tends to be the default or easy option, groups working on team-building exercises saw themselves in competition with each other irrespective of any messages from tutors to encourage or even to contradict it. This meant that groups did not trust each other and were not interested in feedback from each other. They would only accept feedback from tutors. It was difficult to get participants interested in the process. They were too concerned about completion of the task and comparing their achievement with other groups. This default competitiveness was equally frustrating with groups working on academic exercises where the drive to be first with an answer, or more importantly first with the right answer, led to a high degree of competition between groups and a complete absence of helping each other and, in some extreme cases, supporting fellow group members.

When we asked groups to devise an exercise for each other as a way of further developing their group skills, or as a way of learning how to manage group exercises themselves, we observed either one or both of the following:

1.   The group devising the exercise set out to humiliate the other group, by making the task impossibly difficult or by requiring them to do something ridiculous.
2.   The participant group would decide to sabotage the other group's exercise by ignoring rules or constraints, by not participating fully (just going through the motions) or by not doing the exercise at all. Sometimes this was done implicitly – participants were not aware they were sabotaging the other group's exercise until it was drawn to their attention, but on reflection agreed that this did account for odd behaviour during their performance. Often, though, it was done explicitly with participants deciding in advance that their strategy was to make life difficult for the group setting the exercise.

Having made these observations and indeed having had to carry out many difficult plenary debriefings of situations where these types of behaviour had occurred, we felt that something needed to change – the learning experience wasn't quite right.

EFFECTS OF OUR GROUP EXERCISE DESIGN PROCESS

Many of the best ideas often come from the most unusual sources. At this time we were also looking at chaos theory as a way of helping us understand organizational behaviour (Stacey, 1992) and we realized that from chaotic situations a sense of wholeness or order can emerge (Briggs and Peat, 1990). It seemed like an idea worth pursuing. We set about devising a group learning activity where there were many tasks which needed to be completed within a certain time-frame. Constraints were applied such that it would soon become obvious to those participating that they could not accomplish the task as a single group. This was our way of fostering, in an implicit manner, collaboration rather than competition.

However, there were also some surprising (well, they were to us) outcomes from this design. In the final part of the exercise, which was a kind of summative assessment in the form of a group presentation, the energy displayed by the groups was high, and coupled with a great deal of innovation in the style of their presentation which excited and pleased us no end. Much of the presentation was very funny, and they were having fun with each other, rather than at each other's expense. During the exercise we also noted that many groups were prepared to take risks both in terms of doing things differently, and challenging rules or constraints or interpreting them in new and interesting ways – they were certainly displaying considerable development of their creative and lateral thinking skills.

In debriefing this exercise we also observed significant changes from our past experience. The groups were much more prepared to talk about process rather than task issues; they would discuss behaviour and skill and reflect openly and with a great deal of energy on what they had done well, what they could improve on and how specifically they might improve their performance in subsequent exercises, and identifying criteria for recognizing progress.

For us this was a significant improvement and indeed was an unexpectedly successful outcome to our initial design to foster collaboration.

Following the success of this innovation we subsequently introduced a second part to this learning experience, building on the process reflection which our learners really seemed to enjoy.

We got the groups to carry out a mini SWOT analysis (Strengths and Weaknesses of the Team – without the Opportunities or Threats bit) the results of which they displayed on a flipchart. We then invited groups to circulate around the room, read the flipcharts and see if they could find a group whose strengths were their weaknesses and vice versa. After one memorable experience where one group remarked publicly that they 'rather fancied' another group, this part of the process has since become known as 'the marriage ceremony'.

Once married the groups work out a contract with each other covering what they will provide for each other in terms of a learning experience, whether for skill or knowledge development. Again this seems to release considerable energy in participant groups. They will work till very late, indeed occasionally all night to prepare something. They seem to take learning contracts between themselves very seriously indeed, perhaps as a result of a real sense of ownership.

As we observed the process from a distance – after all we are not usually part of the contract – one or two interesting outcomes emerged, again somewhat unexpectedly.

First, the group designing the exercise (to assist the other participant group with a 'weakness') clearly works on its own weakness during the design process, while ostensibly demonstrating its strength. For example, if the designer team has identified 'listening skills' as a weakness, our experience is that this group shows evidence of improving its listening skills more during the designing of an exercise for its partner group than it does by doing any exercise designed for it by its partner. When this phenomenon is pointed out by the facilitator in a debrief, the designing group is usually unaware that they had been doing this. Yet this has happened every time, so we are sure it's not random chance but rather some kind of serendipity (if we go back to chaos and fractal patterns, there is an obvious analogy about the really nice patterns or interesting bits occurring around the edges where you don't expect them!)

Second, as a result of this process, many of the participants (about 10 per cent of the total) declare that they want to do more of this collaborative group learning. When this first happened, the best opportunity for further learning we could envisage was to invite such people to become small-group facilitators at subsequent events. This was a completely unexpected outcome from our standpoint, the net result of which is that a training programme that started with university staff acting as facilitators moved on to have small-group facilitators drawn entirely from students who particip-ated in previous years. In later years it took a further step and those students who were the most competent and motivated small-group facilitators went on to become the lead tutors while other students filled the role of small-group facilitators. For any student development event we run now there is an established team of student facilitators, two of whom will act as lead tutors, and on some staff development events we have student facilitators. Members of this team have become highly competent facilitators and now organize and run other events for students entirely on their own.

SOME THOUGHTS FOR THE FUTURE

It seems to us that higher education is not standing still; increasing numbers of students and diminishing resources are going to be around for some considerable time to come. Employers and government continue to stress the need for better skilled graduates. If the curriculum moved towards group-based learning activities where collaboration rather than competition is fostered, then our experience is that students can and do take considerable responsibility for their own learning. Perhaps it is a way of working with students that more people could experiment with. For us it is a highly motivating way to work with students, and the learners (we include ourselves in this category) seem to gain more from a caring supportive environment than they do from the normal competitive, individualized world of higher education.

Our advice would be, 'Go on try it; dare to be different!'

REFERENCES

Blanchard, K, Zigarmi, P and Zigarmi, D (1986) *Leadership and the One Minute Manager*, William Collins, Glasgow.
Briggs, J and Peat, F D (1990) *'Turbulent Mirror – An illustrated guide to chaos theory and the science of wholeness'*, Harper & Row, New York.
Matthew, R G S and Hughes, D C (1991a) 'Problem based learning – a case study in civil engineering', in Smith, R A (ed.) *Innovative Teaching in Engineering*, Ellis Horwood, Chichester.

Matthew, R G S and Hughes, D C (1991b) 'What's t'do with the sewage', *Simulation/Games for Learning, The Journal of SAGSET*, **21**, 2, 131–40.

Matthew R G S, Sayers, P, Dietz, G and Uppal, N (1996) 'Creating an environment for peer learning – the Bradford Experience of Course Rep Training', *Innovations in Education and Training International*, **33**, 3, 171–7.

Mulligan, J (1988) *The Personal Management Handbook*, Sphere Reference, London, p.146.

Sayers, P and Matthew, R G S (1996) 'Issues of power and control: moving from "expert" to "facilitator"', in Brown, S, Armstrong, S and Thompson, G (eds) *Facing up to Radical Change in Colleges and Universities*, Kogan Page, London, ch.14.

Stacey, R (1992) *Managing Chaos – Dynamic business strategies in an unpredictable world*, Kogan Page, London.

ABOUT THE AUTHORS

Bob Matthew is a lecturer in the Civil Engineering Department at the University of Bradford. He has been using student-centred approaches, particularly problem-based learning, for some nine years. He is a keen cyclist and hillwalker in his spare time.

Pete Sayers is the University of Bradford's staff development adviser. He has worked with Bob for some six years. During this period they have developed a number of training courses with groups as the basic vehicle for learning. Pete is a very keen cyclist.

Address for correspondence: Dr Bob Matthew, Dept of Civil & Environmental Engineering, University of Bradford, West Yorkshire BD7 1DP.

Chapter 4

MERIT 2: A construction management simulation

V Ahmed, A Thorpe and R McCaffer

ABSTRACT

The increase in size and complexity of modern construction projects has encouraged the development of better management training methods for potential construction managers. One such method is the use of simulation and gaming to enable these potential managers to experience the range of typical decisions that senior managers face daily.

MERIT 2 (Managing Engineering Resources Involves Team Work) is a construction management simulation which allows up to 1,000 teams referred to as companies to operate a construction company for up to 16 periods or quarters, representing four trading years. The participants are required to control and manage the direction of their company through inter-related marketing, tendering, overhead allocation, labour and staffing and general financial decisions. The companies operate in a computer-simulated market based on current UK statistics.

MERIT was developed at Loughborough University for graduate civil engineers working towards chartership and it is run annually by the Institution of Civil Engineering. The leading teams are invited to play the final at Loughborough. So far, about 12,000 participants have played MERIT over the last seven years.

This chapter describes the main features of MERIT, the range of decisions to be made, and their implications. The performance indicators which determine the success or failure of each company are highlighted. Finally, the benefits gained from such an approach are reported from an opinion survey of past players.

INTRODUCTION AND BACKGROUND

In recent years simulation and gaming have become widely recognized as particularly powerful tools in the study of a whole range of topics, such as decision making and intellectual communication (Elgood, 1988). There has also been widespread recognition of the powerful features of simulation as a tool of research and as an experimental study aid and a professional training instrument.

In the construction area a number of games have been developed over the years; examples include:

BAILY SIMULATION (Cooper, 1994) which provides a learning experience of the nature of a construction company, the role of company directors, the tasks involved in submitting a tender by a team of engineers such as the creation of drawings, specifications, cost estimates, scale models and other appropriate documents for presentation to the client. It also illustrates the aspects of human relations involved in awarding a tender.

BAUMARK I AND II (Seeling, 1994) simulates different stages in the construction industry and demonstrates the effect of different types and sizes of contracts to be undertaken by a company. It puts players in the decision-making situations of project bidding and tendering and forces them to study their actions in relation to the market, giving them an opportunity to explore the behaviour of a market and its potential instability.

PYRAMID and PYRAMID II (1994) emphasize the importance of group work in experiencing time/cost planning and allow participants to experience the problems of working in a group, delegating and coordinating a construction project.

CONSTRUCTO (Halpin, 1976) is a project-oriented game which gives students the opportunity to develop their own problem response model, by confronting them with simulated situations described in terms of environmental and economical parameters and placing them in the position of being in charge of a construction project facing similar difficulties to real-world managers.

AROUSAL (A Real Organization Unit Simulated As Life) (Lansley, 1982) has been designed to simulate the world of the directors of a medium-sized enterprise. Participants in the simulation form into small teams and take the role of the directors of that enterprise. The game assists in the development of managers and in evaluating the potential costs and benefits of different business and organizational strategies. This game been used by a number of firms in the UK and the USA and has proved a valuable part of their training programme.

VENTURE (Elgood, 1994) was designed as a form of business simulation and a management game that tests strategic perceptions rather than the players' skills in running a production line, in a tightly defined market.

BIDDING SIMULATION

Although there are a number of management and construction games available, there is little reported on the use of bidding simulations in training. Some approaches have attempted to model the way bidders vary their strategies in terms of significant variable characteristics of the contract. Provided reliable models can be deduced, a bidder can investigate minor variations in his or her strategies by simulating the effect of these changes over a period of time. This approach is more concerned with allowing management to explore the consequences of its action than the basic approach which concentrates on providing an optimum bid value for a given contract (Lilley, 1978).

A bidding game described by Torgensen *et al.* (1968; 1970) does not have any competitive element but is concerned with the decision to bid or not and the problem of workloading. A rather more sophisticated game, described by Au *et al.* (1969) incorporates different costs for different suppliers. The features are designed to help managers discriminate between bids, and also to encourage the purchase of extra market information. However, this is still a deterministic game with no element of uncertainty, and uncertainty is one of the major parameters for bidders in cost estimates.

SUPER BID (AbouRizk, 1993) is a project-oriented management bidding game designed to assist in training estimators in developing bidding strategies in construction. SUPER BID teaches the players about various factors to be considered during bidding, to enable the players to observe and experience what is involved in the bidding process such as basic estimating and costing skills, forecasting, financial planning, studying the market and competition trends, decision making under uncertainty, random factors and phenomena such as providing a medium for experimenting with different bidding strategies to achieve a desired objective, and basic financial book-keeping fundamentals (which are required to insure that players succeed in the game).

Due to the shortcoming of these games, MERIT 2 was developed to demonstrate to the players the interacting nature of variables which need to be considered in the tendering and production phases of a construction project.

The simulation which is described in the following sections of this chapter is designed to demonstrate the problems of overall control of a contracting company whose turnover is made up of contracts obtained by competitive tendering of the type commonly found in the construction industry.

OBJECTIVES OF THE GAME

The purpose of the game in general is to give participants the experience of:

- the problem of constantly revising targets and plans;
- the problem of allowing for overheads where workload differs from the forecast;
- the problem of cash restraints on growth;
- the problem of overhead commitments when trying to reduce the size of the company;
- the bidding situation where the actions and estimates of other companies thwart your own plans;
- the pressure of reducing mark-up when insufficient numbers of contracts are being won;
- the problems of allocating, recruiting and laying-off personnel (project managers and labour).

GENERAL FEATURES OF THE GAME

The game was created by the department of Civil Engineering, Loughborough University for Balfour Beatty Construction Limited in 1989. Since 1992, MERIT 2 has run annually via the Institution of Civil Engineers.

The game is arranged so that it can be played by three to six participants in each team of players, where each team represents a company identified by a unique name.

MERIT 2 allows the participants to operate a construction company for up to 16 periods or quarters, representing four trading years from an historical established position of one year. The frequency of the decision periods is restricted by the computer turn round and the time needed for analysis by the players between decisions. Operating at two periods per week, the game can be played within eight weeks, but much faster rates of play have been achieved, with four decision periods per day being the maximum.

The game operates in two modes:

1. A postal mode whereby each up to 1,000 participating companies compete for a number of specified periods, not with each other but against a computer simulation.
2. A competitive mode where at the end of the postal mode, the leading companies compete in a final against each other for a further specified number of periods. This competition is for jobs and available project managers, while continuing to manage the company operations.

The situation in the game involves several bidding companies and participants playing the role of estimators and managers responsible for pricing bids. The objective is to achieve the highest performance indicators score, and the winner of the competitive phase is deemed the overall winner.

INFORMATION PROVIDED BEFORE PLAYING THE GAME

All participants are provided with the following information before playing the game:

1. A briefing manual which introduces and describes the game of MERIT 2 and how it is played. It also gives an introduction to the overall aims and objectives of the game, and an overview of the principal concepts that have to be addressed. It refers to the specific game parameters for measuring the performance and a short description of the market.
2. Company reports which describe the immediate past history of one year comprising ongoing job reports and data for quarters -4 to -1.
3. A list of available project managers and their CVs as provided by the staff recruitment agency.
4. A print-out of a list of the current jobs which are available for tender.
5. Decision forms for submitting bids; labour allocation; project managers allocation; overhead allocation and cash distribution (this may also be submitted on diskette, software being provided for this).

Participants must complete their decisions and return them to the game controller (supervisor). After receipt of the decisions, the results are processed and returned to the participants. They receive a set of reports for the company decision sheets for the next period, and a report of their progress to date.

TASKS

The players are expected to study the manual before filling in the decision forms in order to develop an understanding of the game. All decisions made by the companies are handed over to the game controller (supervisor) to be processed and the results returned back to each company with a set of reports containing decision sheets for the next quarter.

The key decisions required from the competitors each quarter are:

- selection of the sectors of the market in which to apply marketing effort;
- control of the principal company overheads in marketing, estimating, measurement and general head office costs;
- choice of tenders to be submitted together with mark-up and site on-costs required;
- for each contract awarded, allocation of project manager and choice between direct labour and sub-contractors;
- for each current contract, management of the labour force and site staff;
- for the company, control of cash flow, operating profit and other key operating factors;
- use of cash to reduce debt burden, increase the capital base and shareholders' dividend;
- increase of capital borrowing and decision on liquidating assets.

INTERACTION OF DECISIONS

This section lists the main decisions made by the participating companies and the factors that they should consider to remain in a leading competitive position.

Bidding decisions

When decisions on bids are made the following factors should be considered to ensure an adequate supply of work:

- the more jobs available to the company the higher the chances to win more jobs;
- the higher the number of competitors the lower the chances to win jobs;
- the greater the marketing efforts with respect to overheads the more jobs will be offered to the company;
- the company's past history, financial position, level of activities, its geographical location and accessibility to site;
- on-costs; these are the sum of site costs and project managers costs given by the

company. Site costs support on-site staff and services required by the project manager, so the higher the site costs the greater the project manager efficiency;

- increasing site costs – improves efficiency but reduces profit;
- the mark-up the company wishes to apply (recorded as a percentage of the company's cost estimate).

The company's cost estimate does not cover labour pay-off charges, sub-contract premiums, project managers' salary, recruitment or retention penalties, which need to be induced in the on-costs applied to the contract. The remaining profit will be required to fund the company's overheads and finance charges.

Therefore, a low mark-up reduces the project's costs and profits but increases the chance of wining work, whereas a high mark-up increases the profits but decreases the chances of winning work.

If submitting bids in the competitive rounds are close; within 1 per cent, then the client may exercise discretion by taking other factors into account, eg contractors' record for contract completion to time budget. It may therefore happen that the award is not made to the lowest price submitted.

Labour allocation decisions

Players have to consider the following factors when allocating manpower resources:

- if the amount of labour chosen to carry out the work is greater than the planned level (assessed in tender), then a higher rate of completion of work will be achieved, subject to the detrimental effect of too much labour in the same area;
- labour transferred from other jobs will operate at full efficiency, while newly recruited labour results in slower rates of finishing as training is required;
- labour which transferred to the idle labour pool may not be available for reallocation to other contracts until the start of the next quarter. This delay represents accrued holidays and reallocation.

Decisions on project managers

When deciding on the allocation of project managers, the following factors should be considered:

- a good manager with well-matched experience affects the efficiency of the contract and produces more output with the available resources;
- the cost of retaining, recruiting or paying-off project managers should be compared and considered;
- bonuses paid to a project manager increase his or her efficiency and promote loyalty to the company. Under-paying a project manager increases their risk of resigning while a highly paid project manager may be head-hunted by other companies;
- in the first phase all project managers are available. In the second phase the project managers are allocated on a first-come, first-served basis by the game controller.

A company can change the project manager allocated to that job, or even retain efficient project managers for future contracts in the pool, preventing their recruitment by other companies.

Overhead allocation

When making the overhead expenditure decisions the following factors should be considered:

- increasing overhead expenditures on head office services tends to reduce costs by improved buying and head office support;
- increased efforts on marketing in relation to turnover increases the number of jobs available;
- increasing the tendering efforts and/or decreasing the number of jobs bid for, increases the accuracy of estimating these jobs;
- increasing the measurement effort increases the value gained from the contract.

However, increased expenditure on each of these overheads will mean the overheads to be recovered from each operating contract will be greater. Consequently, competitiveness will be reduced, so impairing the company's ability to win contracts.

Cash distribution and borrowing decisions

The factors to be considered include:

- dividend paid to shareholders will affect the share price of the company; insufficient dividend will result in a fall of share price and vice versa (the company share price is one of the performance indicators);
- increasing the company capital base either by retaining profit or by additional borrowing;
- additional borrowing increases the company's capital base and allows turnover growth, but increases gearing and reduces share prices;
- liquidating assets to raise cash will cause a reduction in the company's capital base and its ability to undertake work.

GENERATED REPORTS

After processing the decisions made at each quarter, the following reports are generated by the computer simulation on the jobs being undertaken by the company and are distributed by the game controller.

Job bids and jobs won report – this report gives details of the bids submitted by the company in the last quarter, and whether the company won any contracts. If the client believes that the company is unlikely to complete the contract and doubts the company's financial standing, even though their tender is the lowest, the client may not award the contract. This will be reported in the 'client not prepared to award tender' column.

Each contract won is controlled by an ongoing job report which gives the current position on:

- planned costs – as estimated
- planned value – as estimated
- planned labour – as estimated
- actual labour – total labour allocated
- expected cost – calculated on a pro rata basis of actual labour, adjusted for training of the new recruits and depending on the expenditure of the head office overheads
- total costs – actual costs, additional costs and penalty clauses costs
- actual value – estimated cost plus mark-up depending on the quality of the project manager and the distance between the site and head office
- measured value – depending on the level of expenditure with respect to turnover of the measurement effort element of the overhead
- gross profit – difference between measured value and total actual costs
- percentage completed – measured by achieved actual value (not measured value) as a proportion of planned value
- remaining value to complete – total planned value less the actual value to date.

Additionally the following reports are available to control and monitor the company's performance:

Aggregate cost-value reports – giving costs, value and gross profit from all operating contracts and the gross profit less the company overheads.

Company cash report – which presents the cash calculations on a quarter-by-quarter basis.

Company job status report – giving the cumulative profit less overheads and the company cash flow.

Company overhead report – giving the cost of the individual overheads and the total overhead period-by-period (quarter-by-quarter basis).

Company profit report – for each year giving the profit net of interest charges each year.

Company turnover report – giving the turnover for the company year-by-year.

Forward work report – giving the forward work load for the quarters to come (planned value and planned cost for all jobs which extend beyond the current quarter).

Performance indicators report – this reflects the results of the decision-making process as measured against a set of performance indicators.

PERFORMANCE INDICATORS

The objective of the decision-making process is to achieve the highest performance indicators score as defined below:

Turnover	100
Gross profit/turnover	120
Operating profit/turnover	140

Cash	100
Contract completion rate	100
Order book	100
Forward margin	140
Return on capital	100
Share price	100
	1000

Each of these indicators will be compared with the position at the beginning of the simulation and expressed as the change to a start figure, given relative weighing to other indicators. This is taken as the definitive performance indicator.

DISCUSSION

The MERIT 2 simulation enables players to experiment with their company strategies in terms of significant characteristics of the construction contract variables. The benefits gained from this simulation are in the ability to investigate minor variations in strategies by simulating the effect of changes over a simulated period for four years. MERIT 2 not only illustrates the importance of the contract variables in the overall company strategies, but also the interaction of these variables.

The success of MERIT 2 may be judged by the number of participants who have played the game. However, the game's success or failure can also be gauged by the participants' reaction or enjoyment of the game, and the skills they have acquired. A pilot survey was undertaken to investigate the effectiveness of MERIT 2 as a training tool in construction management. This was done by surveying previous players; from a sample of 600 postal questionnaires, 236 questionnaire were returned. The results showed a favourable response from the players in terms of enjoyment, assessment and value of the game. The players were highly satisfied with the game as a tool for improving their communication skills and leadership skills. The simulation proved most effective for civil engineers (for whom the game was designed) and those who played the game twice gained maximum benefit. About 50 per cent of the participants noted that the game improved their overall professional abilities while 30 per cent had actually used the skills obtained in their day-to-day work.

MERIT 2 was designed to fulfil a specific training need, ie, a greater understanding of management issues by newly qualified civil engineers. The scope for such simulations is large but they need to target specific skill deficiencies and take account of the learning styles of the participants. A further study into this area is now being undertaken by the authors.

REFERENCES

AbouRizk, S M (1993) 'Stochastic simulation of construction bidding and project management', *Microcomputers in Civil Engineering*, 8, 343–53.

Au, T, Bortleman, R and Parti, E (1969) 'Construction management game–deterministic model', *Journal of the Construction Division,* Proceedings of the American Society of Civil Engineers, **95**, 1, 25–38.

Cooper, J R (1994) *'Baily Simulation',* Discovery Learning Engineer and Associates, (promotional material), London.

Elgood, C (1988) *Handbook of Management Games,* Gower Publishing, London.

Elgood, C (1994) VENTURE, *The international strategic management game,* The University of Bradford Management Centre (promotional material).

Halpin, D W (1976) 'CONSTRUCTO – An interactive gaming tool environment', *Journal of the Construction Division,* Proceedings of the America Society of Civil Engineers, **102**, 1, 145–56.

Harris, F and McCaffer, R (1990) *Modern Construction Management,* 3rd edn, BSP Professional Books, Oxford.

Lansley, P (1982) 'AROUSAL; A model to match reality', *Journal of European Industrial Training,* **6**, 6, 17–21.

Lilley, A (1978) 'Discussion of ROAD CONSTRUCTION – Simulation game for site managers', *Journal of the Construction Division,* Proceedings of the American Society of Civil Engineers, **104**, 2, June.

PYRAMID and PYRAMID II (1994) Northgate Training, promotional information, London.

Seeling, R (1994) *The BAUMARK I and II,* Department of Construction Methods and Management, Technischen Hochschule, Germany (unpublished literature).

Touran, A (1990) 'Integration of simulation with expert system', *Journal of Construction Engineering and Management,* **116**, 3, 480–93.

Torgersen, P, Wyskida, R and Yarbrough, L (1968) 'Bidding work loading game', *Journal of the Construction Division,* Proceedings of the American Society of Civil Engineers, **94**, 2, 127–37.

Torgersen, P, Wyskida, R and Yarbrough, L (1970) 'Closure to "Bidding work loading game"', *Journal of the American Society of Civil Engineers,* **96**, 1, 81–2.

ABOUT THE AUTHORS

Ms Vian Ahmed is currently a research assistant at the Department of Civil Engineering, Loughborough University of Technology. Her research interest is in the development of CAL in Civil Engineering

Address for correspondence: The Department of Civil and Building Engineering, Loughborough University, Loughborough, Leicestershire, LE11 3TU. E-mail: v.s.Ahmed@lboro.ac.uk

Tony Thorpe is Professor of Construction Information Technology in the Department of Civil and Building Engineering, Loughborough University. His main research interests are in construction communications and IT, and the simulation of construction activitites.

Ron McCaffer is Dean of Engineering at Loughborough University and formerly head of the department of Civil and Building Engineering. His research interests are broad, covering construction management, construction economics and the effective application of IT in construction.

Chapter 5

SYSTEMIGAME – play the game, learn the process

J M Bulbeck, J T Boardman and S J Wingrove

ABSTRACT

The Systems Engineering Group at De Montfort University is developing a methodology and diagrammatic representation for mapping business processes (Carr *et al.*, 1992); these we call the 'Boardman Soft Systems Methodology' (Bulbeck and Clegg, 1996) and the Systemigram (Systemic Diagram) respectively. A systemigram is a network of prose and graphics which represent a business process or activity (Sherman *et al.*, 1996). Collaboration with a variety of engineering companies suggests that people are unaware of the extent of their relationship with people in other processes as well as in their own process. The implication of this is that a decision or action taken by one group can have adverse effects on another group in another process. These effects are often unpredictable and undesirable.

To help alleviate the problem, the Systems Engineering Group create systemigrams to increase 'shared understanding' within a process. One of the techniques used to educate people about process-oriented thinking is by the use of a game called SYSTEMIGAME. The 'playing area' of a SYSTEMIGAME is a systemigram with some of the key prose removed. The player(s) start with the removed prose (node labels) and the partially complete systemigram. The object of the game is to associate each of the node labels with the corresponding empty node. This helps the players to learn, by trial and error, the relationship of activities and people within a process. SYSTEMIGAME has been developed for use in the Microsoft Windows environment.

INTRODUCTION

Companies need to continually re-examine themselves if they want to be as competitive as possible. They need to know exactly what it is they do and how they do it if they want to prosper and not just survive. Their processes should be as efficacious as possible to ensure they are getting maximum performance from the resources they have available. If companies are to avoid losing money they must reduce or eliminate the inefficiencies inherent within their processes, they need to know that their operations are as optimal as is reasonably possible. By continually re-examining themselves they can reap higher rewards for their effort than if they just continued operating the way in which they always have.

The Systems Engineering Group (SEG) at De Montfort University has talked to industry to discover what they do, how they do it and, if relevant, why they do it (Clegg *et al.*, 1996). We have found that many people within industry often do not know exactly what it is they do; they know generically what the operations of their company are, but they do not know, or appreciate, the details. This void in knowledge can be one of the reasons for company processes running inefficiently, so it is important that company personnel are aware of what it is they do and what other people in their company do.

Modelling techniques

There are a variety of modelling techniques and graphical representations which are available to industry for better understanding their processes. These include Gantt charts, PERT charts, IDEF models, Petri Nets and flow charts. Gantt charts and PERT charts can be used to predict the lifecycle of a single project and to illustrate the precedence of the individual activities within the project (Levin and Kirkpatrick, 1966). However, neither of these techniques is used for illustrating how the processes within a company generically interact (ie, for all projects). Petri nets (DiCesare, 1993; Peterson, 1981; Reisig, 1985) show the flow of information through a process but are inadequate in themselves for learning about the process. Flow charts (Gane and Sarson, 1979) show the order in which activities take place but do not have time associated with them and do not give any real depth or detail, just the sequential order of activities. IDEF0 models (US Air Force, 1981) can show which resources are required for processes, but they can be very difficult to read for someone who is not familiar with them.

From much work with industry we have concluded that processes are not well understood, either with or without models. Companies are trying to examine and re-examine themselves with tools which we believe are not optimum for the job. Even if managers and directors do learn what their processes are they then have to teach the other members of the organization, which can prove to be very difficult.

THE SYSTEMIGRAM

SEG is developing a methodology that abstracts information from within a company and then models the information into systemic diagrams (Boardman and Cole, 1996), which we call 'systemigrams'. These systemigrams are a network of sentences that contain words and phrases which originated from the company being modelled, thus making it easier for people within the company to understand the model. Systemigrams show the individual processes and activities within a company and the relationships between them. Systemigrams can be decomposed into conceptually lower levels (in a similar way to IDEF models and flow charts) which give greater detail about a particular area of interest.

Systemigrams show individual activities, artefacts and agents (people) in English, so special training is not required to read them (in theory, anyone who can read

English can read a systemigram). It is very simple to identify which activities are associated with each process. We have found from experiment that systemigrams are more readable (and understandable) to people without prior knowledge of modelling techniques than IDEF, PERT or Gantt.

Many companies use flow charts (or a variant of) to better understand the execution of their processes. Systemigrams are richer in detail than flow charts and can be used as a catalyst for discussion between decision makers within a company. Systemigrams clearly show the relationship between key entities of the 'as is', and encourage thoughts and ideas about whether the current system could be improved and how it could be improved.

Systemigrams as a teaching aid

Systemigrams can be used as teaching aids within a company, enabling staff to see how they themselves fit into the company as a whole (Ramsay *et al.*, 1996). Systemigrams could also be used to illustrate a new idea concerning how a particular process or system could work. Systemigrams can show great detail without being technical, so an engineer and an administrator (who typically have differing back-grounds) can understand a common systemigram.

Systemigrams are constructed from a variety of sentences which can be story-boarded into an electronic slide show. Currently Microsoft PowerPoint is used to create these slide shows, but SEG may develop a package which is more apt to showing the build-up of systemigrams. These slide shows (SystemiShows) are highly favoured by industry for exposing their people to systemigrams, because they can be fed the information in manageable pieces.

Another technique for educating people within a process about the process is to let them 'play the game, learn the process'. SYSTEMIGAME is a tool created by SEG which allows the players to learn the system using logic, common sense and heuristic thinking (or luck). SYSTEMIGAMEs are still in their infancy and have only been studied in pilot tests, but early indications are that they are a valid tool for educating people about processes.

SYSTEMIGAME – PLAY THE GAME

Introduction

SYSTEMIGAME is the (potentially) classic game of processes which can be played solitaire, in pairs or in groups. Play takes place on a game board which represents an incomplete description of a process or system in the form of an incomplete systemi-gram. The removed components (node labels) of the systemigram are available for placement within the system and must be correctly placed to increase the score.

Winning the game requires all the nodes to be correctly placed; this will give the player(s) a score of 100 per cent. If many errors were made prior to achieving the maximum score, the nodes can be removed and the game replayed, the objective now being to complete the systemigram with fewer errors.

SYSTEMIGAME was originally created with coloured, plastic-coated card and was played on a table top. It has since migrated to the PC and can be played on a desktop or laptop. The systemigrams used in SYSTEMIGAME are created using SystemiDraw, a drawing package developed by SEG for creating systemigrams in Microsoft Windows.

Equipment

One Game Board; one Palette listing removed node labels; one Option Menu. Other equipment required for playing the game includes a PC (with mouse) which has Microsoft Windows 3.1 or later.

The game board is a systemigram with most of the nodes blanked out. The only nodes which are not blanked out are the titles of containment nodes (if present), the first (top left) node and the last (bottom right) node. All the link text is present and the systemigram has a title which gives an indication of the area of interest.

The palette is a floating window which alphabetically lists all the nodes which have not yet been placed on the systemigram. Initially the palette lists all the nodes; at the end of the game the palette is empty.

The option menu allows the player(s) to affect game play by selecting 'notify every attempt'. With this selected, a sound will be played every time a node is placed which indicates whether or not it has been correctly placed. The option menu also allows the 'current score' to be displayed: how many nodes are correctly placed. Finally, player(s) may select 'give up' from the option menu; this will show the solution – the player(s) may want to try again.

How to play

The conduct of play depends on how many people are playing. There are five basic variants, these are:

- Solitaire SYSTEMIGAME – place the node text in the empty nodes and try to achieve the maximum score.
- Team SYSTEMIGAME – a team of two or more can work together to try and find the solution.
- Competition SYSTEMIGAME – players play the whole game on their own without the other players watching. Each player does this in turn, the winner being the person who completes the game with the fewest mistakes.
- Speed SYSTEMIGAME – similar to Competition SYSTEMIGAME, except the winner is the one who completes the game in the shortest time.
- Killer SYSTEMIGAME – each player starts with three lives. Players take it in turns to place a single node label into the correct node. If they make a mistake they must return the node label to the palette and lose a life. When a player loses all three lives they are out of the game. The winner is the last player left.

Objective

The object of the game is to match up the node labels from the palette with the blank nodes on the systemigram game board.

The play

The current player selects a node from the node list and should place it in a blank node where they think it belongs. The player can use the following systemigram features to aid their progress:

- Agent Nodes (people, departments) are shaded red.
- Artefact Nodes (objects) are coloured green.
- Other Nodes (eg, meeting, journey) are white.
- Containment Nodes are (usually) labelled.
- Link text may give an indication of the nodes it is joined to.

Example: by looking at the palette of node labels a player may be able to identify four or five nodes which are agents (people, departments). The player will observe that there are only four of five nodes shaded red on the systemigram, so the number of places that the agent nodes can go is limited.

Monitoring progress

During the game a player may want to check the score, this can be done by selecting 'current score' from the option menu. Players may want to know whether or not a node label is correctly placed immediately, this is possible by selecting 'notify every attempt' from the option menu. A sound will then play each time a node is placed, indicating whether or not it is correct.

EXAMPLE OF LOGIC

Below is a brief example of the logic which can be used for playing a SYSTEMIGAME. The systemigram used is a simplified version of an 'order intake' process created for a manufacturing company in Leicester. The simplified systemigram is used because this is an example of the logic which can be used; it is a demonstration of how a SYSTEMIGAME could be played, not what the process is really about.

In this grey-scale example, the agent nodes are the darker ones, the artefact nodes are the lighter ones. Part of the solution is explained for the lower left segment of the systemigram.

The node labels on the palette can be grouped into two categories for this example; they are agents (Contracts Dept, Programmes (Bid) Dept, Estimating Dept, Purchasing Dept, Test Engineering) and the artefacts (Customer Quotation, Request for Quotation, Purchase Order, Estimate Request, Tooling and Test Requirements, Expensive/Unusual Items, Quotes for Expensive/Unusual Items, Test Estimates).

A good way to start a SYSTEMIGAME is to read all the links and see if any of them give clues as to the nodes they are pointing to. Additional clues can be gained from the first node, last node and any containment nodes.

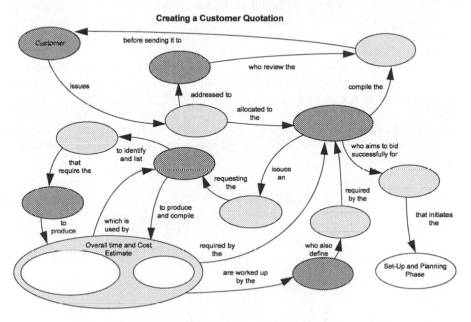

Figure 5.1 A simple systemigram with the node labels removed

Example: The containment node 'Overall Time and Cost Estimate' is produced and compiled by *an agent*. Of the agents listed above, the most likely is the 'Estimating Department', so this can be put into the appropriate node, as shown in Figure 5.2.

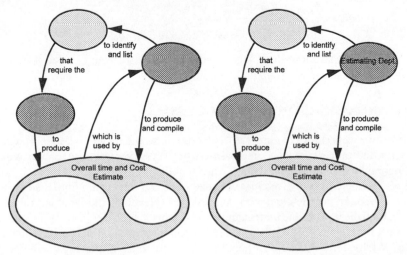

Figure 5.2 Placing the estimating dept in the correct node

We can now read that the 'Estimating Dept identify and list *Artefact* that require the *Agent* to produce *Artefact* which is used by Estimating Dept'. They 'identify and list'; the following artefact must be plural and there are only three plural artefacts, 'Expensive/Unusual Items', 'Quotes for Expensive/Unusual Items' and 'Tooling and Test Requirements'. By knowledge or trial and error, the correct answer can be found – Expensive/Unusual Items.

We know that an agent uses this list to produce something, the obvious answer being 'Quotes for Expensive/Unusual Items'. Now we have to decide who would do this. There are four agents left to choose from, the player of this SYSTEMIGAME would hopefully realize that the agent most likely to be able to get hold of this financial data is the 'Purchasing Dept'. Figure 5.3 shows this part of the systemigram, the role of the Purchasing Dept (note: the purchasing dept would be involved in other processes within the company).

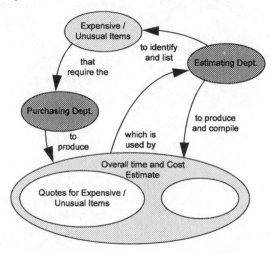

Figure 5.3 The role of the purchasing dept

This small example shows how logic (and trial and error) can be used to find the solution. The final systemigram is shown in Figure 5.4.

SYSTEMIGAME – LEARN THE PROCESS

The real motivation for creating SYSTEMIGAME is so the people who are playing it can learn the process which is represented by the systemigram. A player will be reading the links over and over again, this is similar to logic puzzles found in some magazines where four or five clues are read over and over again until a solution is found. By continually re-examining the links the player should be able to find the logic behind the process and understand exactly what the process does. While playing the game, the players will ask themselves questions such as, 'Who is this? What does he do? What documents does he handle?' Answers to these questions will become clear as the game progresses.

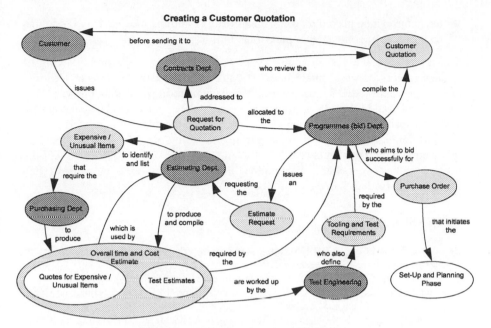

Figure 5.4 The completed systemigram

The player may be able to correctly place some of the node labels on the first or second attempt; these nodes are likely to be parts of the process the player understands and is confident of labelling. In contrast, some of the node labels may take several attempts to correctly place; this would imply that the player is not familiar with this part of the process or does not understand the relationship between the nodes. When a player does correctly match a node label to a node they will then know the relationship it has with other nodes and hopefully understand the systemigram better (and therefore learn the process).

When a player has finished a game he or she may wish to return to the game after an arbitrary period of time and try again. Each attempt at a SYSTEMIGAME should be more successful than the previous attempt as the player becomes more familiar with the process. If the player is really confident they can disable the 'notify every attempt' option and try and get all the nodes right before checking the score.

CONCLUSION

SYSTEMIGAME can be a fun way to learn. It has some advantages over traditional teacher-pupil teaching methods, including:

- the player has to think rather than just sit and listen – some people have trouble concentrating and let their minds drift to other (more interesting) thoughts;
- the game can be played (and the process learnt) at a time convenient to the player, as opposed to meeting a 'teacher' at a certain time;

■ the game can be played on the player's desk (assuming they have a PC), so they do not have to go to another part of the building.

We have found that systemigrams are powerful teaching tools for explaining ill-defined processes; we speculate that SYSTEMIGAME will aid the teaching and learning of these processes. SEG has been working with engineering processes, but we believe the principles and rules of systemigrams and SYSTEMIGAME could be applied to any system (especially ill-defined human systems which are difficult to model).

Consideration has been given to varying the game so that the link labels are removed and the node labels are left showing. This has not yet been tried, but it is felt that the links are richer in information than the nodes, so it is of more use to show the link labels rather than the node labels.

REFERENCES

Boardman, J T and Cole, A J (1996) 'Integrated process improvement in manufacture using a systems approach', *IEE Proceedings Part B Special Issue*, March.

Bulbeck, J M and Clegg, B T (1996) 'A systems methodology for analysing and simulating manufacturing processes', abstract accepted for IEEE Man, Systems and Cybernetics Conference, China, October 14–17.

Carr, D K, Dougherty, K S, Johanasson, H J, King, R A and Moran, D E (1992) *Break Point Business Process Redesign*, Coopers and Lybrand, Arlington, VA.

Clegg, B T, Boardman, J T and Buckingham, A D (1996) 'Factory process improvement using a human-centred approach' for CE '96, Toronto.

DiCesare, F (1993) *Practice of Petri Nets in Manufacturing*, Chapman and Hall, London.

Gane, C and Sarson, T (1979) *Structured Systems Analysis: Tools and Techniques*, Improved Systems Technologies Inc, New York.

Levin, R I and Kirkpatrick, C A (1966) *Planning and Control with PERT/CPM*, McGraw-Hill, Maidenhead.

Peterson, J L (1981) *Petri Net Theory and the Modelling of Systems*, Prentice-Hall, Hemel Hempstead.

Ramsay, D A, Boardman, J T and Cole, A J (1996) 'Reinforcing learning using soft systemic frameworks', *International Journal of Project Management*, **14**, 1, 31–6.

Reisig, W (1985) *Petri Nets: An introduction*, Springer-Verlag, Berlin.

Sherman, D G, Cole, A J and Boardman, J T (1996) 'Assisting cultural reform in a project-based company using systemigrams', *International Journal of Project Management*, **14**, 1, 23–30.

US Air Force (1981) *Integrated Computer Aided Manufacture (ICAM) Functional Modelling Manual (IDEF0)*, Report # AFWAL-TR-81-4023, Air Force Laboratory, Wright Paterson AFB, Ohio.

ABOUT THE AUTHORS

Julian Bulbeck graduated from the University of Portsmouth in 1993 with a BEng in Electrical and Electronic Engineering and is currently studying for his PhD at De Montfort University, Leicester. His current research concerns the simulation of project activities represented as semantic networks to aid process optimization.

Professor John Boardman graduated from Liverpool University in 1967 with a First Class Honours Degree in Electrical Engineering and obtained his PhD from Liverpool in 1970. John's academic appointments have taken him through Brighton Polytechnic, Georgia Institute of Technology and the University of Portsmouth to his present position as professor of Systems Engineering at De Montfort University, Leicester.

Stuart Wingrove graduated from the University of Portsmouth in 1993 with a BEng in Electrical and Electronic Engineering and is currently studying for his PhD at De Montfort University, Leicester. He created the software packages for drawing 'Systemigrams' and for playing SYSTEMIGAMEs.

Address for correspondence: Professor John Boardman, Science and Engineering Research Centre, De Montfort University, Hawthorn Building, The Gateway, Leicester LE1 9BH.

Chapter 6

The Softmatch-method: Enterprise transformation through simulation games

Päivi Haho and Riitta Smeds

ABSTRACT

This chapter describes the participative Softmatch-method which uses, in a systematic way, customized simulation games to achieve successful business process-oriented enterprise transformation. The principles of the Softmatch-method and practical experiences in Finnish case companies are described, and results and experiences are discussed. The method is still in its development and testing phase; the final results and their evaluation will be available at a later stage.

The Softmatch-method is composed of the following interactive elements which involve different organization levels and functions: definition of the scope and objectives based on company strategy, simulation games, team and group work methods, project management methods and training. The participation of employees from the design of the new process to its implementation accomplishes high commitment throughout the whole transition.

Softmatch is being developed in an ongoing Finnish-Swiss Eureka research project with participants from Helsinki University of Technology IIA-Research Centre, consulting companies and industry.

CHANGE ACCOMPLISHMENT

The driving forces of enterprise development are innovations in both products and processes. Innovations stem from the interaction of creative individuals on all levels of the organization (eg, Burgelman, 1983; Moss Kanter, 1983; Van de Ven, 1986). In this innovation process, examples from other enterprises are an important input; this kind of 'benchmarking' has evoked a huge managerial interest during the last years – business process benchmarking is a particularly 'hot' idea at the moment.

However, imitating the competitors or other enterprises in business process redesign does not solve the management of change problem.

'Creating new knowledge is not simply a matter of learning from others or acquiring knowledge from outside. Knowing has to be built on its own, frequently requiring intensive and laborious interaction among members of the organization.' (Nonaka and Takeuchi, 1995, p.10).

Innovation requires implementation. For example, the new production system has to be successfully implemented before it can be called an innovation. Only as an innovation can it improve the profitability of the enterprise.

Enterprises suffer from a lack of strategy-based business process development methods in which, from the beginning, the implementation of the new process is present as a goal instead of only process identification and description. Softmatch has been developed to fill this gap.

Softmatch aims to stimulate the whole organization's creativity, and manage the ideas systematically and efficiently towards a competitive business process innovation. The method combines simulation games, team work and project management in an iterative system of learning. Through acting and experimenting in the cross-functional and cross-hierarchical simulation games, the method brings into the innovation process the tacit knowledge of the organization. Through team work and systematic project management, this tacit knowledge is converted into an explicit new process design. With the iteration rounds between simulations and project work, the innovation process proceeds in a prototyping manner, until a sufficient design is created. The Softmatch-method thus supports an emergent, or learning, change strategy (eg, Mintzberg, 1994; Smeds, 1996).

THE SOFTMATCH-METHOD

Softmatch is a participative method for business process reorganization and change implementation. The method is designed for the rapid and systematic implementation of change projects in industrial companies as well as in service or administrative organizations. Softmatch enables genuine employee participation in the change and significantly increases the motivation and flexibility for change in the organization. Both the top-down and bottom-up approaches are used iteratively in the method to get the best accomplishment in change implementation. A top-down approach is needed in the first phase to select the process and set the development objectives. In the other phases, bottom-up knowledge and abilities become crucial. However, the method starts a business process-oriented dialogue between managers, employees and experts in supporting functions. The method can be used in business process re-engineering as well as in management of minor changes. The method itself balances the range of change with the maturity and capability level of the organization – goals which are too far away are hard to believe! Ideally incremental changes add up to radical business process re-engineering (see also Smeds, 1996).

The method contains the following six phases (see Figure 6.2):

1. Starting the Softmatch project.
2. First simulation game (present process).
3. Development of the new process.

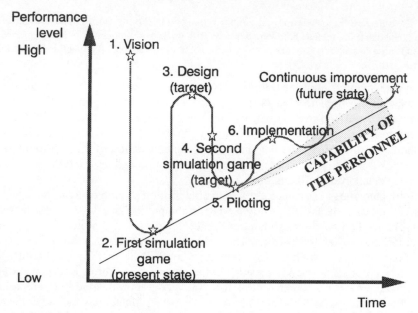

Figure 6.1 The Softmatch-method processes in balance with the change capability
of the personnel

4.   Second simulation game (new process).
5.   Piloting the new process.
6.   Implementation and follow-up.

The first four phases can be realized in two to four months. The duration of the last,
piloting and implementation phase, depends on the range of the change and the size
of the organization. In global organizations this stage can last years, but smaller
organizations can implement the results faster, since the whole personnel of the new
process can experience the new process together in the second simulation game. In
this case the implementation of the new process is in fact already beginning in the
second simulation game.

The Softmatch-method can be adapted to the enterprise's change situation (Figure
6.3). It can be used throughout the transition (a), or only for the first simulation game
phase, when the role of the simulation method is to identify the needs of process
re-engineering or incremental process improvement (b). In this case the process will
be developed according to a strategy, methods and schedule selected later on. The
method can also be applied to test the functionality of a new process before
implementation, or the new process itself can be developed collaboratively in a
simulation game (c). The number of game sessions can be extended from two
according to the needs of the individual change projects to get clear and concrete
results. The method can also be applied in the implementation phase for training and
continuous process development (Figure 6.7).

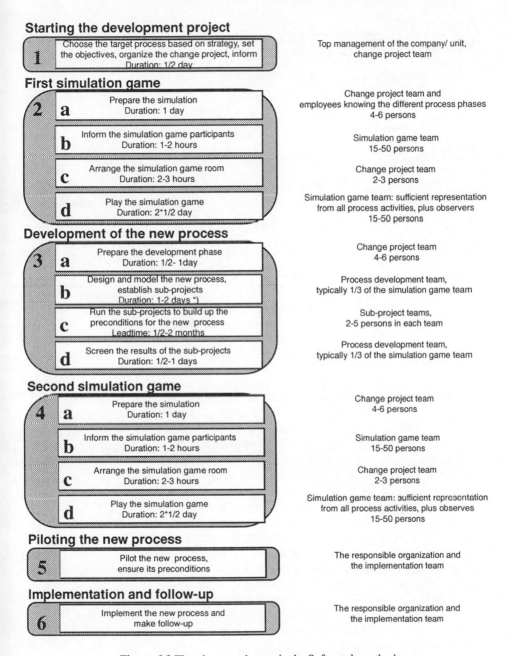

Starting the development project

1 — Choose the target process based on strategy, set the objectives, organize the change project, inform
Duration: 1/2 day

Top management of the company/ unit, change project team

First simulation game

2 a — Prepare the simulation
Duration: 1 day

Change project team and employees knowing the different process phases
4-6 persons

b — Inform the simulation game participants
Duration: 1-2 hours

Simulation game team
15-50 persons

c — Arrange the simulation game room
Duration: 2-3 hours

Change project team
2-3 persons

d — Play the simulation game
Duration: 2*1/2 day

Simulation game team: sufficient representation from all process activities, plus observers
15-50 persons

Development of the new process

3 a — Prepare the development phase
Duration: 1/2- 1day

Change project team
4-6 persons

b — Design and model the new process, establish sub-projects
Duration: 1-2 days *)

Process development team, typically 1/3 of the simulation game team

c — Run the sub-projects to build up the preconditions for the new process
Leadtime: 1/2-2 months

Sub-project teams, 2-5 persons in each team

d — Screen the results of the sub-projects
Duration: 1/2-1 days

Process development team, typically 1/3 of the simulation game team

Second simulation game

4 a — Prepare the simulation
Duration: 1 day

Change project team
4-6 persons

b — Inform the simulation game participants
Duration: 1-2 hours

Simulation game team
15-50 persons

c — Arrange the simulation game room
Duration: 2-3 hours

Change project team
2-3 persons

d — Play the simulation game
Duration: 2*1/2 day

Simulation game team: sufficient representation from all process activities, plus observes
15-50 persons

Piloting the new process

5 — Pilot the new process, ensure its preconditions

The responsible organization and the implementation team

Implementation and follow-up

6 — Implement the new process and make follow-up

The responsible organization and the implementation team

Figure 6.2 The phases and steps in the Softmatch-method

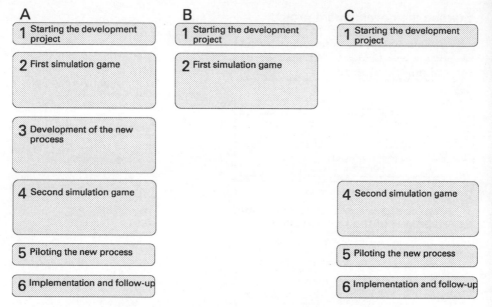

Figure 6.3 The Softmatch-method and change capability

Starting the Softmatch project

The selection of the business process to be developed must be based on company strategy. The selected process should be the object of future development and investment, where the company is clearly looking for growth or better profitability. Usually the core processes like sales-to-delivery process, product processes or the processes near the customer interface are the ones to develop; sometimes even the support processes evolve into a remarkable role. The change project also often leads to the development of other processes or preconditions for change concerning management, control, resources or human aspects. Communication and commitment are especially important prerequisites for successful change.

The selected process should not be too complicated in the first change project. A stepped transition with one process at a time gives the best result. Sometimes support processes can be so closely related to the core process that it is valid to handle them together. In the simulation phases, however, it is advisable to separate the processes from each other and perform the simulations consecutively.

Case studies have shown that the change objectives, and even the definition of the core process, can be unclear and hard to decide at the beginning of the change project. However, it is important to set at least broad goals. The specification of the exact objectives can be done in later stages, especially during the design and modelling phase. The first simulation game will open people's eyes to the necessary goals from the customer's point of view.

Change projects managed with the Softmatch-method require five different types of teams:

- the change project team;
- the simulation game team;
- the process development team;
- the sub-project teams;
- the implementation team.

The change project team is the core team in arranging the change project. It is involved in the whole change project and usually contains about four to eight members. Members are typically from different operational business units and from staff units like business logistics or information technology. The leader of the team runs the practical arrangements.

In *the simulation game team* there are members from the process itself: employees who are doing the real work in the core process like sales people, designers, production planners and assemblers who together come to about 20 people. In addition to these active simulation participants, there are up to 30 observers from different hierarchical levels of the organization, from other core processes or support processes. The simulation situation is a learning situation, so it is possible, and also recommended, that the team is fairly large.

The process development team is built after the first simulation game to design and model the new process. The team consists of about ten members who have been participants in the simulation game. Sometimes one or two members can be called to the group from outside the simulation game team to add some required competence. Each part of the process and all hierarchical levels have to be represented.

The sub-project teams typically consist of two to five people. They will carry out the projects which build up the preconditions for the new process. The members of these parallel teams come partly from the process development team, but new members can be added. The sub-project team leaders should be members of the development team.

The implementation team supports the process owner and the trainers in realizing the change so that the planned new process is taken into full use in the organization. The implementation team consists of people from all organization units that affect the operation of the new process. It is important that the implementation team members are from top management level. The team can continue, during the continuous improvement phase, to support the process owner in decision making and in the realization of small changes even after the change.

Experiences:

1. The Softmatch-method does not substitute the methods used in strategy formation. It is meant to support business process development based on an existing strategy and business objectives. During the change process many questions concerning strategy can arise. In the best case, the Softmatch-project can contribute to strategic changes in business or in business process management.
2. The Softmatch-method can also be used in situations where the personnel will decrease in certain parts of the process. Here the advantage of the method will be its sincerity – the problems in the company and process will be discussed

openly during the simulation session and the participants can begin to prepare for their individual change processes together with company reorganization. The Softmatch-method, however, should never be used for lay-offs – if the need for lay-offs is obvious, it is better to handle them first and start the participative development project thereafter.

3. Organizing the different teams with the right persons is a key success factor in a change project. In all teams, both management and operative-level employees as well as experts have to be represented to get the best result and commitment in change implementation.

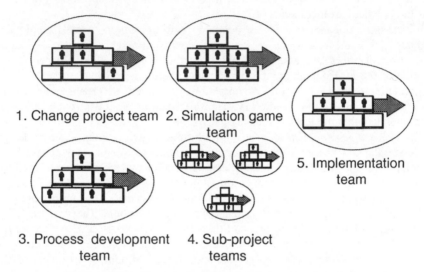

Figure 6.4 The teams in the different softmatch project phases

First simulation game

Change project preparation
The preparation of the change project consists of the following phases:

■ getting familiar with the subject of the process and the Softmatch-method;
■ preparing the process description;
■ selecting the simulation game team;
■ setting the schedule for the change project.

The selected process and the possibilities and advantages of the Softmatch-method should be studied before the project. The Softmatch-method can be applied to many different change situations in companies, but how to use it in the specific case should be discussed carefully before the change project is started in order to understand its possible results.

The process description is participative team work, conducted by the facilitating team with employees knowing the details of the process. Usually this is a half-day task with four to eight people. The facilitator 'walks through' the process by asking what the activities, inputs, outputs, responsible persons and organizations, tools and rules in the process are. A wall-chart of the process description should be put up (Figure 6.5).

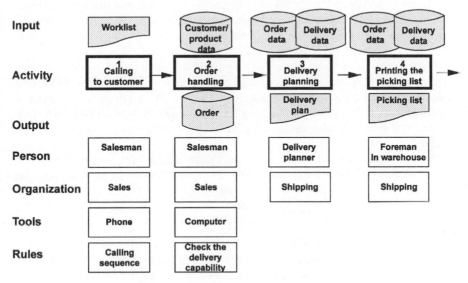

Figure 6.5 Example of the process model

Before the game, the participants and their roles have to be decided. They should represent all the activities throughout the whole process chain. The game is played using a real case, eg, a real order, as an example. The case should be selected carefully to reveal the potential for improvement in the process. The schedule of the project can be quite rough at first: only the first simulation game and the information session should be decided exactly according to the schedule. The first simulation game will reveal the rest after the game; the level of the change can be decided: is the change going to be radical, small or both, what is the role of the next steps, and what can be left outside the change project?

Experiences:

1.   The process description is a tool in the simulation game. It is used as a manuscript during the game session. Therefore, it need not be too complicated or too detailed – the game itself will add the missing details to the process description during the simulation session.

Information session about the change project, and the first simulation game[1]
The information session for the participants is held about one or two weeks before the first simulation. The purpose of the session is to tell people about the forthcoming change project in the selected process and about the method to be used. The objectives for the change project are highlighted and the process descriptions and the selected cases for the simulation are dealt with.

The first simulation game shows all participants the present state of the process. The game provides a common understanding of the whole chain with its strengths and weaknesses. It shows the interdependence between different departments and activities, and stresses the importance of cooperation and communication. The simulation game is often the first time that people from different departments meet and get to know each other, and appreciate their own roles in the whole process.

The game room resembles in its layout the real departments or functions so that actors from one department/function sit around the same desk. The room is equipped with different kinds of gaming material: a big process flow chart on a wall, documents used in the real process, raw materials and products, as well as tools (eg, PCs) used in the process. The gaming material need not to be very sophisticated. The most important issue is that there is something concrete to depict the flow of information and material in the process, not just the verbal explanation (eg, Smeds and Haho, 1995a).

The actors play their actual working roles by explaining their tasks in the process. The game follows the process flow depicted in the flow chart on the wall. The documents and the objects depicting the raw material and the products are passed from actor to actor like in the real process. Each actor explains to the others the following items about her or his own work:

- What she or he is doing. Why.
- Where and how she or he gets and sends the needed information or material.
- What kinds of problems and questions she or he has in the work. New ideas.

The observers, as well as players, follow the game and make notes of improvement ideas, problems, questions and comments that come up during the game. Questions and problems can be discussed as they arise. The simulation is not based on time, but on the process structure with its material and information flows. The aim is to find out what really happens in the process and not what is officially stated in, for example, the quality manual.

During the game, the problems, ideas, questions and comments are documented on stickers, which are then attached to the flow chart on the wall. Afterwards they are grouped for further development by the process development team.

The game is led by an external or internal facilitator who directs the discussion to achieve the objectives of the game. Another important role of the facilitator is to encourage everyone to participate freely in the discussion.

Example:

In a manufacturing company that produces one-of-a-kind products, the selected process to be changed was an order-to-delivery process. The 22 actors in the simulation game were from sales, purchasing, engineering, project management, production planning, production and shipping. Production was represented by both supervisors and operators. The observers came from middle management, production and information system development. A past customer order was selected for the simulation case.

The game material consisted of the real order sheets, technical drawings, schedules and work orders associated with the selected case. Parts and components were depicted by scale models which could be assembled together. The processing of components was simulated by marking the processed components with tapes of different colours. As a result of the game there were more than 150 stickers on the big flow chart. Many of them were small problems, comments and open questions, but there were also lots of concrete improvement ideas.

Experiences:

1. The main purpose of the first simulation game is to highlight a need for change and reach a shared understanding about the actual situation in the process.
2. The simulation game suits different organizational cultures – only the methods of using it as a tool differ.
3. Our experience based on several simulation games is that the number of observers is not limited, in the way that the number of players is. To achieve successful results in the change project, it is better to have many observers, even from top management, to make strategic contributions. The participation of external technology providers and system designers is highly recommended if technological investments are planned for in the change project.
4. The first simulation game can be an excellent approach for decision making: when all participants in the process and also management are present, it is easy to agree upon the rules in the business process chain and make decisions immediately. In one case company, the simulation team was able to make seven decisions during one simulation day, of which two were very important decisions concerning the controllability of the whole process. Fast decision making stimulates great hopes and a positive attitude towards the coming change and change management. In the simulation game, the managers feel the need for decisions, and they have the possibility to use their executive power quickly and efficiently.
5. In the simulation games all players are equal. Nobody is an expert in the method and each player knows best his or her own real tasks. The games are detached from reality, which allows experimentation without fear of real-life consequences.
6. Top management's observation example:

    The planned strategy dies in the originating phase if communication is neglected and strategy is not implemented in the everyday routines of the business processes.

Development of the new process

Based on the results from the first simulation game, the process development team produces the future process description with its detailed objectives. It is now possible to agree on the possible range of changes with qualitative and quantitative targets, since the first simulation revealed the present status of operations management, of process control, functionality and resources. Sometimes minor improvements are enough; in other cases bigger changes are needed.

Often the sub-processes or other preconditions related to the core process are key requirements for the success of the new process. Ongoing crises, for example in the physical processes, management or decision making, could be obstacles for successful process change. At this stage, therefore, the main goal is to balance the rate of change with the change maturity of the organization. By change maturity we mean not only the existing technical and operational ability, but also the managerial and leadership skills as well as the possible resistance to change at all organizational levels.

The process development team analyses the ideas and problems that were found in the simulation game and refines the change objectives. This work helps to focus on the essential issues in the process and builds up the guidelines for the following development. The general objectives are usually the same as in the first phase, but now the objectives receive meaning and can be focused. At this stage it is useful to discuss the level of the objectives – how radical the change should be compared to the present situation (Figure 6.6).

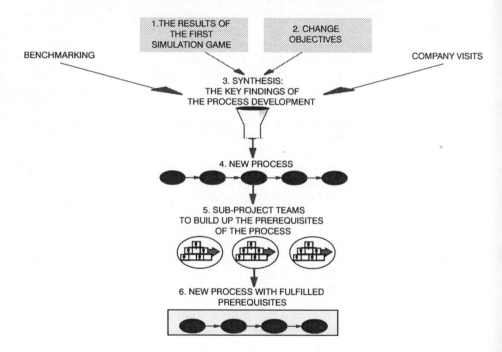

Figure 6.6 Main phases in the design of the new process

The ideal process can be developed by applying the main development trends in the design. Process consulting methods, creativity techniques and benchmarking can be used to support this creative task. The development team should be encouraged to consider radical and completely new ideas to achieve the goals. The main purpose of this step is to open the eyes to possibilities: what could be done to reach the business objectives. A detailed process description of the new process is the final result of the brainstorming. The process description smoothes out the too radical ideas to a realistic level.

After the process description, sub-project teams are established to build up the preconditions for the new process. The teams usually deal with controllability of the process, rules in the process, or technical questions concerning the tools and IT systems. The themes of communication, commitment and new demands for qualifications as well as training are also important.

Experiences:

1. This stage should be implemented as soon as possible after the first simulation game.
2. This phase is very important in the method due its to high creativity level. The first simulation game builds up the need for the change; this stage makes the change in principle achievable. There is a feeling of relief – implementation and its difficulties are not yet to hand.
3. To sustain the momentum of change, it is important to also plan minor, quick changes, even if radical change is foreseen.
4. The sub-projects are usually cross-functional and cross-hierarchical. Based on our experiences in several cases, they broaden and reinforce the understanding of the special topics in the process and increase the learning effects.

Second simulation game

All participants are informed about the results of the sub-projects and about updated plans of the new process. Often the participants in the second game differ from the first simulation game, at least their roles have been changed in accordance with the new process structure. The information session coaches the participants to the next steps and guides their thoughts to the future process.

The purpose of the second and possibly subsequent simulation games is to test the functionality of the designed process before implementation. With simulation games, different process alternatives can be experimented with before the final choice. The game also provides an important learning experience for the actors and observers (compare also Ruohomäki, 1994). The games can be used for employee training before the actual implementation of the new process and for training of newcomers when needed.

Because the actors are often unfamiliar with the designed process, the role of the facilitator in the second game is now different. The facilitator must explain the new process structure and how it affects the actors' roles. At the same time she or he guides the game according to the new rules.

Piloting the new process, implementation and follow-up

The piloting phase is crucial: testing the new process in a limited working environment before full-scale implementation will avoid shortcomings and problems in practice.

The piloting and implementation, as well as follow-up phases, are mainly realized by the line organization rather than business process or IT experts – experts, however, support these phases.

Communication and personnel training have to be arranged professionally. Simulation games or a modified Softmatch-method can now be used for sharing the information and adapting the continuous development for a daily routine in line organization (Figure 6.7). Implementation is the most demanding phase in large organizations with their different subcultures, with standardization demands and the huge workload in implementation itself.

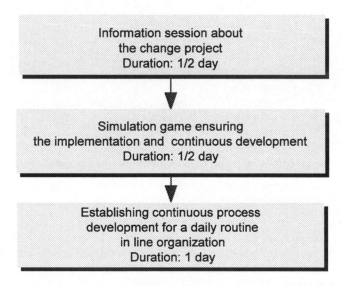

Figure 6.7 The Softmatch-method modified for the implementation phase

The follow-up of the new process should be based on the objectives set during the designing and modelling phase. For practical follow-up, feedback from only two or three process-related performance indicators is reasonable.

Experiences:

1. The involvement of the line organization is crucial.
2. Everyday problems can disturb the implementation very easily.
3. The resistance to change decreases by using the simulation games and piloting as a means for participation and empowerment.

DISCUSSION

Softmatch as a systematic method to support the transformation of enterprises

The Softmatch-method aims to shorten the lead-time of process-oriented transformation. If Softmatch is adopted as management practice, it can build into the organization a capability for continuous development, learning and innovation.

Softmatch contributes to all phases of knowledge creation in companies: to socialization, externalization, and the combination and internalization of new knowledge (Nonaka and Takeuchi, 1995, p.238). The preparation and realization of the first simulation game contains the phases of *socialization* (sharing of individual tacit knowledge in face-to-face dialogues, facilitated by the simulation games) and *externalization* (creating the present process model). The design of the new process with its change objectives, enables and preconditions, taking into consideration 'benchmarked' practices as well as internal and external knowledge, constitutes the systemic *combination* phase. Testing the new process prototypes, and finally *internalizing* the chosen design, is achieved in the second and subsequent simulation games, where the new knowledge can be experimented with and learnt by doing. Internalization of the new process design then proceeds in the organization through the piloting phase into full-scale use, to the full enterprise transformation. The tacit knowledge connected to the new process structure materializes itself in the vision and culture of the company, the explicit knowledge in the new technology, structure, rules and procedures (Nonaka and Takeuchi, 1995, pp.84, 241).

All the different phases in a Softmatch-facilitated change process are linked together through the use of self-organizing, partly overlapping, cross-hierarchical and cross-functional teams with high autonomy, requisite variety and redundancy. Participation and empowerment are important prerequisites for successful enterprise transformation. Not only the concrete solutions, but also their acceptance and implementation within the organization are crucially dependent on broad participation (Smeds, 1996). According to Moss Kanter (1983), change is fascinating if we are doing it ourselves, and threatening if someone is doing it to us.

Softmatch provides a systematic method to combine, in cyclical interaction, tacit and explicit knowledge, analysis and synthesis, and bottom-up and top-down approaches during the change project. In many change management methods, creativity and learning are killed through 'paralysis by analysis'. Unsystematic methods also lead to unsatisfactory results. The results of a Softmatch change project are always real changes: either incremental or radical, depending on the organization's maturity level for change. Ideally, incremental changes add up to radical business process re-engineering (see also Smeds, 1996).

NOTE

1. The principles of tailored simulation games are described in Haho, 1992; Laakso *et al.*, 1995; Ruohomäki, 1994, 1995a, 1995b; Smeds, 1994; Smeds and Haho, 1995a, 1995b.

REFERENCES

Burgelman, R A (1983) 'Corporate entrepreneurship and strategic management: insights from a process study', *Management Science, 29*, 12, 1349–64.

Haho, P (1992) 'Game experiences from Neles-Jamesbury', in Ruohomäki, V and Vartiainen, M (eds) *Simulation Games as Educational Tools in the Learning Organization* (in Finnish),

Helsinki University of Technology, Industrial Management and Industrial Psychology, Report 140, TKK OFFSET, Espoo, 45–9.

Haho, P and Smeds, R (1996) 'Softmatch: enterprise transformation through simulation games, experiences', in Koubek, R J and Karwowski, W (eds) Manufacturing Agility and Hybrid Automation – I, IEA Press, Louisville, pp.571–4.

Laakso, T, Hakamäki, J, Forsberg, K and Smeds, R (1995): 'Process assessment and simulation games – methods and software supported tools in business process re-engineering', Proceedings of the IFIP WG5.7 Workshop, Galway, Ireland, April 20–21, Chapman & Hall, London.

Mintzberg, H (1994a) 'The fall and rise of strategic planning', Harvard Business Review, January – February, 107–14.

Moss Kanter, R (1983) The Change Masters. Innovation and entrepreneurship in the American corporation, Simon & Schuster, New York.

Nonaka, I and Takeuchi, H (1995) The Knowledge Creating Company, Oxford University Press, Oxford.

Ruohomäki, V (1994) 'Participative development and organizational learning with work flow game', in Vartiainen, M and Teikari, V (eds) Change, Learning and Mental Work in Organizations, Working papers of the 3rd Otaniemi-Dresden workshop, Helsinki University of Technology, Industrial Economics and Psychology, Report 157, Espoo, 63–75.

Ruohomäki, V (1995a) 'Viewpoints on learning and education with simulation game', in Riis, J (ed.) Simulation Games and Learning in Production Management, Chapman & Hall, London, pp.13–25.

Ruohomäki, V (1995b) 'A simulation game for the development of administrative work processes', in Saunders, D (ed.) The Simulation and Gaming Yearbook, Volume 3, Games and Simulations for Business, Kogan Page, London, pp.264–70.

Smeds, R (1994) 'Managing change towards lean enterprises', International Journal on Operations and Production Management, 14, 3, 66–82.

Smeds, R (1996) 'Successful transformation: strategic evolution management for competitive advantage', Business Change and Re-engineering. The Journal of Corporate Transformation, 3, 2, 62–72.

Smeds, R and Haho, P (1995a) 'Tailored order-to-delivery process game', in Riis, J (ed.) Simulation Games and Learning in Production Management, Chapman & Hall, London, pp.145–55.

Smeds, R and Haho, P (1995b) 'Simulation games in business process re-engineering', in Saunders, D (ed.) The Simulation and Gaming Yearbook, Volume 3, Games and Simulations for Business, Kogan Page, London, pp.246–53.

Van de Ven, A H (1986) 'Central problems in the management of innovation', Management Science, 32, 5, 590–607.

ABOUT THE AUTHORS

Päivi Haho, MSc (Eng) is responsible for the management of change projects (business process development and customer documentation) in the overall business process re-engineering project in her company, Neles-Jamesbury Group Ltd. She has developed simulation games since 1988 and bases of Softmatch-method (since 1993) in her job. She is also currently working as a part-time researcher in the Softmatch project at Helsinki University of Technology, IIA-Research Centre. Her research interest is participative management of change in enterprise transformation.

Address for correspondence: Helsinki University of Technology, Department of Industrial Management, Otakaari 1, 02150 Espoo, Finland.

Riitta Smeds is Associate Professor at Helsinki University of Technology, Department of Industrial Management. Her current research interests include enterprise evolution, technology strategy, management of process innovations, and participative modelling and simulation for business process re-engineering. She is leading the ongoing EUREKA project Softmatch, 'Social simulation method for the management of techno-organizational change', as well as the Finnish part of the EUREKA project, Time Guide, 'Guiding the evolution of industrial enterprises'.

Address for correspondence: Helsinki University of Technology, Department of Industrial Management, Otakaari 1, 02150 Espoo, Finland.

Chapter 7

Acting to plan and planning to act: An initial exercise in major emergency planning and response

John M Rolfe

ABSTRACT

The exercise explores the activities involved in planning for and responding to an emergency. It also attempts to demonstrate the differences between these two functions and the training implications that arise.

INTRODUCTION

The exercise described in this chapter is used with students coming from a variety of backgrounds to study civil emergency management. It is used at the introductory stage of the course and is in two parts. The first part is an interactive examination of what constitutes a major emergency and the nature of the response that is required. The second part is an exercise in planning and responding which can be related to emergency situations.

EMERGENCIES

The following definition of a major emergency is used as a starting point for an initial discussion:

> 'A situation generally arising with or without warning, causing or threatening death or serious injury to people and extensive damage to property or the environment on a scale that cannot be dealt with by the normal agencies operating alone. The incident requires from the outset the special mobilisation and co-operation of a number of other bodies and voluntary organisations.' (The Society of Industrial Emergency Services Officers, 1993)

To explore the range of situations that could constitute an emergency, the participants are asked to relate the definition to their job and say what would be a major emergency for them. For example, when this chapter was presented at the 1996 SAGSET Conference, all those present at the session were involved in education; consequently the range of emergency situations offered was restricted. Nevertheless, some important emergency dimensions were elicited, such as:

- Life-threatening situations arising within the educational establishment, eg, a fire.
- Situations occurring externally to the educational establishment but producing life-threatening situations within it, eg, serious toxic pollution arising from an emergency at a local industrial site.
- Life-threatening situations occurring externally to the educational establishment but involving its personnel, eg, an accident to a party of students and staff on a mountaineering expedition.
- Non-life-threatening situations which threaten the ability of the educational establishment to continue to function, eg, the total failure of a major administrative computing system.

Having explored the range of events that might contain one or more of the above elements, attention turns to the response and the range of priorities that might be present. The above definition emphasizes that, in a major emergency, those at the centre of the event must expect to seek assistance from a number of specialist full-time and voluntary organizations. The exploration of this feature of emergency response aims for an understanding of the range of agencies which may be part of the response and the reasons for their presence.

When those participating in the session come from a variety of backgrounds it is possible to explore these issues at first hand. When, as in the case of the group at SAGSET 96, the range of participants backgrounds is limited, it is necessary to elicit by discussion a list of the agencies that will be present at an emergency. One way of doing this is to consider the pattern of an emergency response over time. For example, immediately after the event has occurred the fire, police and medical services will be fully involved. They may be aided by the military and voluntary organizations such as the Red Cross and Salvation Army. At later stages of the response insurance assessors, lawyers and forensic scientists may be active.

The different organizations taking part in the response will have specific reasons for being involved. These objectives and priorities may relate to:

- saving life;
- preventing the escalation of the disaster;
- relieving suffering;
- safeguarding the environment;
- protecting property;
- facilitating criminal investigation and public, technical or other enquiries; and
- restoring normality as soon as possible. (The Home Office, 1992)

At the SAGSET Conference the members of the group were asked what their first priority of action would be in the event of an emergency of the kind they had identified earlier. The replies demonstrated that not every participant responding to an emergency would put saving life first. The rescue services would have this objective but others could have different priorities. For example, an educational administrator might see restoring normality a soon as possible as the first priority while working alongside those who are seeking to save life.

A teaching point arising from this discussion is that the management of a major emergency involves not only the number of personnel who will be needed to deal with the event; the range of disciplines also have to be coordinated and controlled. For each of these their role will determine their priorities and how they respond to the emergency. All those participating must know their own role and ensure that it is recognized and accepted by other participants.

In preparing personnel to respond effectively to an emergency the most realistic starting position is that emergency response capability must be based upon day-to-day competences. Consequently, to prepare an effective response requires two sets of information:

1. The nature of the proficiencies that should already be possessed by individuals as a result of performing their normal functions.
2. The additional skill and knowledge that will be needed if they are to perform effectively in an emergency.

Having determined what is different between a normal and an emergency response it is necessary to identify methods of minimizing the difference and maximizing the quality of the response. This objective has two dimensions.

■ *Professional capability*: seeking to ensure that personnel, at all levels, know their roles and possess the proficiency to respond effectively.
■ *Personal awareness*: enabling personnel to understand the impact an emergency is likely to have on them, and help them to do some of the 'work of worrying' before the event.

An emergency training programme has to aim to achieve an effective and efficient response capability. Effectiveness is about doing the right things and involves training in how to plan an emergency response. Efficiency is about doing things right and involves training in how to respond to an emergency.

For emergency planning the objective of training is to acquire proficiency in being able to draw up the plans and procedures that will be followed if an emergency occurs. For emergency response the objective is to exercise these plans in order to be proficient in implementing action. Knowing what to do, and being able to do it, requires different opportunities and strategies for learning and training. To explore the differences between emergency planning and response the following exercise is used.

ON THE DOT: AN EXERCISE IN PLANNING AND RESPONDING

Participants are divided into groups of between six and eight. Each group needs a table, chairs and writing materials. The exercise director needs to have at least one set of dominoes and a means of timing the group(s) activities. The exercise can be completed in an hour. However, longer should be allowed if the introductory discussion of emergencies and an extended post-exercise debrief are part of the session. Forty minutes should be allowed for the planning phase of the exercise. The implementation stage does not usually take longer than two minutes.

Introducing the exercise, the director tells the participants that they have been selected to form an emergency planning team. Their task is to formulate a plan so that the organization they work for can respond effectively to an emergency.

The resources of the organization are represented by a set of dominoes. At this point it is essential to ensure that every group member is familiar with a set dominoes and how the game is normally played. If time is available it is recommended that the set of dominoes is produced and the participants play one short game. This familiarizes them with the set of domino pieces and the way in which they are normally used. A brief description of how a short game can be played is contained in Annex A.

The director then explains that if an emergency occurs the organization must be able to contain the problem as quickly as possible using all its resources, ie, the full set of dominoes. To do so the group must be able to build a hollow square of dominoes (Figure 7.1) where the sum of the dots on each side add up to the same amount. The square must be as large as possible and the dominoes must be placed face up so that their values are easily seen.

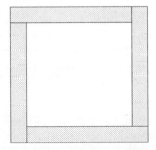

Figure 7.1 A hollow square made with dominoes

The director then explains that the organization's normal operations must continue while the emergency plan is being worked out. This means that the dominoes will not be available until the participants have a response plan. When their plan is ready they must ask for the dominoes and build the square. The time taken to build the square will be a measure of the effectiveness of the emergency plan.

The director concludes by saying. 'As I have my own job to do I am going to let you get on with the task. However, I am available if you need any more information about the organization'. The director should then retire to a position within call and sight of the group(s) activities. The director should note the time at which planning starts and how long it takes the group to be ready with a plan and ask for the dominoes.

The group's first objectives will be resource definition and task feasibility. They need to know how many dominoes there are in a full set and the sum of all the spots. They may ask the director for this information, in which case it should be given to them, or they may attempt to work out this information for themselves. There are 28 dominoes with a total of 168 spots. The teaching point is that planning is likely to require information which already exists somewhere in the organization and it has to be collected and used. Generating information from scratch takes time, wastes limited resources and is often inaccurate. A real-world parallel with the dominoes is the need for detailed staff lists on which to base an emergency plan.

The group must now determine if the task they have been set is feasible (are both the above values divisible by four into whole numbers?) and should conclude that it is. Each side should consist of seven dominoes having a total number of 42 spots.

The group's next task is the formulation of a response strategy for assigning the dominoes to meet the criteria for side length and dot value. This is likely to be the longest part of the exercise. There are several different methods that can be used but all will be based on the group knowing the sum of the dots on each piece in a set of dominoes. With this information a number of strategies may be adopted to reach a solution to the task. Two examples are:

1. *The statistical method*: this is based upon determining the mean value of the dots on an individual domino, ie, six, and putting together pairs of dominoes which make up twice the mean value. These pairs are allocated to one of the four sides in a balanced order. After having put three pairs to each side the remaining four dominoes should each have a value of six and can be used to complete the sides.
2. *The analogue method*: the group will make a set of dominoes from paper and by trial and error, or possibly the use of the statistical method described above, arrive at a solution. This approach to the problem has the interesting property of being a simulation within a simulation. As such it provides a teaching opportunity to introduce a discussion of the value of simulations and table-top exercises as an aid to planning.

If the group is a large one, sub-groups may form to explore alternate methods. These options then have to be evaluated by the group.

During the planning stage further teaching opportunities arise which can be discussed and related to the participants' own work experience. The group is told that its task is to build a square that meets set criteria but they are not told whether the rules for the game of dominoes still apply, ie, that the dominoes should be laid out so that dot values on adjoining pieces correspond. If they ask the director they will be told that this rule does not apply. A teaching point is that, in some emergency circumstances, it may be important to change or suspend normal procedures. If this is the case it is essential that all those involved know this, along with the procedures that will apply in an emergency. An actual example is that under normal conditions means of access to a building may be restricted, often for security reasons. In an emergency it may be essential to use other entrances to facilitate speed of entry and exit.

At some point the group will realize that their calculations and planning must take account of what happens at the corners of the square. The value of the domino at this location will count on both sides. The best solution is to use zero value pieces at each corner. The teaching point is that there are interactions between different responding groups in an emergency. These can cause friction and result in reduced effectiveness.

One function of emergency planning is identifying sources of potential conflict between responding groups and ways in which they can be resolved. An example of a source of potential conflict in a real emergency is who handles requests for information from next of kin about possible victims of an emergency. The organization directly involved, for example an airline, may see it as their responsibility, while the local police authority may insist that it is their duty.

Having decided on an agreed solution the participants must next find a method of implementing it. When given the dominoes they will have to be sorted and distributed to one of the four sides. The sides will then have to be built and finally joined together. This is a resource management task which includes deciding on the number of participants who will be involved in the task, specifying their individual functions and how to coordinate their response.

After some discussion the group will probably agree on a structure in which one person takes overall control of the task, one person sorts and allocates the dominoes, and up to four others assemble the sides. With a group of eight there will not be roles for every person.

Having reached this point the group will call for the dominoes and set about building the square. This task should take about one minute. The exercise director should measure the time taken to build the square, check that the sum of the dots on each side is correct and that the corners of the square are correct.

When the task is completed it is not unusual for the group to start their own exercise review. This may lead to them wanting to repeat the square-building task using a different method or discussing how their performance could be improved. In any case it usually helps the director to initiate a debrief where the following teaching points can be discussed:

Group structure. In the planning phase the group is likely to have very little vertical management; every member contributes on an equal basis as ideas are exchanged and evaluated. When the task changes to implementing the response, the structure of the group also alters. A more rigid and hierarchical structure is likely to be agreed, or imposed. One person will coordinate the function of the others who either have specific roles or no function at all. The point can be made that emergency management requires command, control, coordination and communication. The game permits a discussion of how these functions are defined, allocated and resourced.

Resource management. In the planning stage everyone in the group can be involved. When the implementation phase is reached the group may be too large. Decisions have to be taken about who actively takes part in building the square and who remains inactive. This facilitates a discussion of the resource requirements for the planning and performance of an emergency response. Those who make the plan may not be the same personnel as those who will have to carry it out. Additional personnel may be involved in the actual response and changes of staff may be inevitable due to fatigue.

Time to plan and time to act. In this exercise it takes considerably longer to plan the response than to carry it out. This point can be used to initiate a discussion of whether this is likely to be so in everyday situations and the resource implications associated with emergency planning.

Delaying action. Once a potentially workable plan has been produced there can be an unwillingness on the part of the group to take the decision to call for the dominoes and test the solution. Minor revisions are proposed and there can be concern that the solution may not work. There may come a point where the group is told that it has to act. This gives a lead in to the discussion of how emergency responses are initiated and subsequently evaluated.

CONCLUSION

Although relatively simple, the exercise provides the opportunity to identify some of the issues associated with developing an emergency response capability. Moreover, the exercise is usually sufficiently demanding, both as a task and as an exposure to managing personal interactions, to generate feelings and emotions among those taking part. These can also be considered in a debriefing session and related to the management of personnel in real emergency situations.

ANNEX A: A BASIC GAME OF DOMINOES

The dominoes are shuffled face down and all players draw an equal number as their hand. Any remaining dominoes are left face down on the table. Players may look at the dominoes they have. If there are any dominoes left over on the table the director turns one over. If all dominoes have been dealt the player on the left of the director lays a domino face up on the table. If the next player in clockwise order has a domino having an end with the same number value as one of the ends of the first domino, it is laid against it on the table. If this is not possible the turn passes on until one of the players can do so. The game continues with players putting down dominoes when they can. The winner of the game is the first player to have played all their dominoes.

REFERENCES

The Home Office (1992) *Dealing with Disaster*, HMSO, London.
The Society of Industrial Emergency Services Officers (1993) *Guide to Help in a Major Emergency*, Paramount Publishing, Borehamwood, Herts.

ABOUT THE AUTHOR

John Rolfe retired from the Ministry of Defence in 1994 where he advised on psychological issues relating to military training. He was the first chairman of the RAeS Flight Simulation Group and continues to be a member of the group. He is a visiting professor at the College of Aeronautics, Cranfield University. At Cranfield he is involved in developing crisis management simulations for the training of aircraft accident investigators and airline operators.

Address for correspondence: Orchard House, The Thorpe, Hemingford Grey, Cambridgeshire PE18 9DA.

SECTION 3: Role playing

Chapter 8

From game to success

Eugenijus Bagdonas, Irena Patasiene and
Vytautas Skvernys

ABSTRACT

The methodology of the organization of learning business basics has been suggested using an existing computer business game. The structure of the business game organization and input-output forms have been shown in the report. Depending on the given teacher data, created software can be applied for training or for examination. An analysis of the game's application for first-year students of Kaunas University of Technology Faculty of Administration has been presented in the report. The results obtained are compared with the parameters of other known computer business games.

INTRODUCTION

After long years of a planned economy our country has witnessed the first steps in the development of private business. Most of the Lithuanian universities, higher schools and private colleges are training people ready to work in the free market economy. All would-be professionals learn basic business principles.

Last year the Faculty of Administration of Kaunas University of Technology began using the computer game HARD NUT in the course 'Introduction to business' which is given to first-year students. The idea and the aim of this game is to systematize theoretical knowledge and to help the students understand the impact of managerial skills and of the chosen strategy on the financial standing of the enterprise.

The game imitates the management of a firm in a competitive environment. The initial condition of the enterprise and its annual development are periodically evaluated, ie, the players participate in the management process. The academic groups of students are split into separate small groups (firms). Members of each small group elect a manager (director). One period of the game symbolizes a year. It takes about one to two weeks to imitate this time period. During this time the players have to:

- analyse the standing of the enterprise on the basis of the documents they have;
- form a general enterprise development strategy on the basis of its performance;
- make major decisions concerning production, personnel, financial, marketing and sales management;
- enter these decisions on to the decision sheet from which the data are transferred into the database.

Object

The simulation software is designed to train students in understanding and analysing real financial statements. Usually the simulation game session covers the period of five fiscal years. The aim of the game is to show the interdependencies between different managerial functions, related to various aspects of company activities, such as production, personnel, commerce, marketing and finance. The simulator has 20 input variables to control the decision-making process.

Educational aspect

The simulation game provides the players with a background for understanding managerial decisions made under free market conditions. The software allows for adjustments according to the educational background of the players, ranging from high school to university.

DESCRIPTION OF THE GAME, HARD NUT

The main enterprise is split into branches which can compete with each other. Each group of players (four to five people is recommended) is in charge of one of the branches. These people have to report periodically on their performance to the board of directors. At the end of the 'year' each group has to present an annual report on the results their firm achieved (Bagdonas, 1995; Bagdonas *et al.*, 1995a, 1995b, 1995c).

The software programme HARD NUT determines the position of the firm in the market at the end of the year on the basis of the competitors' decisions and social and economic conditions. The results of the firm's performance at the end of each year are presented in various forms which are similar to those required by the government.

Management of the firm starts at the beginning of the year. The starting situation is fixed in the instructor's file. Before starting the game the instructor enters initial data (Table 8.1). These data can be classified into: general, market parameters, personnel, equipment, sales and financial data.

The general data include the investment capital, the firm's credit which has to be repaid in five years, the initial number of employees, the type of output, coefficients of elasticity, etc. The instructor may adapt the game for independent learning, ie, when the market does not exist, choosing a certain parameter to allow imitation of competition. This programme may be used for the assessment of students' learning progress.

Table 8.1 The screen for the data entered by the instructor

Year of the game	1	Equipment price	40000
Joint-stock capital	100000	Depreciation rate	20
Overhead expenses	60000	Equipment service expenses	10
Equipment loan	120000	Equipment production CC	0.5
Number of employees	15	Product materials #1	300
Price coefficient of elasticity (CE)	0.84	#2	600
Advertising CE	0.383	Suppliers credits in days	60
Distribution CE	0.35	Paying at once	5
Credit CE	0.525	Storage expenses	#1 20 #2 50
Demand for one firm #1	6336	Loan interest rate	10
#2	2880	Bank interest rate	15
Permission to produce two kinds of articles	2	Interest on deposit	8
Demand increase index	#1 1.04 #2 1.04	Customer int. rate	0.025
Price average	#1 700 #2 1400	Suppliers' int. rate	0.025
Payment to employee	10000	Taxes	34
Payment to sales agent	12000	Payment for query (PQ) of Demand	3000
Admission expenses	10	PQ of Competition	2000
Firing expenses	15	PQ of Position (state)	3000
Temporary workers payment fund	50	Annual inflation rate	1.3
Number of sets	4	Game type (0 or 1)	1
Service margin	5	Max. growth rate	120
Labour hours	#1 5 #2 9	Profit seduction reserve	10
Year-machine hour fund	800	Name of #1 product	Kaitra150
The equipment production decrease index	0.5	#2	Kaitra200

The model allows production of two types of products. The instructor can decide which parameters to change and which to leave standard. According to the market model, production is sold through sales agents who receive a certain salary. The forecasts of potential annual demand, price per unit and coefficient of demand increase are made. When entering initial data the marketing parameters are determined.

Personnel data include the salaries of sales agents, annual wages of the employees, employee recruiting/firing expenses, and the payment fund for temporary workers. For each product the instructor determines the required labour hours, the coefficient of decrease in equipment productivity, the depreciation rate and the coefficient of equipment productivity. In the sales area the instructor enters the data about used raw materials and supplies, the suppliers' credit and the storage expenses. Financial data include the interest rate on the loan and on bank deposits, as well as the interest rate paid by customers and to suppliers.

The decision sheet (Figure 8.1) is used by the players for entering the data concerning production (equipment acquisition, sales of obsolete equipment, wage index, social security budget, production volume), financial management (capital increase, dividends, the loan of the main enterprise, repayment of the loan, suppliers' credit in days), personnel management (recruitment and firing of employees, recruitment and firing of seasonal workers), marketing management (selling price, advertising expenses, customer credit in days, market research information: demand, competition and marketing).

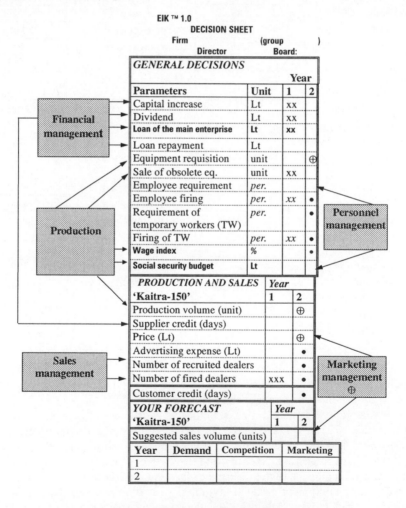

Figure 8.1 Part of the decision sheet

The best performing firm is that which accumulates the highest level of capital during the entire period of four to five years. The analysis of the firm's performance is done by students independently using suggested methods. The projects are presented to the audience.

In order to better understand the game variables, before the real game the students carried out three laboratory assignments which helped them to get acquainted with managing production, marketing, sales and finance.

Production management

Output level depends on the equipment and number of employees. Each set of equipment requires five workers. In the first year of use, one set of equipment can produce 334 first-grade and 186 second-grade output units per shift. Due to depreciation, in each following year the output level decreases by 7 per cent. The level of output produced by one set of equipment can be increased by hiring an extra five workers to work in the second shift and five more in the third shift. These workers are paid 50 per cent higher wages since they work at night. Changes in the wage index (from 100 per cent to 120 per cent) and social budget cause changes in productivity and output level.

Marketing and sales management

The sales level depends on output price, advertising expenses, number of sales agents and buyers' credit (the number of days in which the buyers have to pay for goods). While making decisions it is necessary to take into account that advertising expenses and big numbers of sales agents increase the cost of output. Buyers' credit brings in 0.025 per cent interest per day, however it diminishes working capital. Unsold goods remain in the warehouse, thus increasing operation costs and freezing working capital.

Financial management

In the case of insufficient working capital, each enterprise can borrow money from the mother-company for buying equipment. The mother-company is represented by the game leader. The loan repayment schedule and level of interest rate should be negotiated with the game leader.

Financial capital can be increased by paying equity dividends to the shareholders. Part of the profit can be shared between shareholders in cash dividends. That increases the firm's stock value in the market.

Lack of working capital is covered by a bank overdraft, loan or suppliers' credit (by postponing payment for raw materials for an agreed number of days). The annual bank interest rate on the loan is 15 per cent, and the suppliers are paid 0.025 per cent per day. If the suppliers get paid for raw materials at once, they grant a 5 per cent price discount. A large number of variables in the management of the enterprise are predetermined by an attempt to make the game similar to the real management environment. According to the survey results, 67.8 per cent of players would like to have more management variables, particularly from the area of finance, such as the possibility of investing free funds in shares of other enterprises, buying shares of bankrupt enterprises, participating in securities exchange, etc. We believe that the number of variables could be up to 30. It should increase in the course of the game and should depend on the level of the players' education. The last semester's work with students revealed that it is reasonable to give them several tasks to help them to determine the impact of single variables on the performance of the enterprise. The students are given special assignments aimed at the development of their skills in production management, financial management and marketing management.

Organization of the course

The course is split into three stages:

1. solution of the problems given by the instructor (laboratory assignments) under monopoly conditions;
2. simulation of a five-year performance period of the enterprise in a competitive market;
3. five-year performance report preparation and defence.

In the first stage the students prepare two groups of instructor's assignments working with the student's version of the game ($EIKST^{TM}$ 1.0) which simulates the operation of an enterprise under monopoly conditions and releases students from routine calculations. The first group of assignments are 'cognitive'. They help students understand the impact of a single specific variable on the performance of an enterprise. Several of them are:

■ to determine the relationship between production cost, total output costs and output level while it increases from 900 to 1,400 units. Other variables are indicated by the instructor and fixed;
■ to determine the changes in production cost and total costs while advertising expenses increase from 10,000 to 30,000 litas;
■ to determine the relationship between production cost, total costs, profit from financial activities and buyers' credit.

The second group of problems is related to decision making in the management of specific areas of performance. Solutions to these problems require corresponding groups of variables. Examples of these assignments are:

■ to ensure certain dynamics of production for a period of several years, possibly minimizing the cost of output. In solving this problem students are supposed to use the group of production management variables (equipment acquisition and selling, hiring and firing employees, wage level, social budget);
■ to determine the break-even point, ie, the minimum output level sold which brings no loss (profit is equal to zero) at a given level of production;

■ the buyers' credit in days is given. The students are required to determine the level of suppliers' credit which would ensure the balance between received and paid out cash.

In the second stage students make decisions for a single fiscal year under conditions of competition. For this purpose they use the student's version of the game EIKST^{TM} 1.0 which allows one to evaluate the previous year's performance in a competitive market and to analyse the current year's performance of an enterprise.

In the third stage students present the results of the five-year performance of their enterprise. The report should include the strategy of the enterprise and the main business indicators which, during the defence of the report, are compared with those of the competitors. This allows one to compare the financial standing of competing enterprises at the end of the five-year period. During the defence, each member of the board of directors has to justify his or her decisions concerning their specific areas of responsibility (production, finance, marketing). In this way team-work is evaluated. Experience suggests that not all students are able to work in a team. We do not know how to help them.

As a result of this work we expect a better evaluation of the course 'Introduction into Business'. The main problem is that the students have difficulties in understanding the impact of the parameters entered into the decision sheet on the final results.

RESULTS OF APPLYING THE GAME HARD NUT

While ascribing the students to a certain group (firm) an attempt was made to achieve the highest efficiency of the group through appropriate appointments to the board of directors. For this reason, before starting the game the students were asked to answer a questionnaire. The questions were designed to determine the personality types of students, business ideas, interests in certain areas, etc. For determination of the personality type, the classification of American Professor I Adize was chosen. According to him, personalities can be classified into executives, entrepreneurs, administrators and integrators.

The personality analysis results indicated a strong dominance of the administrative type. The survey results made it clear that 50 per cent of the elected directors of enterprises do not have any business ideas (Figure 8.2). This also applies to most of the board members. Although the performance of group activities can be evaluated only after the game is over, it is obvious that it will be more difficult to succeed for the boards which have directors without business ideas.

For more exactly determining the degree of entrepreneurship, the test developed by John R Broun, psychology professor at the University of Bridgeport, was used. The results of this test, used on 180 students, are shown in the Figure 8.3. About 65 per cent of our students have entrepreneurial possibilities.

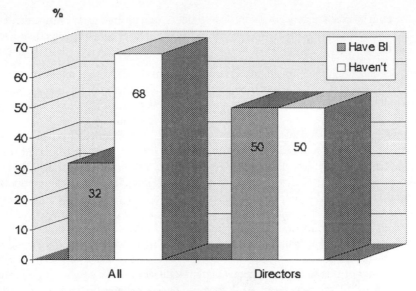

Figure 8.2 Possession of business ideas (%)

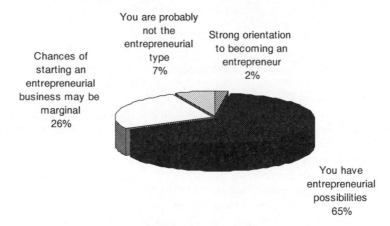

Figure 8.3 The test results

At the end of the game the students were asked to answer one more questionnaire in order to get an evaluation of the game and of the course 'Introduction into Business'. The questionnaire included 18 questions. The first 14 were valued on the scale 0 to 10, the rest in percentages (0 means the answer is absent). It can be concluded that after the first year the course is evaluated as good. Some of the survey results are presented in Figure 8.4.

a) Did the course help you to
understand about future studies?

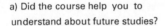
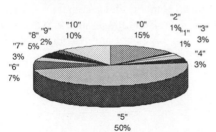

b) What is your individual benefit?

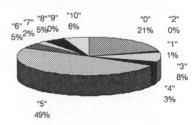

c) What is your opinion about the relation between the book and the game?

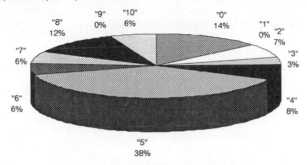

Figure 8.4 The results of the survey on usefulness of the course

Deeper analysis will become possible when each student is able to use a PC for independent studies and can perceive the impact of his or her decisions on the financial performance of the firm.

Business schools around the world employ a great number of business games for teaching economic principles (Ayal and Zif, 1989; Cadotte, 1995; Smith, 1987). One could ask why they were not applied in our course. We carefully examined the JUNIOR ACHIEVEMENT computer game which is excellently designed and accessible. The main differences between the game described in this chapter and JUNIOR ACHIEVE-MENT are:

- the latter uses only five variables, the former 20;
- in JUNIOR ACHIEVEMENT the instructor is not allowed to change the starting values, ie, it is impossible to regulate market parameters, while our game grants this initiative to the organizer;
- our game result sheets comply with regulations of the Lithuanian government; this is not the case with JUNIOR ACHIEVEMENT.

EVALUATION

The HARDNUT simulator was used in teaching management-related courses at Kaunas University of Technology and at eight technical schools in Lithuania. The evaluation results for the courses prove that the students' involvement and participation has increased due to the highly interactive nature of the simulation game.

The second version of this software based on more detailed financial and market management models is under development.

REFERENCES

Ayal, I and Zif, J (1989) PRODUCT MANAGER, *A simulation,* Prentice Hall, New Jersey.

Bagdonas, E (1995) *Biznio ivadas,* Technologija, Kaunas.

Bagdonas, E, Patasiene, I and Skvernys, V (1995a) *Biznio zaidimas 'Kietas riesutas'*, Technologija, Kaunas.

Bagdonas, E, Patasiene, I and Skvernys, V (1995b) *Kompiuterinio dalykinio paidimo taikymas,* Kompiuterininkø dienos '95, Birðtonas, 130–31.

Bagdonas, E, Patasiene, I and Skvernys, V (1995c) *Computer game for teaching business principles,* Upgrading of the social sciences for the development of post-socialist countries, Kaunas, 19–26.

Behrman, J N and Levin, R I (1984) Are Business Schools Doing Their Job?, *Harvard Business Review.*

Cadotte, E R (1995) *Business Simulations: The next step in management training,* Selections, Admission Council, pp.8–19.

Dauderis, H (1994) *Financial Accounting,* Concordia University, Holt, Rinehart & Winston, Toronto.

Smith, J R (1987) MANAGER *A Simulation,* Houghton Mifflin, Boston, MA.

Summers, E L (1991) *Accounting Information Systems,* Houghton Mifflin, Boston, MA.

ABOUT THE AUTHORS

Eugenijus Bagdonas is the Chair of the Department of Service Management at the Faculty of Administration, Kaunas University of Technology. His research interests include the analysis of simulation business games and applying them at different levels of the education system of Lithuania.

Irena Patasiene is Assistant Professor in the Department of Service Management at the Faculty of Administration, Kaunas University of Technology. Her research interests are in the areas of simulation modelling, service operation management and information systems.

Vytautas Skvernys is Assistant Professor in the Department of Service Management at the Faculty of Administration, Kaunas University of Technology. He researches into simulation modelling and accounting.

Address for correspondence: Department of Service Management, Faculty of Administration, Kaunas University of Technology, Donelaicio 20, Kaunas, 3000, Lithuania. Tel: 370 (7) 201849; Fax: 370 (7) 207232; e-mail: eubag@adf.ktu.lt or Irena.Patasiene@cr.kktu.lt

Chapter 9

Simulating laboratory teaching for graduate teaching assistants

Sinclair Goodlad

ABSTRACT

For many years postgraduate students and post-doctoral researchers have assisted with the teaching of undergraduates in science laboratories. What is new is that increasing attention is now being given to ensuring that these graduate teaching assistants (GTAs) receive some formal instruction before being let loose on students. For three years, experimental workshops have been offered at the Imperial College of Science, Technology and Medicine, University of London, to address relevant issues. Preliminary research revealed that GTAs' main concerns are about their own knowledge of the subjects they teach and about coping with students. This chapter describes a simulation exercise developed to assist physics GTAs who have to supervise laboratory teaching.

INTRODUCTION

For many years postgraduate students and post-doctoral researchers have assisted with the teaching of undergraduates in science laboratories. What is new is that, with Audit and Teaching Quality Assessment teams swarming over universities, increasing attention is now being given to ensuring that these graduate teaching assistants (GTAs) receive some formal instruction before being let loose on students.

Several recent surveys have studied the deployment in universities of postgraduate students as teachers: see for example, Attfield *et al.*, 1993; Irvine and Darwen, 1994; Knottenbelt and Fiddes, 1993. Other studies have concentrated more specifically on the type of training the GTAs receive, see for example, Elton and USDU Task Force 3, 1994; Morton, 1994. The requirement for proper training has also been stressed by the National Postgraduate Committee (NPC, 1993) which has promulgated guidelines on the use of postgraduates as teachers.

At the Imperial College of Science, Technology and Medicine, University of London, surveys were undertaken to discover the felt needs of GTAs and experiments were mounted to examine the extent to which workshops would address these needs.

THE USE OF GTAs AT IMPERIAL COLLEGE, LONDON

Some 600 GTAs take part in the teaching of undergraduates at Imperial College. All departments use research assistants and most also use postgraduate students in parts of their teaching. GTAs are usually selected by the department Director of Undergraduate Studies (DUGS) with advice from the GTAs' supervisors who are best placed to know the needs and capabilities of individuals.

The most common use of GTAs is in laboratory classes to help supervising staff, but most departments also use GTAs in individual and group tutorials and as extra helpers in problem classes. Typically, GTAs are required to familiarize themselves with the theory and practice of the laboratory experiments they are going to supervise, in many cases by actually doing them in the weeks before the undergraduates return to college. Training in teaching techniques as such has, until recently, been on-the-job, with advice and support from academic staff supervising particular laboratories, from DUGS and/or from departmental senior tutors.

EXPERIMENTAL WORKSHOPS FOR GTAs

Under the auspices of Imperial College's two principal quality control committees, the Undergraduate Studies Committee and the Graduate Studies Committee, workshops were provided in 1993, 1994 and 1995 for GTAs. In 1993 and 1994, the workshops had two basic objectives: (a) to offer some instruction to GTAs and (b) to discover whether or not the procedures used were suitable for future use. In the light of experience, similar workshops were offered in 1995. Participants were nominated by their departments. A total of 327 GTAs attended (see Table 9.1); 298 questionnaires were returned, an overall response rate of 91 per cent.

Table 9.1 Experimental workshops: numbers

Year	Participants	Questionnaires
1995	141	119
1994	117	112
1993	69	67
Totals	327	298 = 91% response

Participants were offered reading suggestions (specifically Ramsden, 1992, and more recently, Goodlad, 1995a). The workshops in each year consisted of a number of activities of the type that might be included on a regular basis in future workshops. Some of these were modifications of techniques I used to prepare undergraduate students to act as tutors in local schools in Imperial College's scheme known as 'The Pimlico Connection' (see Goodlad, 1979, 1995b; Goodlad and Hirst, 1989). Participants were invited to comment on them and on some documents designed to help them to build upon the teaching offered to undergraduates by the academic staff in their departments. More importantly, before they attended the workshops the GTAs were asked to write down what they anticipated to be (or if they had already had experience as GTAs, what they had found to be) their greatest problem. Three types of problem far outweighed all others (see Table 9.2), namely: coping with students who are inattentive/disruptive/refuse to take advice; not knowing the answer to students' questions/not knowing the material; and not being able to explain things clearly/interestingly.

Table 9.2 Problems reported by GTAs in pre-workshop questionnaires

| Problems | Percentages of mentions | | |
	1995 %	1994 %	1993 %
1. Coping with students who are inattentive/ disruptive/refuse to take advice	27	30	19
2. Not knowing the answers to students' questions/not knowing the material	25	23	30
3. Not being able to explain things clearly/ interestingly	23	18	27
4. All other problems	25	29	24
Totals	100	100	100

In the first two years, and for most GTAs, workshops of five hours duration were provided with the following ingredients:

- a nominal group ('brainstorming') session on GTAs' own experience of the conditions that most affect their ability to study effectively;
- a simulation exercise on one-to-one tutoring;
- a short talk on frames of reference in technical communication;
- a role-play exercise on the restraint of traffic in towns;
- a short talk on research on student learning;
- discussion with departmental tutors about how the ideas examined in the previous sessions might feed into their teaching.

Participants were asked to rate the workshops as wholes on a five-point scale and rate specific items. The ratings record:

$$\frac{\text{Score given} \times 100}{\text{Maximum possible score}}$$

Such a rating system is a stringent test of appreciation, with neutral responses resulting in zero ratings, and minus ratings (which can be and are given) offering the possibility of an overall negative response to an item. In every workshop for academic staff and GTAs at Imperial College interest and enjoyment are examined as well as usefulness on the assumption that if participants find items interesting and/or enjoyable, they may come to perceive their usefulness later. Fortunately, in both 1993 and

1994, the GTAs found the workshops interesting (ratings of 78 and 73 respectively), useful (69 and 68), and enjoyable (72 and 65).

In line with what they had revealed in the pre-workshop questionnaires, the GTAs in these first two years showed most appreciation of the interactive components of the workshops (see Table 9.3). However, qualitative comments from GTAs from the physics department indicated that they would have preferred a role-play/simulation exercise on the supervision of laboratory teaching (of which they did a great deal) rather than of small-group teaching (of which they did less). Accordingly, I sat in on a number of laboratory sessions, observing and listening, and interviewed GTAs and their supervisors about the types of problem that GTAs encountered in supervising undergraduates. These studies indicated that there were a number of interpersonal 'situations' that caused trouble to GTAs almost independently of the content of the specific laboratory experiments. The simulation exercise described below was devised for use in the 1995 workshop for physicists.

Table 9.3 Ratings of individual sessions in the workshops

	Interest		Usefulness		Enjoyment	
	1994	1993	1994	1993	1994	1993
1. Nominal group/ 'brainstorming' exercise	50	55	52	50	35	37
2. Simulation of one-to-one tutoring	71	84	57	68	66	77
3. Talk on frames of reference in communication	61	63	40	41	49	52
4. Role-play exercise on small-group tutoring/ demonstrating	66	78	61	72	50	63
5. Talk on research on student learning	67	64	54	53	43	45
6. Discussion of specific problems	51	55	53	54	36	37

FEATURES OF THE SIMULATION EXERCISE

In the workshop session previously occupied by the role-play, two 'laboratory' sessions were held each with:

■ one roving 'tutor';
■ six 'students' – in pairs at three benches;
■ each 'laboratory group' given a bag of 'Scrabble' tiles and a board;
■ each participant given a role sheet: ('non-players' were 'observers');
■ discussion after each 'laboratory session' in which each study group writes down a list of dos and don'ts for laboratory supervision.

The 'Scrabble' tiles were the apparatus. The instructions to all concerned were as described below. Everyone was given the instruction sheet shown in Figure 9.1.

IMPERIAL COLLEGE OF SCIENCE, TECHNOLOGY & MEDICINE
USC Workshop C for Physics
Exercise on laboratory supervision

The object of the exercise is to simulate laboratory demonstrating. There will be two short sessions, each of 7 minutes duration, in which six 'students' working in pairs will attempt to complete the task outlined on the laboratory instruction sheet below. In each session, a 'demonstrator' will be present. All those not assigned specific roles of student or demonstrator are asked to watch the exercise and to note down problems of being a demonstrator that the incidents portrayed bring to mind; after the exercise, each study group will be asked to identify three problems and list solutions.

Laboratory Exercise

1. Background
As language becomes more complex and specialised, it may become necessary to redesign the keyboards of word-processors. Your lecture course on linguistic probability theory examines how, using advanced computational procedures, it is possible to calculate the frequency with which specific letters occur in words of the English language used in various contexts. Past experience suggests that students do not appreciate the power of these modern analytical tools until they have had direct experience of creating words in conditions of constraint.

2. Aim
The aim of this exercise (experiment) is to give you practical experience in linguistic analysis.

3. Objectives
By undertaking this exercise, you will

- increase your knowledge of the English language by collaborating with other students;
- improve your skill in composing text under constraints of time and space;
- develop your capacity to analyse probability in the field of word analysis.

4. The task
Using as much of the equipment provided as you wish:

- organise the letter tiles into four-letter English words (no proper names).

5. Assessment
Each person is required to submit for assessment a laboratory log book (a copy of the grid on the sheet for the specific session and group) recording the disposition of tiles, and listing any not built into words.
   You will be assessed on the following criteria:

- your competence in meeting a specific time deadline – 7 minutes;
- your skill in creating interesting and/or unusual four-letter words;
- your capacity to use all the tiles in the bag: one mark will be deducted for each letter not used in the grid.

Figure 9.1 Laboratory instruction sheet

The participants were given the instructions with the (usual) injunction not to show their sheets to anyone. For Session 1, the pairs of 'students' had the following instructions:

Session 1, Group 1

You have not yet had any lectures on linguistic probability theory, so you are not sure what to expect. Spread out all the tiles face up, and start to make up four-letter words. If you find something wrong with your 'apparatus',* do not admit it because you may be 'marked down'. Fiddle about as best you can (ie start trying to set out words on the bench, leaving gaps for any missing letters) but without telling the demonstrator what is wrong. Keep your heads down to the task and try to avoid catching the demonstrator's eye. If you get help, try to complete the task in the 7-minute deadline.

* What the 'students' did not know, but all the observers did know, was that all the tiles with vowels on them had been removed.

Session 1, Group 2

You have not yet had any lectures on linguistic probability theory, so you are not quite sure what you are to do. You recognise that the tiles are 'Scrabble' tiles. You are not supposed to see the tiles until you take them out of the bag one-by-one. (Start doing this – and making up four-letter words, some on the bench and some on the Scrabble board.) Keep doing this until help arrives – but do not ask for it. If you get the necessary help, try to sort out words and enter them in the grid within the 7 minutes allowed.

Session 1, Group 3

You have heard the first two lectures on linguistic probability theory and realise that the complexity of words relates to the specific social contexts of their use. The task as set is clearly boring and uninvolving. The laboratory demonstrator should tell the students to use the 'Scrabble' board for the four-letter words, giving extra marks for extra points – e.g., as in the game 'Scrabble' by landing high-scoring letters on triples. Get the demonstrator's attention and argue your case vigorously and for as long as you like about what should be done.

The 'demonstrator' had these instructions:

Demonstrator

You are the Demonstrator for today's exercise/experiment. The instructions given to students are as on the Laboratory Exercise sheet.
• When the workshop organiser starts the exercise, do exactly as you would do in a normal Laboratory in Physics.
• Be ready afterwards to say what problems (if any) you experience.

In Session 2, the 'students' had these instructions:

Session 2, Group 1

One of you (decide between you which one) has arrived very late for this laboratory session.

On time student: By the time your partner arrives, you have already done a good deal of the work (taken a large number of readings as recorded in the grid below); why should your laboratory partner be allowed to copy these results down having done none of the work? *Late arrival student:* The 'results' of your partner are useless because none of the 'difficult' (infrequent) letters have been incorporated in the grid. Point this out and persuade your partner to start again.

Session 2, Group 2

Unlike the members of Group 3, you have not yet heard any lectures on linguistic probability theory; those who have heard the lectures will be at an unfair advantage in the laboratory experiment. Make up four-letter words without reference to your partner. (Do not enter anything in the grid in your 'laboratory notebook'. Go over and try to find out from group 3 how they have tackled the problem.) Discuss with your partner how to get out of the mess you have created for yourselves. Could the laboratory demonstrator do the work for you? Group 3 has an unfair advantage over you; the demonstrator should be told this.

Session 2, Group 3

Having heard the first lecture on linguistic probability theory, you have hit upon the idea of using up all the 'difficult' (infrequent) letters first (Q, Z, X, J, etc) so that you are not stuck with them at the end of the 'experiment'. You have rapidly generated the configuration below. [See Table 9.4.] (Please set out the tiles on the bench, not the 'Scrabble' board, in the configuration below.) You are anxious that other students should not get marks, as you see it, 'at your expense'. You object strenuously to the laboratory demonstrator about the unfairness of other students being allowed to 'pinch your ideas' and then get marks as if the work was their own.

Table 9.4 Configuration generated in Session 2 by Group 3

Q	U	I	Z		E	X	I	T
J	U	N	K		S	H	E	D
B	U	L	B		C	R	E	W
V	I	C	E		P	E	L	T
N	A	I	L		M	O	P	E
T	E	A	R		R	A	I	D
W	A	N	T		F	E	L	T
F	R	O	G		T	E	N	D
R	O	A	M		G	R	E	Y
S	H	O	E		V	E	I	N
G	A	I	N		S	O	Y	A

Letters remaining: A O O U I O Blank Blank

Again, a demonstrator was assigned, with instructions similar to those given in Session 1.

Everyone who was not assigned a role in each session was given a sheet containing transcripts of the instructions given to the 'students' and the relevant 'demonstrator'. They were asked to consider: 'If you were the demonstrator, what would you say/do?

What problems do the incidents call to mind?'

After each session, the GTAs (who conferred throughout the workshops in study groups of eight to ten, each with a member of the physics staff as leader) were asked to discuss how they would have felt as students in each situation and then how they would have coped as demonstrator. They were also asked to write on acetate sheets a list of dos and don'ts for laboratory teaching which were then shared in plenary.

EVALUATION

The qualitative comments of the GTAs (and of the staff acting as study group chairs) indicated that the issues of laboratory practice raised by the simulation had led to fruitful discussion; but the ratings of the simulation were lower than those in the previous two years when simulations of group tutorials had been run; see Table 9.5.

Table 9.5 Physics GTAs' rating of the simulation on laboratory teaching (N = 18)

Interest	Usefulness	Enjoyment
61	50	61

The defects of the simulation, as identified by the participants and by participants in the SAGSET 1996 Annual Conference to whom the exercise was described, were mainly these:

- there were two quite separate problems for the 'demonstrators' – management of their time and coping with interpersonal conflict;
- only two participants actually experienced directly the stresses of the situation: for the 'observers' it was vicarious experience.

Both of these problems will be addressed as the exercise is developed.

On the plus side, it seems that the use of 'Scrabble' tiles as 'laboratory equipment' was a simple and effective way of enable participants to simulate and/or observe the types of situation they have to deal with as laboratory demonstrators.

ACKNOWLEDGEMENTS

It is a pleasure to acknowledge help and advice received in developing this exercise: Dr Roy Burns of the ICSTM Physics Department, and participants at the 1996 SAGSET conference: Claude Bourles, Marty Fallshore, Elyssebeth Leigh, M McCarthy, Bob Matthew, Mieko Nakamura, Chris Percy, Pete Sayers, Morry van Ments, Peter Walsh and Tina Wilson. Any improvements that future versions of the exercise may have will flow from their guidance; any defects that remain will result from my not having listened to good advice!

REFERENCES

Attfield, J, Hughes, P and Wareham, T (1993) *Developing Support and Training for Post-graduates Employed as Tutors/Demonstrators* , University of Lancaster Unit for Innovation in Higher Education, Lancaster.

Elton, L and USDU Task Force 3 (1994) *Staff Development in Relation to Research,* Occasional Green Paper No. 6, CVCP Unit for Staff Development, Sheffield.

Goodlad, S (1979) *Learning by Teaching,* Community Service Volunteers, London.

Goodlad, S (1995a) *The Quest for Quality: Sixteen Forms of heresy in higher education,* SRHE and Open University Press, Buckingham.

Goodlad, S (ed.) (1995b) *Students as Tutors and Mentors,* Kogan Page, London.

Goodlad, S and Hirst, B (1989) *Peer Tutoring,* Kogan Page, London.

Irvine, J and Darwen, J (1994) 'The use of postgraduate students as teachers', paper presented to the Annual Conference of The Society for Research into Higher Education.

Knottenbelt, M and Fiddes, N (1993) *Postgraduate Tutoring: A survey,* Edinburgh University, Centre for Teaching Learning and Assessment.

Morton, A (1994) 'Development and implementation of a scheme at the University of Birmingham to train postgraduate students in teaching skills', *Journal of Graduate Education,* **1**, 2, November.

NPC (1993) *Guidelines for the Employment of Postgraduate Students as Teachers,* National Postgraduate Committee, London.

Ramsden, P (1992) *Learning to Teach in Higher Education,* Routledge, London.

ABOUT THE AUTHOR

Dr Sinclair Goodlad is Director of the Humanities Programme and Senior Lecturer in the Presentation of Technical Information at Imperial College. He has written and edited books on theories and methods of higher education and was for seven years editor of the international journal *Studies in Higher Education.* He is a Fellow of the Society for Research into Higher Education whose publications committee he chairs.

Address for correspondence: Humanities Programme, Mechanical Engineering Building, Imperial College of Science, Technology and Medicine, Exhibition Road, London SW7 2BX. Fax 0171 594 8759; e-mail s.goodlad@ic.ac.uk

Chapter 10

Managing an open-ended manufacturing design case study

Doug Love and Peter Ball

ABSTRACT

This chapter presents aspects of a novel case study structure for teaching the process of manufacturing system design. The approach used for the case study removes many of the limitations of traditional methods of teaching the design process. It has been used successfully for a number of years and proves to be both enjoyable and valuable to manufacturing engineering students. In particular the method by which the case study is introduced and administered will be described.

The approach used is to actively involve students in a design problem. The problem is defined using a modified industrial example and is open-ended in nature. The students must define the boundaries of the problem and seek the necessary information to be able to offer a solution.

INTRODUCTION

In the process of teaching manufacturing system design the use of lectures is an efficient means of conveying the theory, but the method of application and the problems associated with it are extremely difficult to convey using lectures alone. The assumption that armed with the tools of the trade, students can go on to apply manufacturing theory without first practising some of the basic concepts is a false one; this is supported by the views of experienced engineers and observing students tackle design problems such as the one described in this chapter.

One approach to providing the experience of applying engineering theories, as advocated in the Finniston report (1980), is via laboratory experiments, design projects and case studies. Laboratory experiments are normally and deliberately limited to the illustration of a particular principle and not intended to develop the student's understanding of the context in which the principles might be applied. For example a student might develop model-building skills during a simulation exercise but fail to gain any understanding of the circumstances in which such a model should be used in manufacturing system design. Case studies, particularly those based around a design task, are obviously better suited to providing an understanding of context and application (Gilgeous, 1995). To be effective it is important that the design task is set in a context which is convincingly 'realistic' and that it is of sufficient complexity to challenge students' analytical skills and avoid the rapid assumption of an obvious solution.

Providing an example that has sufficient complexity will expose students to a number of potential solutions which have to be analysed and tested for acceptability. Such analysis will not only enable students to improve their understanding of the practical application of the techniques involved but also allow them to realize that selecting the 'best' design is not a trivial process. The selection of the best design requires a broader understanding of the contribution of manufacturing to the performance of the business.

This chapter will discuss these issues in the teaching of manufacturing systems design and will describe the 'yoke flange' case study that has been developed to meet the extended requirements mentioned above. In particular the method by which the case study is introduced and administered will be described.

JUSTIFICATION FOR AN OPEN-ENDED CASE STUDY APPROACH

Hands-on approach

It was stated earlier that while lectures are an effective means of conveying theoretical information they are less effective at conveying practical information and certainly fall short of providing applications experience. By introducing the approach of 'learning by doing' (Gibbs and Habeshaw, 1989) not only can the learning process by made more effective it can be made more interesting and enjoyable.

By allowing students to work at their own pace on a case study they will build up their own mental model of the case. This model is effective at providing understanding of the case itself and provides a platform on which to understand the links between other concepts they have been introduced to (Gibson, 1993). Related to this is the requirement to develop related skills such as communication, information retrieval and documentation which are not core learning objectives.

The approach of 'learning by doing' makes activities such as manufacturing system design more memorable. The necessity to get involved with a detailed design task will result in design techniques and problems being more easily recalled than something read in a book or heard in a lecture. Furthermore, in becoming actively involved in a problem and seeking out potential solutions students will inevitably make mistakes either in the application of a technique or concept. This is an important part of the learning process that aids understanding.

Finally, when applying a method or technique to solve a problem students will become more aware of why it exists and how it can be used. Students will achieve a better understanding of the fundamentals of a technique and the principles surrounding why it needs to be applied.

Establishing the boundary of design work

When tackling a design problem, engineers must not only understand the theories and know where to apply them but they must also be familiar with practical considerations. These may include understanding the limitations of techniques, knowing what assumptions are reasonable, being able to compare options to judge which one is superior and being able to approximate certain aspects of the problem to simplify and expedite the process.

Within a lecture environment many of the subtleties are difficult to convey. A tutorial approach usually involves applying techniques to tightly defined problems that, while they help students apply techniques, fail to build up a student's understanding of when a technique should be applied and what care should be exercised in applying it.

The use of a practical exercise improves on the tutorial approach. Students become involved in a problem over a longer period, allowing more time for reflection. The route forward is not always obvious and therefore students develop their understanding of how to progress a solution.

If the practical exercise is open-ended in nature an added dimension can be brought to the work. Students must then develop their understanding of the value of particular solutions and how one solution can be superior to another. A further step can then be made to force the students, not the tutor, to evaluate the suitability of a solution and the point at which to stop design work. These are steps that students are initially apprehensive about (Edge and Coleman, 1986) but afterwards in retrospect feel that it was a hurdle well worth jumping.

KEY FEATURES OF THE YOKE FLANGE MANUFACTURING DESIGN EXERCISE

The yoke flange manufacturing system design exercise was born out of a real-life design problem in which a company needed to rearrange its manufacturing facilities. One of the company's products was being replaced, namely the yoke flange, and subsequently over a period of years demand for the product would fall. Students are given the task of relocating the machine tools to a smaller area and deciding which machinery can be discarded. The case is complicated by a shortage of space, physical obstructions such as pillars and little initial information.

Open-ended approach

The students' remit is to redesign the manufacturing area to achieve a certain level of output. Since the initial information given is minimal two beneficial consequences arise. First, the students must decide what information they need and then request it. Second, by forcing the students to obtain extra information they quickly realize that the boundaries of the problem have not been set.

When embarking on such a design exercise the students will at times experience a sense of bewilderment and insecurity in that they may not know how to carry out a certain type of analysis or when the analysis should stop. To counter this the tutor plays two distinctly separate roles: an adviser and an information provider.

Figure 10.1 illustrates the structure of the design exercise. A number of student teams are given the design task and they can seek help and advice from the tutor. The tutor's role is to help the team with their problems but not to provide any information concerning the company. Using a second mechanism students can request information on the company (sales history, machine breakdown patterns, absenteeism rates, union opinions, costs, etc).

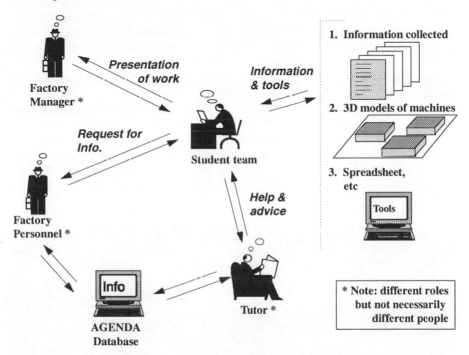

Figure 10.1 Overview of the yoke flange case study

The students will have been introduced to a variety of other information and tools. For example, 3D models of the factory are available for use. Access to computer software such as spreadsheet and simulation tools is provided to enable students to carry out adequate analysis of their designs. At the end the teams present their work to the factory manager. This will either be in the form of a report or oral presentation.

Features of the design exercise are such that from the outset the students must give thorough consideration to the approach and boundaries of the problem. They must decide when to stop asking for information and when to stop analysing the data. Students use spreadsheets and simulation software to provide evidence that their design is fit for purpose.

Obtaining information

The information requests are addressed to specific managers within the company and the mechanism for requesting (either paper memos or e-mails) brings in the added dimension of delays in replies (perhaps a couple of days) and misunderstandings in what data were actually requested. The roles of the individual managers are usually played by the tutor.

A database (see Figure 10.2) is used to retrieve all the necessary information. A database is used due to the amount of data that are potentially available for the students to request, the ability to provide consistent replies across the teams and the ability to quickly transfer the data back via memo or e-mail. The data are organized as questions and answers by manager/department. For example, for the Training Manager there are a number of sections such as 'operator training' and 'operator ability'. The specific question highlighted in Figure 10.2 is the training time for operators. Behind this question is a note containing the answer.

When a request for information comes in the tutor first looks up the manager and then searches for the question. Where information does not exist the data are 'generated' (with knowledge of all the other data, the tutor invents a reasonable reply to the question). A further advantage of the database is the ability to record what questions groups have asked. This helps in monitoring groups to check they are actually requesting information and that the requests span a reasonable number of areas.

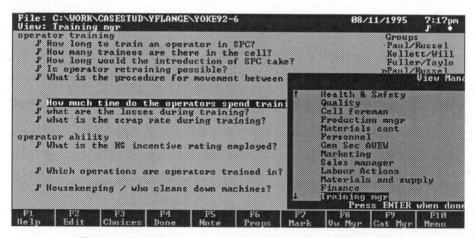

Figure 10.2 The yoke flange data held in a Lotus Agenda database

Obtaining advice

The tutor's face-to-face role with the students is to provide help, advice and encouragement where necessary. Encouragement is particularly important during the early stages of the exercise when those who have not been asked to carry out an open-ended case study before experience difficulties.

The tutor's role is also to provide help in the practical application of engineering techniques using the data they have obtained. Typically the data they are provided with are in a raw format and difficulties may arise in ascertaining whether more data are required.

In general the tutor operates an 'open door' policy for obtaining advice in which students can turn up at any point. Due to the time required to administer the design exercise when large numbers of students are involved, some consideration has been given to scheduling sessions in which students have a limited amount of time with the tutor (acting as various company personnel) to obtain information.

Assessment

The design exercise raises some questions regarding the nature of assessment. Some of the problems arc: the exercise is team-based, the exercise aims to foster understanding of the practical process of design, and the open-ended nature of the exercise.

The design activities such as data collection, synthesis and analysis can be written up by each student in the form of a report or cut down into a presentation. This process can be used to consolidate the student's understanding of the activities and techniques involved and should include a review of the quality of their design. Assessment here is balanced between the actual performance of their design and the standard of discussion based on how they went about the design process and the problems they encountered.

To tackle the problem of identifying individual performance in a team-based environment peer assessment has been used in some instances. The peer assessment is used to establish the relative amount of work each of the students within a team put in and is then used to obtain individual marks from the overall group mark. The peer assessment has two benefits. First, it allows a more representative mark to be given to each of the students and second, it provides a carrot to individual members of the team if they know that they could be marked down at the end.

FEEDBACK FROM STUDENTS

Reaction to the open-ended case study

Student feedback has shown that participation in the case study is worthwhile and enjoyable, both in terms of designing a manufacturing system, and also of the element of competition that arises between different design teams.

The students must decide when approximations are justified and can test their assumptions in a safe environment. The extra organization required and the open-ended nature of the investigation can lead to some students spending an excessive amount of time on the exercise. This risk is minimized by contact with the tutor. While the case represents an additional burden compared to conventional tutorials, students report a clearer understanding of the principles of manufacturing system design and experience suggests that this is reflected in improved examination performance.

Benefits to related lecture material

The open-ended nature of the case study and the origin of the case data provide a good preparation for students to tackle real industrial problems. During the process of design they will have gained a good appreciation of the difficulties of obtaining data and the often vague format they are supplied in. They will have practised the sequence of a number of design tasks and will have an understanding of the difficulties involved.

The need to apply particular techniques forces the students to realize the advantages and disadvantages of using them. The students quickly gain an appreciation of the difficulties and time-scales of using tools such as simulation. More importantly insight into the whole of the manufacturing system design process is gained; the necessity to work effectively as a team provides an important learning experience. A possibly underrated effect of using this approach is it reinforces an understanding of some of the more basic manufacturing principles such as bottlenecks and dynamics. Gibson (1993) noted that one of the problems with undergraduate teaching programmes is that the curriculum is seen as compartmentalized and as a result knowledge can be bundled separately. It has been noted that towards the end of this case study there is a greater appreciation of how many of the manufacturing principles (often taught separately in different lecture modules) interrelate.

CONCLUSIONS

This chapter has argued for an improved method for teaching engineering practices, in particular that of manufacturing system design. The approach of 'learning by doing' was described and shown to have the benefits of not only enabling students to apply engineering techniques but also providing them with valuable experience of working in an environment in which there is no obvious solution.

The yoke flange manufacturing system design case study has been developed over a number of years to provide a valuable open-ended practical exercise. The case study enables a good balance to be achieved between providing students with a challenging practical exercise and providing structured support. In terms of the overall effect, the student feedback is very favourable and exam results have shown an improved understanding of manufacturing principles and their application.

REFERENCES

Edge, A G and Coleman, D R (1986) *The Guide to Case Analysis and Reporting*, System Logistics, Honolulu, Hawaii.

Finniston, M (1980) *Engineering our Future: Report on the Committee of Inquiry into the engineering profession*, HMSO, London.

Gibbs, G and Habeshaw, T (1989) *Preparing to Teach: An introduction to effective higher education*, Technical & Educational Services, Bristol.

Gibson, I S (1993) 'Teaching engineering design through project management', *International Journal of Engineering Education*, **9**, 2, 143–7.

Gilgeous, V (1995) 'Teaching operations management: experimental learning, games and workshops', *Proceedings 13th International Conference on Production Research (ICPR)*, Jerusalem, Israel, Freund, London, 106–8.

ABOUT THE AUTHORS

Dr Doug M Love is a lecturer in the Aston Business School at Aston University, UK. He has worked in production control, as a product manufacturing manager and as an industrial engineer designing group technology cells. His research interests concentrate on the design and operation of cellular manufacturing systems. He has developed a number of novel case study approaches to teaching manufacturing systems principles and behaviour to undergraduate and postgraduate engineering students as well as practising engineers. He is a member of IEE (Manufacturing Division).

Dr Peter D Ball is a lecturer in the department of Design, Manufacture and Engineering Management (DMEM) at the University of Strathclyde, UK. He holds a BEng in mechanical engineering and a PhD in manufacturing simulation from Aston University. His research interests cover manufacturing system design and the development and application of simulation tools. He is an associate member of IEE (Manufacturing Division).

Address for correspondence: Dr Peter Ball, Design Manufacture & Engineering Management (DMEM), University of Strathclyde, Glasgow G1 1XJ. Tel: 0141 552 4400 (Ext 4548); Fax: 0141 552 0557; e-mail: p.d.ball@dmem.strath.ac.uk or p.d.ball@iee.org.uk, Web: http://www.strath.ac.uk/Departments/DMEM/MSRG/peter.html

Chapter 11

Developing tourism in Erehwon: An interactive case study approach to strategic planning for hospitality management

Mac McCarthy

ABSTRACT

This chapter outlines an interactive case study simulation exercise designed to teach the basic principles of strategic planning to final year students on the Hospitality Management programme at the University of Central Lancashire. The design encourages groups to think and act strategically, first providing them with basic information and then giving additional information as the simulation progresses. Reflection is encouraged on both the process and the difficulties involved. The discussion includes the reflective problem-solving model that informs the teaching and learning methodology.

INTRODUCTION

A fictional, emergent East European state is faced with a number of economic and social problems following independence and the departure of a dominant section of society as a result of the split into two nation states. The impact of this emigration on education, welfare and general national wealth in the weaker state leaves it with a major strategic review and exploration of options on the agenda as a matter of urgency.

Students work in groups as a think tank to explore how a minor tourist industry might contribute more fully to the country's development. Their task is to conduct a strategic review and analysis, to identify key questions that need to be asked and to establish an action plan as a way forward.

The case study introduces fourth-year undergraduates to the concepts of strategic planning at the beginning of a strategy module on a hospitality management programme. In carrying out the task, the students must act as a strategic group. A part of the feedback process focuses upon the team issues that emerge.

Students present their findings, suggestions and issues map for consideration by their peers. The discussion focuses upon:

- the problems of strategic planning;
- the impact of uncertainty on their interactions and their approach to planning;
- the interrelationship of issues identified;
- team development issues;
- the creativity-analysis mix.

THE CASE STUDY

The case study (Annex 1) presents an overview of the state of affairs in Erehwon, with particular reference to the tourism industry which is of very minor importance at the time that independence is declared, and relevant natural resources. Additional general information is provided concerning the state of affairs in Erehwon.

The students are then presented with the task of thinking about the strategic development of the industry for the benefit of the emergent state of Erehwon. At various stages throughout the process of their working together, they have a set of envelopes which they are required to open, each containing new information or reflective questions about their process.

The process

Following an initial lecture which presents an overview of strategic planning and introduces students to a strategic planning model (Pfeiffer *et al.*, 1984), they are invited to form groups and begin work on the case study immediately. Support material is provided on strategic planning tools and techniques, together with input on concepts, applications, and the difficulties of strategic planning. Considerable weight is placed upon the need for strategic thinking and discussion focuses upon what this is, the skills and capabilities required and the importance of team work to achieve appropriate inputs for the strategic planning and management effort.

The group sessions

Working in groups, students are required to think about producing a strategic plan for developing tourism in Erehwon; in particular, they should identify:

- the key questions they need to ask;
- the assumptions that need to be made;
- the areas that require creative thinking compared to those that can be analysed.

It is envisaged that they will work together in blocks of three hours (three blocks in total before the plenary) over a period of two weeks. The time outside group activity should be used to research aspects of tourism development and strategic planning.

This exercise takes up the first three weeks of the module and is concerned with principles and concepts of strategic planning as a whole. It is their first encounter with strategy and is the final core module of a four-year programme. Students spend their third year on placement, usually overseas, and they are encouraged to draw upon aspects of this experience in tackling the Erehwon case study.

The feedback session

At the plenary, each group must make a presentation on their approach to the problem, indicating:

- key questions;
- outline strategic plan;
- mission statement for the State Tourism Office;
- outline of the initial market strategy.

Following the presentation, each group will be required to answer questions concerning the material presented, the rationale and assumptions behind it and the implications that they think it has for the development of Erehwon.

Additional questions will be concerned with:

- the group process and the difficulties in trying to establish a strategic focus;
- the assumptions that needed to be made;
- the difficulties and necessity of mixing creative and analytical thinking in order to produce the level of strategic thinking necessary;
- gaps in knowledge, skills and confidence.

The final part of the discussion is focused upon the key question: where do we go from here? The purpose of this is to seek to clarify learning needs for the rest of the course. Blocks of study following this overview phase are concerned with:

- marketing;
- finance;
- IT;
- HRM.

In the final phase of the course, students are encouraged to adopt a multidisciplinary approach to their study of strategic hospitality management.

THE LEARNING MODEL

The approach is based upon a reflective problem-solving model, and draws on the work of Kolb (1984) and Revans (1980) for its conceptual base. A reflective problem-solving model seemed to offer possibilities of integrating skills development and critical thinking, rather than viewing them as parallel learning paths that had to be developed (at times, as separate entities) as part of the new demands within teaching and learning policies. A criticism often levelled against problem-solving approaches is that they are essentially pragmatic and therefore tend to be weak in the area of conceptualisation and critical thinking beyond the conceptual model of problem-solving itself. The strong emphasis on reflection and exploring assumptions (models of the world) seeks to mitigate this.

The model encourages problem exploration, in the first instance, in part as a means of understanding the problem *per se* and in part as a means of identifying the range of issues. By extension, this leads to an early formulation of the conceptual areas involved within the learning arena suggested by the problem. Further examination extends into two directions: the analytical (and, therefore, critical analysis and conceptualization) and the exploratory (a consideration of broader issues through generative or creative thinking). This latter process involves investigation of connections between aspects of the problem, related concepts and implications for any proposed solution. It is, essentially, an iterative process. In this way, the boundaries of the problem are tested and clarified in preparation for the generation of solutions. The conclusion of the problem-solving task follows. However, it is important to ensure that opportunities for reflection on both the problem-solving task and the learning process are included to ensure learning occurs. There are challenges here to the ideology underpinning teaching and to the structuring of it. In particular, the following seem to me to be important:

■ Perceptual repertoire affects analytical capability – thus, an uneasy combination of challenging existing maps of the world and of patience is required.
■ Argument is limited by mutual acceptance of a paradigm; exploration goes beyond it – thus, one will frequently draw upon meta-models to clarify meaning.
■ Thinking modes can be represented by an analytical metaphor or by a design metaphor; the latter invites consideration and tolerance of ambiguity.

The model is outlined in Figure 11.1.

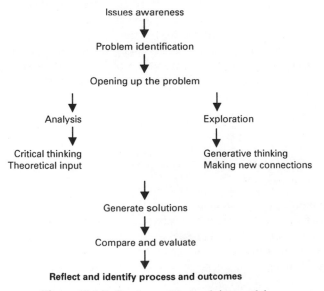

Figure 11.1 Reflective problem-solving model

Students are requested to behave as a consultancy team charged with the strategic planning task for Erehwon's tourism development.

Reflecting an adaptation of the action learning model (Revans, 1980) and, to an extent, the Kolb learning cycle (Kolb, 1984), students are pushed into an interactive problem-solving exercise with limited theoretical knowledge together with the case material, and instructed to develop an action plan for the state of Erehwon.

Up to this point in their studies, students have done little, if any, work on strategic management and so immediate input is necessary. This input focuses on:

- strategic planning concepts;
- a planning model;
- relevant tools and techniques;
- difficulties associated with strategic planning;
- strategic thinking.

Discussion is largely focused on the demands of strategic thinking, together with some clarification of the concepts and techniques.

Students are then given the experiential exercise to complete in teams in the following two weeks. Team selection is made by the students themselves, based upon prior knowledge and associations. Although the students are not made aware of the Kolb learning cycle during the input phase, they are introduced to it as part of the plenary phase in an effort to help them to develop a model of what was taking place in the groups. They are also encouraged, at this stage, to re-examine earlier work on group dynamics, notably work on group development (Tuckman and Jensen, 1977).

Parallels are drawn between the demands of developing strategic thinking and the learning process. Thus, aspects of the discussion provide comment on mental models and changing patterns of thinking to accommodate new concepts and new forms of action (Kostere and Malatesta, 1990; Zuber-Skerritt, 1992).

This early introduction of experiential learning proves to be quite challenging and a number of students express their concerns about their capability. Interestingly, most of the students have just returned from a year's placement when they are introduced to the module. In consequence, many of their concerns are linked to their practical experience, with responses such as:

- denial of their own ability;
- claims of insufficient experience;
- lack of knowledge 'at that level of the industry';
- a degree of uncertainty and confusion as they try to relate placement experiences to the simulation.

The group meetings are conducted among the student groups without the presence of a tutor to facilitate. However, there are two opportunities during the study period to meet with the tutor to discuss problems and issues arising and to seek clarification of the material provided in the envelopes, which simulate shifts in circumstances over time. These facilitative meetings are an adaptation of the action learning set model and the role of facilitator as defined by Revans and others.

THE STRATEGIC PLANNING MODEL

The model adopted is that developed by Pfeiffer *et al.* (1984). The model was chosen for its widespread acceptability and for its applicability to both private and public sector organizations. In addition, it is useful because it accepts as fundamental the need to consider the importance of organizational values, an issue which the groups were encouraged to take into account by examining their own values, the values they encountered during placement and the problems of identifying and coming to terms with potentially conflicting values within the case study. The model also emphasizes the need to examine environmental factors as an ongoing aspect of strategic planning and review. Aspects of the model had to be played down at this stage because of the technical demands they created; most notably, performance audit and gap analysis presented difficulties which the students could not be expected to tackle at this stage. Even so, the model provides a good overview of the strategic planning process and students are thus very aware of those areas that have to be skirted over or omitted. Developing an approach which is an approximation of the model seemed to me to be quite acceptable on the grounds that, from my own experience, organizations tackling strategic planing for the first time operate along iterative lines, moving more closely and accurately to a truer reflection of the model that they adopt.

LEARNING OUTCOMES

The learning outcomes that are recognizable in the short term are:

- identification of the problems of strategic planning;
- experience of the impact of uncertainty;
- analysis of the interrelationship of issues;
- recognition of team development issues;
- examination of the creativity–analysis mix.

Others are signalled by students as they progress further into the module on strategic management. These include:

- a shift in their thinking, which is often difficult to articulate but which is concerned with the need to take account of wider issues as well as both to acknowledge and challenge theory;
- a greater sense of pragmatism;
- greater confidence;
- acknowledgement of the need for creative thinking alongside analysis.

DISCUSSION

Many students spend a lot of time in the early phases of learning an academic discipline trying to discover how to learn it and what the expectations of the tutor are, in terms of interaction and understanding. Following the interactions and plenary relating to the case study, an explicit statement of some propositions and some room for both exploration and negotiation seem to be in order. It is useful to articulate these through group discussion, drawing upon the experiences of the exercise. Inevitably, some students recognize the emergence of some of these and struggle with others. In particular, the value of those omitted by them is sometimes questioned, not least for their practicability in working life following graduation. A useful but by no means exhaustive list would include the following propositions concerning learning:

■ Problem-solving offers an initial perspective for all students tackling a new subject.
■ Critical thinking is another skill.
■ Problem-solving itself is a complex mix of skills and functions at different levels.
■ Levels of abstraction and conceptualization will vary between students and this is acceptable.
■ Levels of problem-solving equate with levels of learning.
■ Learning styles are an important part of the interaction and are context-bound.
■ Learning is not just a cognitive activity.
■ Students arrive with many of the core skills; the task is development.
■ Within the problem framework all learning is valuable.

Implicitly, these propositions and the use of a problem-solving approach suggest conditions for effective learning.

The notion of a learning milieu has gained ground over the last decade. In many organizations this notion is developing credence, especially as they explore the value of moving towards being a learning organization, itself a strategic development. The sense of what that is, is suggested below:

■ Relationship (trust, empathy, unconditional positive regard).
■ Dialogue.
■ Reflection.
■ Opportunities for self-examination.
■ Sharing and examining cognitive maps.
■ Feedback.

The value of exploring such issues and their relevance both conceptually and in practice is at least as great as the explicit learning outcomes concerning strategic planning.

Tutors and students work in partnership and share their models of the world and of learning about the world as part of the process. These maps will, after all, be called into question as the relationship progresses and more ground is covered. Old questions may well be revisited as part of the process, as both students and tutors are challenged in their understandings and beliefs.

ANNEX 1: THE CASE STUDY

TOURISM IN EREHWON

Background information

Population
24,678,492.

Geography
Bordered on three sides by other states, including Erehwesle, from which it has just split, in the south and Nabisa in the Northwest, which has a seven year history of political unrest and military activity. The western edge is an incredibly beautiful elongated coastline, dramatically rocky in the north with attractive sandy beaches in the south. There has been no development of the coastal region and even the farming has been on a smallholding basis. The lack of development has been due to the lack of piped water along the coast and the reluctance of the government of Erehwesle to spend money on the infrastructure of the region. Over half of the coastline is the habitat of some of the world's most unusual seabirds and marine life and is of special interest to conservationists; indeed, the University of Central Lancashire has a conservation centre and laboratory on the outskirts of one of the coastal towns. Much of the countryside is pleasant farmland with some interesting villages; the mountains in the east are picturesque rather than spectacular.

The capital, Sivad, has a Jewish quarter dating back 400 years and famed for its architectural interest and its cultural and artistic activity. Situated in the Northeast, it is also the base for the international airport. It has a population of four million.

Niwde is the main sea-board centre and, indeed, the only port, with a population of 2.5 million. Its shipping businesses declined rapidly in the 1950s and then levelled out as it became a key traffic centre for landlocked Eastern states in the '70s and '80s that were beginning to develop new trading links with the West.

Economy
Mixed but with a strong rural emphasis.

Industry & commerce
Mostly agricultural, some mining although this is dying out. It is thought that there may be an off-shore oil field but there has been no serious exploration and interest from the oil giants has been mild, to say the least. Historically, the country was a major trading nation in dyes, semi-precious stones and marble. Presently, these have no importance economically although they do attract passing interest from tourists looking to get off the beaten track. Tourism as an industry is totally unimportant despite the numerous natural attractions and temperate summers and autumns. Only a trickle of visitors have ever made Erehwon their final holiday destination and few use it as a stopover point on the way to points further east.

GNP
Erehwon is in the lowest 25% in the world's league table.

National debt
It has the third highest debt in Europe and the World Bank is anxiously observing the effects of independence on the country's future. The new government is being closely watched with regard to its handling of the country's economic and political development.

Political stability
Erehwon is a breakaway state from Erehwesle, having gained its independence in what political pundits are describing as the most peaceful revolution in world history. In fact, there was no revolution; in the redefining process that has characterised the politics of Eastern Europe in the last few years, Czechoslovakia and Erehwesle have managed the process peacefully and constructively. Others have been less fortunate.

The government of Erehwon is a coalition; amongst the Western powers it has been described as left of centre. Its primary concern is to ensure that the economy does not suffer now that it no longer has the support offered by the industrial base of Erehwesle; opportunities are being sought to develop the economy in ways that both protect and reflect the culture, history and traditions of its people. At the same time there is a recognition that the country must now stand on its own feet in a modern world that almost passed Erehwon by. There is a mood of cautious optimism and people are getting used to the fact that they are no longer dominated by a majority from their neighbouring state.

The fact that the new prime minister is a university professor and national poet has not added to the country's immediate credibility overseas. However, he is overwhelmingly popular with the people and his liberal views have been received with excitement and anticipation.

Communications
It is well linked to other Eastern European countries via good rail networks, reasonable roads and an adequate airline service. It is also linked to the Far East and, indeed, the capital's airport is a stop-over point for major airlines refuelling on far eastern routes. While the road network and standards of driving surface are adequate rather than good, the volume of traffic is not problematic so the system works well.

All public utilities have remained functioning following independence, with the exception of radio and television. Programming was an offshoot of the Erehwesle network and so stations in Erehwon were staffed only by technicians and a handful of presenters who have now returned to their native state. On independence day, therefore, the radio and television station effectively closed down. The technicians are able to broadcast a very limited diet of Australian soap operas and satellite programmes for about six hours per day. Three national newspapers are the only source of communication at the moment.

Education
Until the break away from Erehwesle the universities and schools were dominated by academics from the neighbouring state. Independence has seen the withdrawal from Erehwon's two universities of 25% of its academics; the number of school-

teachers has been depleted by 15%. This is a major crisis. An additional problem is that Erehwesle has initiated a plan for the gradual withdrawal of its financial support for these institutions over the next ten years; Erehwon is already faced with finding 30% of its education budget compared to previous years' figures of 20%.

Training and development is well established in Erehwon but is focused upon its traditional industries and electronics. There is a newly established Ministry for Educational Development but most of its efforts are being concentrated upon support for the schools and universities because of the crisis there.

The brief

Introduction
It is now just a year since the declaration of independence. The government is deeply aware that the lack of effective television services was a national crisis and dealt with it immediately. Reinstatement of these services was seen as a pre-requisite for dealing with a number of the other key issues, including educational and economic problems. Transport systems have been tackled efficiently and networks are operating reasonably well. Western business leaders are finding their way to the country on exploratory missions and commenting favourably on accessibility, if less so on the standard of accommodation and leisure activities available.

The task
You are required to outline a strategic plan for developing the national tourist industry. Much of your plan will inevitably be *in the form of questions* to be answered at this stage but it is important to be able to identify the right questions to ask. Many of these questions will be concerned with government policy, particularly in relation to broader economic, developmental, educational and training issues. Nevertheless, these questions are an important starting point in developing any strategic plans.

You should write a mission for the State Tourism Office, for whom you are providing advice and guidance to reflect the role that it will play in the forthcoming development of the country.

You should also prepare an outline of your first market strategy to demonstrate how you are going to raise awareness and begin the revitalisation of the industry in a way that reflects the country's needs and interests.

Work schedule
The task should be approached in three blocks of group work:

■ session one 3 hours.
■ session two 4 hours.
■ session three 3 hours.

Total time spent: 10 hours
Each of the accompanying envelopes should be opened at the time indicated. They contain review questions or additional information that you should now take account of in developing your strategic approach.

Envelope 1: To be opened after working together for three hours

Individually and then collectively consider how effective you have been as a group.
Spend 30–40 minutes sharing your views on this.

Key questions:

- Has a leader emerged?
- If so, on what basis?
- How and why have roles been assigned?
- Are there alliances forming?
- Are they productive and helpful?
- How has conflict been handled?
- What does the group need now to develop a successful outcome?

Envelope 2: To be opened after working together for another two hours

More problems have emerged which you need to take into consideration. The World
Bank is less than happy about the lack of modernization in the country and a perceived
lack of initiative. The prime minister has received reports that the bank is considering
stopping all further loans to Erehwon as a result of its declining confidence in the
country's ability to revitalize itself.

The tourism initiative is likely to need significant loans to succeed in its plans.
Information discovered from research indicates that:

- business visitors are finding the country attractive as a meeting point for
  representatives from other East European states, because of its central location
  and political stability, with Savid attracting a growing number of delegations
- leisure trips to the coast are beginning to prove popular with those visitors who
  are spending some time in the country
- most visitors are still only staying for less than a week
- the domestic market is extremely limited with many people unaware of the
  attractions of their own country within a leisure and tourism framework
- almost a third of the homes in Erehwon do not have a TV set.

Taxation is already high and so is inflation.

Envelope 3: To be opened after working together for another three hours

Chumrod International Leisure has approached you with an offer of considerable
funding in return for a 30% stake in the development of a hotel chain and control
over 80% of the management. They have an international reputation for providing
rapid turnover package holidays and developing holiday resorts to a highly commercial level. Their approach is highly standardized and focuses upon the 'get away from
it all' holiday. Their commitment to local culture in the past has been largely
cosmetic. Indeed, some resorts that have been developed under their influence in
Southeast Asia have been the target for pressure groups, who have resented the loss

of identity accompanying development. Their representatives have said that they will change their policies to meet the needs of Erehwon.

Both Piphill Electronics and Syon Electrics, two international electronics companies, have expressed an interest in providing low cost TV sets in return for an interest in the technical development of the network and possibly later in its programming development.

Envelope 4: To be opened at the end of the ten hours working together

You should spend an additional 30–40 minutes discussing the following:

- What are the limitations of your strategic plan?
- What would you need to develop it further?
- Where do you think its weaknesses are?
- What are the critical success factors for the plan?
- Where are the key risk areas?
- How do you feel about the plan and about the team's effectiveness?

REFERENCES

Kolb, D (1984) *Experiential Learning: Experiences as the source of learning and development*, Prentice-Hall, New Jersey.

Kostere, K and Malatesta, L (1990) *Maps, Models and the Structure of Reality*, Metamorphous Press, Portland, OR.

Pfeiffer, J W, Goodstein, L D and Nolan, T M (1984) *Applied Strategic Planning – A how to do it guide*, University Associates, San Diego, CA.

Revans, R (1980) *Action Learning – New techniques for management*, Blond and Briggs, London.

Tuckman, B and Jensen, N (1977) 'Stages of small group development revisited', *Group and Organisational Studies*, **2**.

Zuber-Skerritt, O (1992) *Professional Development in Higher Education*, Kogan Page, London.

ABOUT THE AUTHOR

Mac McCarthy works at the University of Central Lancashire and as an independent management consultant, in the areas of strategic change, team development and creative problem-solving. He has many years' experience of using student/client-centred approaches to teaching and learning through problem-solving methodologies, and is currently researching into accelerated learning.

Address for correspondence: Mac McCarthy, Dept of Hospitality and Tourism, University of Central Lancashire, Preston, Lancashire. Tel: 01772 893900.

Chapter 12

Educational technology in the making of a crop pest management game

Scott Miller

ABSTRACT

The Centre for CBL in Land Use and Environmental Sciences (CLUES) has found that a systematic method is vital for the production of good computer-assisted learning (CAL) courseware. The development protocol for courseware at CLUES provides a series of discrete stages. The conclusions drawn following evaluation of one stage are used to improve the next iteration of the courseware. As the process continues, the package steadily approaches the goal – of achieving the desired learning outcomes when embedded within a course. This systematic approach to CAL courseware development follows the work of Rowntree (1982). The development of the CLUES module BEET is described as an example of this process.

'BEET – *a crop pest and disease management game*' is a CAL module presented as a simulation game. A simulation was adopted because it is the only way to provide students with an alternative to the kind of experience that they can acquire through the practical management of a beet crop. A comprehensive manual accompanies the CAL module. It provides advice on how to use BEET in a course, explains the underlying model, and details successful playing strategies.

INTRODUCTION

At the Centre for Computer Based Learning in Land Use and Environmental Science (CLUES) the development protocol for computer-assisted learning (CAL) courseware follows a series of discrete stages. Formative evaluation improves the next stage of the courseware. This approach to CAL development follows the concept of 'educational technology' as outlined by Rowntree (1982). The lessons learnt will help others to develop effective CAL courseware.

This chapter outlines the CLUES protocol for courseware development, and demonstrates how a systematic methodology forms a crucial role in the development of educationally effective CAL courseware.

An overview of the CAL module, BEET

BEET is a simulation game in which players manage a 40 ha sugar beet enterprise on a 120 ha arable farm. Sugar beet is one component of a three-year crop rotation. Players are responsible for managing the beet crop over a simulated 15-year period. The other components of the rotation are cereal crops and these are managed by the program, without action from the player.

The main educational aim of this package is to provide students with the experience of crop protection. It gives students the opportunity to learn from mistakes which would be very costly in the real world. While the focus is sugar beet, it teaches principles of crop protection that can be applied in other crops. The game is played with one of two aims. Players must either *maximize profit* or *minimize the impact of pesticide use*. In playing the game the participants must develop strategies for meeting the set objective. Playing with these different objectives demonstrates how crop protection decisions are influenced by a particular farmer's objectives.

BEET is a Windows™ CAL courseware module. The development of the current version of BEET was funded by the UK higher education funding bodies under their Teaching and Learning Technology Programme (TLTP). The academic concept for BEET and the original DOS-based program was developed by John Mumford at the Centre for Environmental Technology at Imperial College. Subsequently it has been developed for the Windows environment by Mumford and Miller (1996).

Rowntree's 'educational technology approach' to curriculum development

Rowntree (1982) describes a systematic process of curriculum development. The process is cyclical, with a number of stages. Figure 12.1 is adapted from Rowntree (1982) and shows four phases in the cycle, with feedback loops involved. These are ringed by the constraints of the real world.

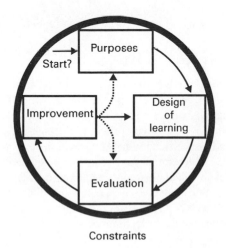

Constraints

Figure 12.1 The four phases of the curriculum development cycle

The four phases repeated constantly throughout the lifetime of the curriculum development process are:

1. *Purposes*. This is an analysis phase where the needs of the user are addressed, and the purpose of the curricula is stated in terms of aims and objectives.
2. *Design of learning*. The means of achieving the desired purpose are drafted and implemented in a form that allows evaluation.
3. *Evaluation*. The curriculum is tested to determine if it meets the stated purpose.
4. *Improvement*. The results of the evaluation are used to improve the design of learning so that it meets the stated purpose better. The aims and objectives or evaluation techniques may also be refined if necessary.

The 'improvement' box is linked to 'purposes' and 'evaluation' by a dotted line, because while these can be refined, the ultimate goal is to improve the 'design of learning'. While the aims of the course are usually the starting point, it may be necessary to start at another point in the cycle, for example when reviewing an existing course. If this methodology is adopted it should ensure that no aspect of the process of curriculum design and implementation is haphazard.

Rowntree uses the term 'educational technology' to describe the technology *of* education, but there is also technology *in* education, such as the use of computers and audio-visual aids. CAL is one example of technology *in* education, but CAL is ineffective unless the technology *of* education is addressed properly.

THE DEVELOPMENT PROTOCOL AT CLUES

The development protocol mirrors Rowntree's cycle, with the following stages:

1. Determine the purpose of the CAL material.
2. Design the learning material.
3. Evaluate.
4. Improve the CAL material based upon the evaluation results.

Purposes – analyse user needs

At CLUES the educational needs of the student are addressed by a group of academics from the subject area. This expert group is aware of the difficulties students have with the curriculum, and they meet with the CAL developer to discuss whether CAL can help their students. For team development projects at CLUES, the CAL courseware developers attend a specification meeting with the expert group to discuss the instructional design and to determine the purpose of their curriculum. Lecturers need to identify educational aims and objectives and examine the teaching resources that are currently available. For models used in education, they focus on what tasks the students will need to undertake with the model to achieve these objectives. This leads to a more detailed analysis of the tasks that the user will carry out with the software.

Design – draft screen designs

Once the tasks to be carried out with the application have been clarified, the designer must think about how they will be implemented in the software. Again, potential users of the software are consulted about these ideas. At this stage, it may be useful to make sketches on paper of the alternative screen designs to help reach agreement on the most suitable designs. This is analogous to 'storyboarding' in filming. The best ideas are retained and the others discarded.

Software development – design, evaluate and improve

The design of the software goes through several versions before it is acceptable to the end-users. These versions are described below.

- The *prototype* is the software implementation of the draft screen designs. It has little or no functionality and is typically a rapid development. The first prototype may be a fairly rough version with only a partial interface. The prototype is tested by observing the group of academic authors interacting with the software and by soliciting their views on the interface. The design of the interface is revised as a result of this user feedback.
- The *alpha* version of the program is 'in development' and is circulated to expert group members for comment. The interface is nearly complete, and there is substantial functionality. The expert group evaluates the usability and its effectiveness with a selected test group of students. The results of the evaluation help to improve the design of both the interface and the educational content.
- The *beta* version has a complete implementation of the interface and nearly complete implementation of the functionality. The Beta version is distributed within the academic authors' group and to specific evaluation sites. This is the first time evaluators external to the project are involved in the evaluation.
- The *pre-release* version has all the functionality and interface completed to a specification agreed by the expert group. It is tested at specific evaluation sites. The purpose of this version is to trap finally any usability problems or bugs.

Version 1.0 is for release outside the expert group. The package is ready for re-testing as Version 1.0 after all the changes to the interface and functionality indicated by the post-evaluation feedback have been implemented. *Version 1.0a* consists of specific adaptations of Version 1.0 for individual sites within the expert group. *Version 1.1* has any bugs fixed and may have some minor changes to functionality. *Version 2.0* is a major change to the interface or functionality.

The CLUES software development process consists of a number of steps that must be completed before a piece of software is released. The progression from one step to the next involves evaluation feedback and the overall development forms an iterative cycle. There are five stages in the software life cycle (draft, prototype, alpha, beta, and pre-release) before Version 1.0 of the CAL courseware is first released for general circulation, so there is ample opportunity for staff and students to influence the design.

Develop supporting materials – using the same cycle of development

Software is only one part of the package in computer-assisted learning. Other media may be required to complete the learning experience. The other media, such as relevant background information, overhead projection slides and student workbooks, are presented in the lecturer's manual that accompanies the software. It also contains advice about how to embed the package in teaching.

A first draft of the manual usually accompanies the beta version of the software. Revisions from the expert group's comments are included in the version that goes out with the pre-release version of the software. Any refinements suggested by the pre-release reviewers are included in the version that goes out with Version 1.0.

DETERMINING THE PURPOSE OF THE BEET CAL MODULE – ANALYSING USER NEEDS

Content analysis

CLUES assembled an expert group of four academics who teach crop pest management. They reviewed available resources and determined that there was a need for CAL in their subject area. One item they reviewed was a DOS version of BEET used only at Imperial College. They agreed that the game format was worth building upon. CLUES and the expert group evaluated the version of the game and a specification meeting was held to determine the content of the new version. Each expert contributed some material and verified the content of the new version.

Who will use BEET?

BEET is extremely flexible. It can be used from basic introductory courses to advanced postgraduate teaching. The game can be run with students from a range of course subjects; for example, agronomy, applied ecology and crop protection. BEET has been used with expert sugar beet farmers, and with students who had a very limited understanding of crop pest and disease management. Much attention was given to making the game easy to use, because there is potential for a wide range of users. The game is simple enough to use with secondary-level school children, but can raise issues sufficiently complex to stimulate discussion at a postgraduate level. The debriefing session held after playing the game should focus on the experience and needs of those present. Lecturers using BEET receive support and advice in the documentation because the debriefing session is so important.

A game format is used because it proves effective in presenting the problems of crop pest management in an interesting manner, and motivates the students to learn.

Considering the aims

There is a hierarchy of aims to be considered:

1. Aims of the TLTP programme.
2. Objectives of TLTP-CLUES.
3. Aims and objectives of the individual CAL module.

Items 1 and 2 set the context in which the courseware has been developed.

1. The principle aim of TLTP was to make 'teaching and learning more productive and efficient by harnessing modern technology'.
2. To meet the aims of TLTP, two of CLUES objectives were:
    ■ *Objective 1* – to specify, develop, pilot and evaluate a library of CAL courseware modules that will increase the resource efficiency of teaching and enhance student learning in land use subjects.
    ■ *Objective 2* – to ensure that, through shared needs analysis and CAL courseware specification, the modules meet the criteria of resource efficiency, general utility and transportability across higher education institutions in the UK.

Aims and objectives for BEET
The expert group, which was sourced from different institutions, agreed the aims and objectives, and many institutions were involved with the development and evaluation of the courseware. This should avoid the 'not invented here' syndrome that has prevented other CAL from being used widely.

BEET is one package from the library of CAL courseware produced by TLTP-CLUES. To increase uptake of the modules it is assumed that it would be better to focus on discrete topics (lessonware) than produce one all-encompassing package. CLUES has based its strategy around the lessonware concept because:

■ the lessonware approach is much easier to incorporate into existing courses because where there are a number of CAL products that cover similar areas, a site may choose from these to enhance their provision;
■ discrete CAL modules that focus on small areas allow different institutions to teach the material in the order and emphasis of their choice, and thus preserve their individuality;
■ CAL that is easy to embed in existing courses should be transportable to new institutions readily. This will also alleviate the 'not invented here' syndrome.

Students work in small groups and learn from their peers. This helps to teach larger numbers of students more effectively.
BEET aims to:

■ teach about sugar beet pests (insect and disease) and their control;
■ demonstrate the stochastic element present in pest management;
■ show the limited information available to decision makers;
■ demonstrate the decision-making problems that farmers face in pest management;
■ teach about the risks and economic consequences of decision making;
■ encourage students to explore pest management strategy and develop a strategy to meet farmers' objectives.

When writing a CAL module that only presents educational content, the learning objectives are agreed with the subject expert who is preparing the content for that section. These are presented to the student in opening screens that say, 'When you have concluded this section you should be able to…'. This contrasts with a simulation where example learning objectives are provided in the documentation and the lecturer can decide the specific objectives for his or her lesson.

BEET will enable a student to develop a cost-effective strategy for the control of a pest in a crop. The recommended learning objectives for BEET are that the learner should:

- appreciate the importance of weather in any control decision;
- adjust their spray strategy according to the type of pesticide used;
- appreciate the importance of pesticide resistance and how to avoid it;
- calculate the cost : benefit ratio of a given control action.

Skills, knowledge and attitudes required for entry to the learning experience

Skills
The site using the CAL package is responsible for ensuring that the students have the necessary computing skills. It is assumed that students have the basic skills required to switch on the computer, use Windows, locate the software and use the mouse successfully. A checklist of required computing skills is in the documentation.

Prerequisite knowledge
The prerequisite subject knowledge required to begin using a CAL module is decided at the specification meeting. At this meeting, they have to fill in a document titled 'Specification of a TLTP-CLUES Module' (Young and Heath 1992) which helps to define the aims, objectives, learning outcomes and prerequisite knowledge of the module.

A simulation allows for multiple levels of ability, so the degree of interpretation can vary and its use is flexible. The simulation BEET has been used with school-children and postgraduates; both sets used the simulation in the same way, but the discussion after the game would obviously be very different. If there are very different levels of ability in the same class then it may be advisable to hold a remedial session for those who need it before using a CAL package.

Before playing BEET, students should have some knowledge and understanding of the following:

- probability and uncertainty;
- risk and uncertainty in crop management;
- management and biology of sugar beet;
- models and modelling;
- limitations of models;
- general epidemiology of plant diseases;
- cost-benefit analysis;
- COSHH regulations.

Although lecturers in crop pest management may be expert in their field, they may not know much about the specific crop of sugar beet. The lecturer's manual contains information about the crop to help such a lecturer, and any lecturer may wish to copy and distribute this to the students before running the game.

Attitude of the students
The students should be comfortable working with computers. Some are technophobic, as are their lecturers. If the lecturer running the course is uncomfortable with computers he or she can project this unease to the students, and cause them to do badly.

A degree of maturity is needed to use CAL, since the students are taking more responsibility for their learning. The dedicated ones will stay and work, while some will just skip over the material and leave. The best CAL packages are fun to use and motivate the students to persist.

Is software appropriate in this teaching context?

To determine whether the use of software is appropriate, it helps to ask: what is the advantage of using software rather than another medium in this case?

Other media such as books and films provide factual information, but do not allow:

- the user to make decisions;
- experimentation of the type offered by the replay option that allows students to re-run a particular year;
- the facility to review previous choices, which may affect current decisions;
- players to see the long-term effects of fluctuating pest populations and weather, from the perspective of an active participant.

Software design features include:

- an uncluttered display of crop management decisions and their effect on the crop;
- relevant information readily available to assist decision making through the context-sensitive help system;
- data files to provide information about the effects of the pesticides. As product formulas change or new products come on the market, the data files can be easily updated.

In most CAL simulations the user can experiment within the modelled system and observe the effects of varying inputs. The 'replay' facility within BEET offers similar opportunities for experimentation, but BEET differs from traditional CAL in two important ways:

1. In BEET the student is required to respond to events as they occur – as in real life decision making.
2. Decisions made in one 'year' affect all future 'years'. Students must therefore 'live' with the consequences of any decisions they make.

BEET provides experience of a type that would be hard to develop except through actual farming. It simulates the real world by making players take decisions that determine a farm's income. In effect, there is a dialogue between the player and the game. Players are able to learn by testing hypotheses and by making mistakes.

SOFTWARE DEVELOPMENT IN THE BEET CAL MODULE

This section will use BEET as a case study to demonstrate the evolution of a CAL module through Rowntree's educational technology cycle. The problems encountered and the resulting changes are documented.

The first cycle through the phases: evaluation, improvement and purposes

The development of the CLUES BEET CAL module started with an *evaluation* of an existing package. The expert group and I evaluated the DOS version of beet and identified areas for *improvement*. These were mostly to do with usability and presentation.

The *purpose* of the existing package was to help teach crop pest management to students at Imperial College. The experts decided what extensions and improvements were necessary to reach the wider audience.

Improving the design of learning – designing the new package

Choice of software tools
There were many software tools available for the new Windows version. Visual BASIC was chosen for the development tool because there was already a DOS version of BEET written in BASIC. It was hoped that portions of the code could be transferred directly to the Windows version. Unfortunately, the code had to be completely re-written because the archaic version of BASIC did not fit well with the structured programming language of Visual BASIC and the event-driven environment of Windows. The Windows environment provided a platform which was much easier to use than the previous version, enhanced graphics, and standard windows help. A feature called 'context-sensitive help' allowed specific items in the help file to be displayed in response to a click on a screen item. This enables students to receive help when they most need it.

Evaluate the look of the new design
Computer simulation models must be easy to use so that the user focuses on the model and not on manipulating the package. The interface must be easy to use if others are to benefit from the model. Guidelines and standards provide a useful framework for designing an effective interface, but to achieve good design, in practice usability testing must be an integral part of the development process (Tidball *et al.*, 1996).

Many of the usability problems in the existing DOS program could be alleviated by programming BEET to run under Windows, where it could use features of the standard windows interface. The DOS version of beet could be treated as a prototype design, but paper sketches and Windows prototypes were still needed.

The evaluation of the prototype interfaces was an informal discussion with the expert group. The screen metaphors were discussed in a number of prototypes. The 'look and feel' of the alpha version was agreed from the example interfaces exhibited.

Evaluate the output of the new design
The model's output was verified by checking a functioning Windows prototype. The prototype version of BEET's model was a straightforward port of the code to Windows. All the decisions were made by dialogue boxes and this posed a serious usability problem. In Windows, the active window has the 'focus'. The portion of the screen where the student makes choices was a modal dialogue box. (Modal means that it must be dealt with before any other action can take place, that is, it holds the focus until it is dismissed.) The main window for the game was updated by the program to display information and only had the focus long enough to do so, before another dialogue box required action. Therefore it was inactive most of the time and no menus on it could be accessed. This caused the users a lot of confusion.

I was aware of these problems and a programming solution to the problem was distant. The only goal of the prototype model was to mimic the output of the DOS version. The experts agreed that it did so, so it was a successful prototype model, even though there were obvious problems.

Continuing the software development

Alpha
The technical difficulty of the inactive main window was settled by using a programming feature known as an 'idle loop', to allow the system to respond to the user and halt the underlying sequential model. The interface was completed, with the screen metaphors of a diary, notepad, yellow band postcards and an aerial photograph of a field.

The evaluation of the alpha stage was an informal discussion with the expert group, and the corrections suggested were mostly spelling mistakes.

Beta
The chemical data were now held in separate data files that are plain text format. This allows the chemical formulations to be changed independently of the program.

The evaluation of the beta stage consisted of observation of classroom trials at one institution, and questionnaires to staff and students at three pilot institutions. The expert group provided a substantial number of revisions to the academic content, which were implemented. These were mostly to make the terminology consistent within the game, and to make the economic terminology consistent with modern farm practice.

Pre-release
In the beta version, the choice of chemical was made from a 'combo box', but this was changed to a 'list box'. A combo box allows the user to type in an entry, but a list box only allows the user to choose from a specific list. Combo boxes allow default text to be present, but if the user's typed entry did not correspond with an item

available, then the program viewed this as 'no application', which was not satisfactory.

The visual display of the virus yellows were phased in gradually, and the plants in the field grew in size throughout the season.

The evaluation of the pre-release version comprised observation of classroom use, structured interviews with lecturers and selected students, and questionnaires to lecturers and selected students. The issues raised by the evaluation were resolved for Version 1.0.

Version 1.0

The practice year was enhanced to draw the users attention to the help file – in particular the context-sensitive feature. This was because evaluation of the beta version showed that users did not know the feature was available.

The package includes evaluation forms to be completed by staff and students. Users are encouraged to provide feedback to enable the package to be improved in the future.

The supporting material

I wrote the first version of the Lecturer's Manual, using material from the expert group. The aim of the lecturer's manual is to:

- provide detailed playing instructions;
- aid the lecturer to embed BEET into a course;
- provide background information for a crop protection lecturer who is not familiar with sugar beet as a crop.

This was passed to another member of staff who reviewed it and revised it with a substantial edit. It was passed to another member of staff who made some minor revisions. Comments from staff involved with the beta and pre-release testing have helped to improve the documentation.

Summary of improvements to the original

The current version of BEET has many extensions to the previous DOS version:

- The use of an all-year model helps to set the context better than the previous version that only showed what was happening during the beet growing season.
- The new version includes a training year, which gives the students familiarity with the interface and introduces them to the game.
- The use of separate data files for chemicals allows the lecturer to set up the program with different default sets of chemicals and avoids the problem of using branded chemical names.
- Displaying a graph of the annual profits and costs allows the lecturer to see how different groups are performing and it is also valuable to students.
- In the simulation, the display of the virus yellows comes in gradually from July onwards, which is more realistic than the previous version where the yellows appeared as a dramatic once-only change

- The game has standard Windows help. This is important because users should be familiar with help and once a user knows how to use it for one package, it can be used in the same way for any other package. The help file for BEET can be used conventionally, or it can be used in a context-sensitive manner.
- It is possible to call up pages from a diary to see the previous regimen for a field.
- Crop rotation is explicit, by using a farm map that shows the field currently in use.
- A calendar shows the simulated time of year.

Possible extensions for the future

From the information gathered so far in the evaluation of Version 1.0, these are the possible future additions or enhancements to BEET:

- An option to re-start the game from a saved file if the user does not have time to complete the whole game in one session.
- Enhanced help file with more pictures of the pests and diseases.
- Inclusion of the output data in a spreadsheet style format, and a program to analyse the class results. The analysis program will process the results from different 'farms', to give the 'winners' for each strategy from each group of students. This will collect the output from the program for each set of players and find the 'best' and 'worst' examples. This would reduce the delay in the feedback session after the game and mean less work for the lecturer running the course.
- An 'undo' feature to allow the user to retract some actions.

ANALYSIS OF THE CAL DEVELOPMENT PROCESS

A systematic approach is vital to produce good CAL. When planning CAL, it is important to know the intended learning outcomes and the prerequisite knowledge. Analysing these indicates the required content and aids the design of effective CAL. The finished courseware should state the learning outcomes clearly, so that the course organizer and the students both know what they should receive from the courseware. One of the principle advantages of the educational technology approach is the setting out of aims and objectives. Ideally, the aims and objectives should be measurable in terms of student behaviour or attitude, to ensure effective curricula.

Without aims and objectives, evaluation has no reference points. Before production starts, the objectives should be clear, and an evaluation strategy chosen. Evaluation shows how well the courseware achieves the stated aims and allows it to be corrected if it is shown to be inadequate. The content in the courseware should follow directly from the aims and objectives and the material should be refined by formative evaluation as the project continues. It is only through a rigorous cycle of testing and implementation of enhancements that quality of teaching can be assured.

The scope of the aims and objectives must be broader than a focus on the assessment of students. Some would argue that by focusing too much upon the aims and objectives that are set for the lesson the teacher may miss out on something unexpected that happens spontaneously in the classroom. This is not the case with BEET because although the courseware is unchanging, the teachers use of it is not. Good teachers will be free to pick up on the spontaneity of a classroom situation.

Although CLUES can produce a series of 'plug in' courseware modules that are easy to use and academically correct, these are of little use if the course organizers do not use them effectively. There is a danger that a hard-pressed lecturer will abdicate their teaching responsibility and expect the computers to do the teaching for them. Similarly, some lecturers may feel that their jobs are threatened. I have consistently referred to CAL as 'computer-assisted learning'. This is the preferred terminology, because computers can only *assist* learning; they cannot replace the human element completely. Unless the lecturers who will use CAL courseware receive help with embedding it into their courses, it is just another teaching resource doomed to failure.

The courseware development protocol adopted at CLUES ensures that there is sufficient effort put into the accompanying documentation, and that advice on embedding the CAL is made available. Evaluation feedback is used to improve the advice. When the 'educational technology cycle' of continuous evaluation and refinement continues after the CAL is produced, it should ensure that the CAL is properly embedded into the curricula of the teaching institutions.

Improved teaching quality should be welcomed. The educational technology cycle of purpose, design, evaluation and improvement has been adopted at CLUES, because this provides CAL courseware of a proven high standard. The adoption of CLUES CAL courseware should help to raise the standard of teaching in tertiary education.

REFERENCES

Mumford, J and Miller, S (1996) *BEET – a crop pest and disease management game, Version 1.0*, MERTaL™ Courseware, Heath, S B (ed.), University of Aberdeen, Aberdeen.

Rowntree, D (1982) *Educational Technology in Curriculum Development*, Harper & Row, London.

Tidball, J F, Milne, J D and Miller, S H (1996) 'Developing the human/computer interface to facilitate the use of models', *Aspects of Applied Biology 46, Modelling in applied biology: Spatial aspects*, The Association of Applied Biologists, Wellesbourne, UK.

Young, C and Heath, S B (1992) *Specification of a TLTP-CLUES module*, Centre for CBL in Land Use and Environmental Sciences, University of Aberdeen, Aberdeen.

ABOUT THE AUTHOR

Scott Miller was the senior courseware development officer at the Centre for CBL in Land Use and Environmental Science, where he was responsible for the design and implementation of a number of CAL modules. He is now the Technology Based Learning Specialist at the University of Essex where his duties are primarily to promote the use of computer, network, audiovisual and multimedia technologies in teaching and learning across the university.

Address for correspondence: Scott Miller, Technology Based Learning Specialist, University of Essex, Wivenhoe Park, Colchester CO4 3SQ.

Chapter 13

Fun and games in operations management: Running a course with games every week?

John Bicheno

ABSTRACT

In common, it seems, with several undergraduate business courses, many students at the University of Buckingham are not initially interested in operations management. Several approaches can be adopted, ranging from 'Just do it; it's good for you!' to, 'We will show you how much fun operations can be'. Over eight years at Buckingham, operations management has evolved from the former but now attempts the latter. A prime tool, but not the only tool, for this has been games. This chapter will briefly describe the games used (including the chain game, a layout game, an MRP game, various OPT games, a JIT game, quality games, supplier partnership, and a business process re-engineering game), and mention the fun and the failures. Over the eight-year period, class sizes have increased which has made the use of games more difficult, but has led to the use of some innovations such as parallel games and computer games, which has met with mixed success. The overall experience will be evaluated. I have also run many of the same games in industry, and a comparison with the industrial experiences will be given. Generally, games seem to work better where there is a real situation to refer back to, leading to the desirability to combine games with other activities such as visits.

INTRODUCTION

The University of Buckingham is Britain's only independent university with a Royal Charter. Student fees are approximately £9,500 per year excluding accommodation. What allows Buckingham to be competitive are two main 'selling points': the two-year undergraduate degree programme (during which time students attend class for the same number of weeks as students reading a conventional three-year British degree), and small group tutorial teaching (tutorials have a maximum size of eight students). As will be appreciated, most Buckingham students come from well-off families, and see their future in finance and marketing rather than operations.

There are two common problems faced by many teachers of operations management (OM) in Britain. These are the perceptions that OM involves factory operations and that OM is a quantitative subject. Of course there is some truth in both perceptions. For the average Buckingham student this is particularly important: the vast majority do not see themselves working in factories and are probably weaker than average in quantitative ability. However, this latter shortcoming is often compensated for by the fact that many Buckingham students are the children of entrepreneurs, and come to the university with an entrepreneurial attitude. Most students have never seen the inside of a factory, and often have an image of grease, noise and boredom. Today, of course, such factories are rare; there is often considerable change, excitement and challenge. On the other hand, all students have had exposure to 'front line' service operations, for example in hotels, airlines, or restaurants but lack an appreciation of 'back office' operations and the complexities thereof. So here the requirement is to change the mindset to the realization that factories and service operations have much in common and are, if not actually fun, at least very interesting and dynamic.

Then there is a perceived problem with quantitative ability. OM has been seen by students as a subject involving considerable quantitative requirements. Indeed, this suspicion is confirmed by flicking through many current texts in OM. Teachers of OM know that today there is far less quantitative material in the average course than there was, say, 15 years ago, but students still perceive it as a quantitative subject. But in OM quantitative skill should be secondary to conceptual understanding: it is positively dangerous to calculate economic order quantities unless one understands the assumptions built into the calculation. So the problem is twofold: one, to change the preconceived notion that operations is exclusively about factories (which are dirty and boring and in which they have no intention of working, anyway), and two, to change the image of OM as being a quantitative course (which they feel uneasy if not hostile about, because of a lack of quantitative ability).

OM has been a core requirement for undergraduate business studies at the University of Buckingham for ten years. Today four courses are offered: 'Operations Management' and 'Quality Management' are required courses taken by around 80 students each, and 'Logistics' and 'Integrated Operations' are electives taken by around 20 students each. OM at Buckingham has evolved from being almost totally manufacturing-oriented some ten years ago, to an approximate equal balance between service and manufacturing today.

For several years now surveys of student opinion about OM at the beginning and end of each course have been taken. These have revealed strong negative perceptions of OM at the beginning of the course. Looking back it is clear that I used to have the attitude that 'OM is good for you, an understanding of it is vital to any manager, so just shut up and listen'. Coming from an engineering school where most students actually wanted to take courses in OM (because many saw their careers developing into this field) it was a shock to encounter the boredom if not hostility of students to the subject before it had even begun. So over the years a number of changes have taken place:

- The name has changed. Formerly the courses were known as 'Production and Operations Management', now they are simply 'Operations Management'. A similar change has taken place at many universities; the intention being to de-emphasize 'production' and to convey the message that it is one integrated field.
- The core OM course has been split into two segments: Operations Management and Quality Management. Surveys have show that students have a far more positive initial perception of Quality Management than OM. The first operations course taken by students is Quality Management, and during that course emphasis is given to the fact that operations is about products and services.
- There is far less quantitative emphasis. The choice of textbooks reflects this. Yet OM can never be non-quantitative; a good way to bring in numbers is to relate them to actual experiences through games.
- Attempts have been made to integrate OM with other courses, particularly marketing and strategy. (It is interesting to note a tendency to reverse the traditional order in which operations is taught – first general OM, followed by operations strategy – to the reverse as, for example, advocated by Professor Terry Hill of London Business School during a workshop on Manufacturing Strategy conducted for the European Operations Management Association, December, 1995.)
- And finally, the use of games and simulations. The remainder of this chapter will describe the games undertaken at Buckingham, but first a comment about case studies. Our experience with manufacturing case studies has been poor, simply because our undergraduate students find difficulty in relating to them. Service cases, however, tend to work quite well.

THE COURSES AND THE GAMES

The use of games in OM has developed over several years. Eight years ago at Buckingham there were no games; only lectures, tutorials and some case studies. The first game used, the JIT GAME, grew out of experience of using the game in industry. It worked well in class, leading to more games being introduced. In 1995 the use of games had grown to an extent where a game, long or short, was used every week on courses I taught. (The Business School at Buckingham has grown and in 1996 not all OM courses were taught by me. I was, however, involved in running a few games for courses I did not run.) During this period, my mindset has changed from 'delivering' to 'selling' OM. This reflects the belief that OM is an essential subject for business, so students need to be motivated rather than told.

The typical OM course at Buckingham comprises a weekly lecture (of one or two hours), a weekly tutorial, and a bi-weekly seminar. Games are played in tutorial and seminar sessions, but some demonstrations and exercises take place during lectures.

An important issue is mark allocation. Buckingham has a general policy of not awarding more than 25 per cent of marks from coursework, which limits the number of games which can attract marks. Thus the games have to be sufficiently motivational in themselves. One way around this is to make reference to the games in several examination questions. But marks should not be the object; learning should be.

THE CORE OPERATIONS MANAGEMENT COURSE

The games used are as follows. They are presented in the order in which they are usually run.

The CHAIN GAME

This competitive game is used as the 'icebreaker'. The aim is to link operations with marketing and accounting and to introduce quality (particularly conformance with specification), productivity (particularly work standards), and capacity issues (particularly trade-offs in technology and bottlenecks), and to get teams working together. The game involves making paper chains with scissors, glue or a stapler. A feature is that the team size is not specified so teams must work out the optimal size themselves to fit in with the chosen technology. There is no specified length of time to make the 20 chains, but time costs 'money' and profit and customer satisfaction are the objectives. Innovation is encouraged; materials have to be supplied by the students.

The game emphasizes the integrative nature of OM: customers, accountants and marketing must all be kept happy.

The game takes an afternoon to run for a class of 60, and usually teams time each other while the lecturer is the final arbiter of quality. A debrief is held at the next class meeting; it is an opportunity to link in all the topics that will be covered in the OM courses, and to discuss the huge variation of results, leading to the realization that good OM can have a large impact on the success of an enterprise. This should lead on to discussion of the strategic issues of time, cost, quality, innovation and flexibility.

Forecasting, inventory and aggregate planning ('master planning'): the WITSIE game

Forecasting and aggregate planning are related topics that can be combined well in a simple business game lasting over much of a typical OM course. (The name of the game comes from Witwatersrand University Industrial Engineering, where the game was developed.) The aim of the game is to develop students' forecasting skills and to illustrate the trade-offs inherent in aggregate planning – namely between inventory, normal time capacity, overtime, customer service levels, and 'hiring/firing' and training costs. It takes time and cost to train a new employee and to acquire new capacity. Students are given a history of demand for a single product and information on the costs of the factors mentioned. Then, each week each student team must produce a decision on normal time production, overtime, hiring and firing, capacity, and raw material purchase. When the students' decision is handed in they are given information on the actual demand for the period. Sales and profit are calculated on a computer program run by the lecturer. Although the actual demands are initially broadly in line with forecasts, they diverge at some point. The teams do not compete for the same market, the assumption being that they are the sole supplier. The objective is profit maximization, and the skill is the optimal trade-off between the factors of production. One problem, however, is sustaining interest among all teams: those that fall behind tend to lose interest.

The game is started early on in the course, before theory has been discussed. This is deliberate. As the course progresses and the topics are discussed (the leading teams at least) pay more attention and are often at a more advanced level than the lectures. This in turn improves tutorial discussion.

Although it is essentially a manufacturing game, it is possible to change it to a service game by rewording for a fast-food operation.

Project management and critical path analysis

Two games and activities have been used here. The first involves developing a flowchart for a simple activity such as getting up in the morning, estimating times for the activities, and calculating the critical path. Although this is a simple activity, when done in groups it illustrates the diversity of possibilities and the fact that the major benefit of networks is developing them in the first place rather than calculating the critical path.

The second game is run given a particular network (usually a construction project is chosen). Each activity has estimated times and required resources. Groups are provided with notional resources and asked to plan the project. Then, week by simulated week, groups are given an update on revised activity times and available resources. This reflects the reality of changing weather, shortages and absenteeism. The winning team is the one that completes the project first. This game can be undertaken at various levels of sophistication; it is possible to use project management software to analyse the situation, but more commonly this is done by hand calculation. Teams have to prove to the lecturer that available resources are not being exceeded. The disadvantage of this type of game is that it usually requires several weeks to run: one cannot have too many simultaneous games in progress.

The OPT game

The OPT game is a commercially available computer game produced and sold by Creative Output Inc. It deals with scheduling and capacity considerations, especially as they relate to job shops. All students taking OM are expected to read the book *The Goal* by Goldratt and Cox (1984), which for those not familiar with the OM area is actually a novel as well as being the all-time bestseller in the area of production management. The OPT game gives players the opportunity to apply the OPT principles that they have learned from *The Goal*. It is a difficult game so we usually allow students to play in pairs. A considerable advantage is that the game does not require supervision and can be played in the computer room at any time. It is also addictive – one student is known to have spent over 80 hours on it.

Perhaps the OM principle that gets indelibly burned into players minds is that of the importance of bottlenecks to productivity and profit. This is a principle which also has application in service, so that once the point has been made it is easy to talk about it in other environments.

Layout game

The layout game aims to illustrate the improvement potential of layout – a central issue in service and manufacturing. The game can be played with either a service or manufacturing orientation. The competing teams begin with a 'job shop'/functional layout, first trying to make an improved functional layout, and then to create cells. Performance is measured by the length of the flowpath and by the total space occupied. Routing and volume information is provided, as well as restrictions as to departmental proximity.

The game is best played with blocks, such as Lego or more substantial pieces of wood. (A computer version is also available, but unfortunately is subject to the occasional 'crash'. In any case, the computer version emphasizes individual play rather than team play.) The layout game was developed in response to student difficulties in undertaking the quantitative CRAFT-type analysis or the analysis needed to form manufacturing cells.

An individual game takes about an hour, and is therefore playable in a tutorial session. Groups of four are possible, which means two groups per tutorial.

Material requirements planning

The MRP simulator is a computer game or exercise developed by me with assistance from a research student for use in professional seminars, and is used regularly on the 'Hands-on MRP' course run by the Institute of Operations Management. The computer program contains many of the features of a full commercial MRP system, but takes only minutes to learn to operate. The program begins with the user entering a master production schedule for two products over a ten-week horizon. In each simulated week the program performs a complete 'regeneration' making recommendations as to the actions that should be performed by the material planner. At the end of each 'week' all the events that took place during the week are presented. The planner can either go with the recommendations or make his or her own. These are entered into the system, and the cycle of regeneration is repeated.

The full range of exercises available on the MRP simulator takes about six hours to go through, so for the core OM class only a small proportion is dealt with. One problem with the simulator is that learning is maximized when progress is discussed with an instructor. The experience is that about eight terminals (or 16 students) at once is the maximum that can be handled. This is a drawback; it may well be the case that most OM teachers cannot afford to spend so much time on this topic unless it is being taught to students who are likely to actually use MRP, for example production engineers. Students learn rapidly about the advantages but also the disadvantages of MRP (which in my view is not only a good thing, but something that most OM courses tend to give too little attention to).

MRP is the core module of a full manufacturing planning and control system. I prefer to teach this topic from the inside out, beginning with MRP and expanding out to the other modules of MRPII. The good grasp that students gain of MRP from the simulator makes this a much easier task for both students and instructor.

The Buckingham JIT GAME

The Buckingham JIT GAME was developed for industrial training purposes, and was run scores of times in that setting before being tried out on students. The game can be played by six to 15 players and illustrates JIT techniques and how they work together. The game uses three products with known demand proportions but a variable sequence of demands. Products are 'manufactured' on a sequence of processes – machine, assembly, and heat treat before moving on to the warehouse. Between each ten-minute round the team decides on what changes to make from layout, set-up reduction, smaller batch sizes, small machines, rebalanced line, and quality improvement. Performance is measured by profit, delivery, inventory and lead time. When run for students, the time for the game is around two hours, but takes up to four hours in an industrial setting. Clearly the longer period is more satisfactory, but with a class of 60 split into four or five groups time and timetabling are constraints.

There is also a computer version of the JIT GAME which allows a single user to experience much of the interest (but not as much of the fun!) of the manual version. The computer version features parameter changes to vary, for instance, inventory levels and speed of working. This means that literally hundreds of different games are possible. For both industrial and student purposes, the computer version should not be run before the manual version. Occasionally we have set an assignment based on the computer version.

One interesting point is to compare the performance of various groups. Although this has not been systematically undertaken (due to continuous improvement to the game itself), in general some student groups perform better than either production managers or factory shop-floor staff. The second best group is shop-floor staff, with production managers (having preconceived notions or a traditional education?) performing worst. The implications are interesting: clear-thinking graduates are at least as good as experienced managers in the newer world of JIT!

A GAME EVERY WEEK?

The aim has been to run a game for every section of the course. Thus far this has not been achieved. What has been achieved is that OM games are in progress every week by virtue of the games such as the CHAIN GAME, the OPT GAME, the PROJECT GAME, and the WITSIE GAME which run over several weeks. In any one year not all of these will be run. This is because some games count for coursework assessment and, even with data changes, there are similarities from year to year. Communication between first- and second-year students, particularly in some groups such as the Germans or

Indians, is strong, so the second year students can act as advisers. This can be beneficial, of course, but where marks are involved there are issues of unfair advantage. In one year there were actual complaints. The result is that games that carry marks are not run every year. Of course, similar remarks could be made with other forms of assessment, for instance case studies. The ideal, however, is to run games which do not count for marks, which is the situation for the many of the games such as the Buckingham JIT GAME.

GAMES ON THE QUALITY COURSE

We now move on to the area of Quality Management. Here there is one major game and a number of short games or exercises.

The ADMISSIONS GAME

To illustrate process principles and process re-engineering, a game based on university admissions is used. The aim is to respond correctly to student applications as fast as possible. The game creates interest because all students have experienced the outputs of the process, and some have strong views. The basic round reflects the movement of forms between several departments. There is duplication, delay and invariably errors. Some 'students' are rejected when they should be accepted and vice versa. Others are lost. Most are subject to considerable delay. Players are required to draw a flowchart of the process. In the second round, simplification is allowed but no departmental changes or responsibility changes. In the final round all constraints are removed. A follow-up discussion period concludes. No student preparation is required. Three hours are needed, and the game is played early on in the course, not for marks.

The game illustrates process thinking, the use of the 'seven tools of quality', and 'Hammer's Principles' of process re-engineering (see, for example, Bicheno, 1994). A discussion on what is meant by 'quality' in service operations is a natural follow-on.

Unlike the OM course, apart from the ADMISSIONS GAME there are no longer or ongoing games. 'Games' tend to be very short, and some are demonstrations. These include:

- An exercise where students are asked to count the number of occurrences of a letter in a paragraph. Miscounts are common. This is used to illustrate the problem with inspection-based quality.
- 'Customer Laws' where groups are asked to devise the 'laws' of everyday service frustrations. For instance the 'law of the library' may be, 'The book I want is always out'. This leads into discussing ways of monitoring, measuring and improving customer satisfaction.
- The well-known old woman/young woman picture to illustrate that two people can perceive the same thing differently.
- Deming's coloured bead game to illustrate variation and to introduce Deming's 14 points.

- The use of a 'Quincunx' (a device that generates binomial distributions of marbles) which is used to conduct various live experiments in statistical process control.
- Benchmarking game. A short exercise where groups are first told to move cards to the other side of the table according to certain rules. They are then told it is possible to do the task in under ten seconds. A creative explosion results.

THE LOGISTICS COURSE

The Logistics course is an optional course taken by some 15 to 20 students. This makes the running of games much easier. Being a new course, only two games are run.

The SUPPLY CHAIN GAME

Like the JIT game, the SUPPLY CHAIN GAME was developed originally for industry. Unlike the JIT game however, running the game through student groups has led to much faster improvement than would have been possible in industry alone. Interest in supply chains has mushroomed over the past few years, a trend that is also reflected in student interest in the topic. Supply chain logistics have traditionally been closely linked with marketing, which is probably one reason why this is a popular topic among students. The Buckingham version of the SUPPLY CHAIN GAME is a modification of the classic BEER GAME developed by the Systems Dynamics group at MIT. Products are passed along from supplier to manufacturer to distributor to retailer and finally to customer. Information flows in the opposite direction. Players make decisions as to the amounts of inventory to order from the previous stage, the objective being to maximize customer service while minimizing inventory holdings. In the first round, invariably students experience the difficulty of controlling inventories and of the magnification of small changes in customer demands as they get passed down the supply chain.

The Buckingham SUPPLY CHAIN GAME is run over several rounds with students choosing the configuration of the supply chain each round. The choices include introducing JIT at the supplier and manufacturer, synchronized manufacture between supplier and manufacturer, simulated electronic data interchange (EDI), or improved communication, cross-docking, and so-called 'quick response' or 'efficient customer response' (ECR). Students can select these independently or in combination. Performance is measured on inventory levels and customer service.

The game is played by a dozen students and takes up to four hours. Usually it has to be curtailed after three hours. This poses difficulties for a class of 60 students: unless there is assistance, a single lecturer would find the time involved prohibitive. Unfortunately assistants have to be good facilitators and be experienced in the game.

The RED BLUE GAME

This long-established game makes several powerful points relating to supplier relationships, but probably the main one being that a manufacturer and their supplier should in fact be partners working against third parties rather than seeking advantage between themselves. The game is based on classic game theory and teams must simply select either a red or a blue play each round. Points are scored depending on what both sides decide. It is best to play this game for real money – say a pound per participant. The games takes a maximum of 90 minutes. Teams can get very excited and angry in this memorable game, which usually is good.

A MULTI-CHOICE QUESTION GAME

Multi-choice questions are provided in support of many OM and quality textbooks. For assessment, one has to be careful not to repeat questions so as to avoid possible hand-down advantages. For revision purposes, we use a Trivial Pursuit-type board subdivided into the main course categories. Trivial Pursuit rules are adopted with groups reading out questions to the opposing team. A small prize or bonus mark is awarded to the first team to finish. Students have found this much more interesting than going through lists of questions.

GENERAL COMMENTS

Visits as a counter to games

It is fun to play games every week, but the link with reality must be established. This is essential to counter the sceptics and the critics (for example, many economists still do not regard OM as an academic subject, and games are the 'proof'), but more important is to demonstrate that what is being learned from games has real academic and practical value.

The best way to do this, I believe, is to run visits to both manufacturing and service sites during OM courses, and to hear from practising managers and see for themselves. Buckingham has arranged regular visits to Rover Cars and to various local companies as part of the course. Unfortunately, once again, there are problems with the size of the group; 60 students is too large a group for a visit so we have failed to achieve visits for all students.

The scheduling of games

Scheduling presents one of the most difficult problems for the adoption of games. Some of the best games take two or three hours and are limited to a dozen students. We have found that running many of the games with graduate students is unsatisfactory. The time load on a lecturer can easily increase to 15–20 hours per week for a single course, which has direct implications for research activity. Fortunately, Buckingham has had a balanced policy with regard to recognition of teaching and research which has certainly encouraged the development of games. Where pressures for research are higher, a 'game every week' may not be possible except if games are themselves researched, for example for teaching effectiveness. Thus far this has not been done at Buckingham. Pressure for research is increasing at Buckingham; ways must be found to accommodate both.

Another issue is finding slots in the timetable. This has proved difficult because game groups are not necessarily the same size as tutorial groups, and may vary from game to game, so it is difficult to arrange times when all can be present. The result has been that many games have had to be scheduled in the early evening, which is not popular. This detracts from the value; an important idea is to make learning enjoyable, not to return to the old attitude of 'It's good for you, and you must do it'. One possible solution is to run courses in blocks of one or two days full time, during which time nothing else is scheduled. This has proved impractical for first-year courses, but some second-year and MSc courses have been run in this way.

EVALUATION: AN OPEN QUESTION

Have games been a success? Evidence from several sources suggests that, at least, games have improved the OM courses. Four indicators are: first, the level of student satisfaction with the OM courses has shown an upward trend, although not continuously upwards. Second, the numbers and proportion of students taking the optional advanced courses has improved, although they are still below the marketing and advertising optional courses where no games are played. Third, external examiners have occasionally remarked on the high standard of work achieved by some students in the examinations. Fourth, student surveys which monitor attitudes before and after the courses have shown reasonably steady improvement. In particular, the proportion of students who say, after the course, that they would consider a career in OM has risen from near zero to around a third of the class. Of course, none of these improvements can be attributed specifically to games. Perhaps nothing is due to games, and everything is due to, for instance, more employment pressure. A control group might give answers, but we have not been willing to experiment.

Student surveys do reveal that games are popular and appreciated. What is not clear is whether the optimal level of game playing has been achieved. There appears to be no (easy) answer. Some students have complained that the amount of time spent on the OM course is excessive, well above the level spent on other courses. The Buckingham two-year degree programme has the reputation of involving hard work, so games have been a source of approval but also of complaint. Lecturers from other fields have also complained about students taking too much time on games, and timetable disruption. Certainly there are still students at Buckingham who regard any time spent on OM to be a distraction away from 'what they came for', namely marketing and finance.

Perhaps the answer lies with longer-term retention: at alumni meetings five or so years after graduation students still remark upon what they learned, or perhaps how much fun they had, playing a particular game. For Buckingham students, that is a transformation.

REFERENCES

Bicheno, J (1994) *The Quality 50*, Picsie Books, Buckingham.
Goldratt, E and Cox, J (1984) *The Goal*, North River Press, New York.

ABOUT THE AUTHOR

John Bicheno is Reader in Operations Management at the University of Buckingham. He was formerly Associate Professor of Industrial Engineering at the University of the Witwatersrand, Johannesburg. He has particular interests in the implementation and integration of just-in-time/ lean manufacturing, quality management and team working, and has developed and used several games for practitioners and students, to this end.

Address for correspondence: School of Management, University of Buckingham, Buckingham MK18 1EG. Telephone and fax: 01280 815023; e-mail: picsie@axiom.co.uk

Chapter 14

Using multimedia to present case studies for systems analysis

Brian Farrimond, Sheila Lynch and Marti Harris

ABSTRACT

Case studies form an important and valued resource in teaching and learning, traditionally being presented as text, with the possible addition of simple role playing. The advancement of multimedia techniques provides us with the opportunity to extend this approach to teaching and learning and we propose that current paper-based case studies be transformed into interactive multimedia simulations to capture the students' imagination and consequently enrich student learning.

This chapter relates research in the development of interactive case study simulations (ICSS), together with a case study language (CSL), to enable the production of multimedia case study scenarios for students of system analysis. The goal of the interactive case study is not to teach or argue the student towards a specific goal but to provide a context in which to explore the 'real' world. The CSL environment includes a mark-up language (CSL), a scene librarian and a text editor to enable the user to create case study scenarios containing scenes, people and documents using images, video clips, sound clips and text.

Research continues at Liverpool Hope with the study of virtual reality (VR) techniques to aid in the realism of the case studies, and the addition of a knowledge-based system to add 'intelligence' to the actors in the case study. Suggested future directions for ICSS involve the use of simulations via the Internet or CD-ROM for applications in distance learning.

INTRODUCTION

It has become generally recognized that people reason or problem solve based on cases, examples and experiences, not by learning rules. Case studies have therefore become an important and valued resource in teaching and learning. The use of case studies provokes the learner to identify decisions, justify choices and evaluate the consequences of their choices.

Traditionally, case studies have been presented as text, with the possible addition of simple role playing, yet the advancement of multimedia techniques provides us with the opportunity to develop and enhance this approach to teaching and learning.

Researchers at Liverpool Hope University College have extended this method of active problem solving by investigating and applying current multimedia techniques to transform current paper-based case studies into interactive multimedia simulations, the principal aim being to capture the students' imagination and, consequently, enrich student learning.

To test this potential, work began on the development of interactive case study simulations (ICSS), together with a case study language (CSL), to enable the production of multimedia case study scenarios for students of systems analysis. An ICSS is a mouse-driven virtual world which students are able to observe, study and analyse. The ICSS environment includes a generic mark-up language (CSL), a scene librarian and a text editor. The CSL enables the creation of case study scenarios containing scenes, people and documents using images, video clips, sound clips and text. Case studies can be updated easily to incorporate new scenarios and new information.

ICSS is intended to provide a vehicle for active participation in the systems analysis, rather than the passive interpretation of text-based data. The goal of the ICSS is not to teach or argue the student towards a specific goal but provide a context in which to explore the 'real' world. The use of case studies in the form of ICSS makes the system accessible to students and gives them a better picture of the nature of real systems analysis. Students construct their own meaning by interacting with the material rather than by being taught something explicitly.

This chapter relates the development of a prototype ICSS software package, together with the generic CSL to enable the production of ICSS. The following section discusses the CSL in detail; the next section relates the creation of an ICSS scenario using the CSL. Then we detail the results of a pilot study conducted at Liverpool Hope University College among former system analysis students using a prototype version of an ICSS. Finally, we discuss how the current prototype version of ICSS may be further developed to create a professional standard software package.

THE CASE STUDY LANGUAGE

The world of an ICSS is a set of interconnected rooms which are populated by people, documents and other objects such as chairs and desks. The case study creator must specify these objects and their interactions in a precise, unambiguous manner. The student must be able to investigate this world by moving through the rooms, investigating the people, documents and other objects they meet.

Visual representation of the world of the case study is at the heart of the simulation. The use of virtual reality (VR) is currently being investigated and developed in the course of developing a professional standard software package. However, much useful experience can be gained from investigating simpler (and cheaper!) mechanisms using still images and video clips.

It was decided that the mouse was the best means for the student to interact with the simulation since it would be familiar to all students using the simulations and has a great deal of support on most platforms. The student would be expected to navigate their way through the simulation by means of mouse clicks on hotspots on the still images. The hotspot mechanism should not cause the students too much difficulty, especially since navigation by hotspots is the navigation method of choice on the World Wide Web.

Requirements

In the light of these objectives, the following set of requirements were derived for a system to create and run interactive case studies:

- a common format to specify the case study;
- tools to allow the designer to create and edit the objects (rooms, people, documents, etc) within the case study;
- a process that creates the student user interface on the target platform.

A fundamental principle was to make everything as generic as possible. This would allow the ability to add new features and port to different hardware and software platforms smoothly.

Meeting the requirements

The case study specification is a text file that can be read by all systems. The text file is written in a new mark-up language called CSL. All keywords in CSL are problem-specific as far as possible. This has a two-fold advantage:

- it hides implementation details from the non-specialist user;
- it allows different implementations to be created without changing CSL programs.

The concept of the case study scene is the basic building block of the case study. A scene consists of an image with associated hotspots. Each hotspot can be assigned a particular purpose within the CSL specification. To simplify the specification of scenes a scene librarian is provided which stores scenes in a set of scene libraries. The CSL specifications can then refer to the scene libraries.

When a case study is executed, a CSL compiler reads in the CSL specification and the appropriate scene libraries and, from them, creates an internal representation of the case study as a data structure. The user then enters the case study world via the student interface. As the user walks around the world, they are actually walking around the data structure.

The complete system is represented in the Data Flow Diagram in Figure 14.1. The components of the diagram and an example CSL file are described below.

Processes

Scenario editor
This is a simple text editor used to create CSL source files.

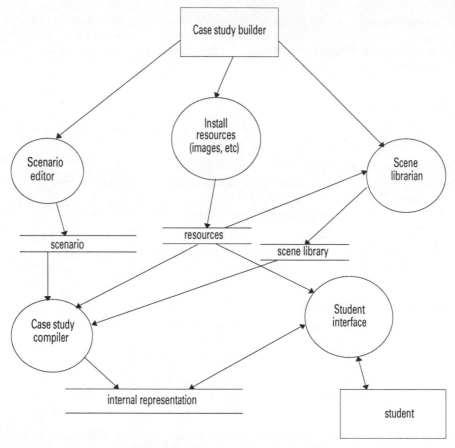

Figure 14.1 The visual case studies system

Scene librarian

The scene librarian enables the case study designer to create and edit scenes and store them in a library. A new scene is created by selecting a name for the scene, selecting an image for the scene from the resources then adding hotspots to the image. Hotspots are drawn by pressing the left mouse button down for the start corner of the box then releasing the button at the end corner of the box. The box is then drawn in on the image. Each box is saved as a numbered hotspot. The hotspots are saved in numerical order: in ascending order from the top followed by ascending order from the left. The purpose of the hotspots (ie, whether they link to other scenes, people or documents) is specified in the scenario CSL file. The libraries are stored as text files with the extension .lib.

Install resources

Resources such as images, video clips, sound clips and documents are installed on the system. The CSL scenario program uses the paths to these resources.

Case study compiler
The case study compiler reads in the CSL file and corresponding scene libraries. It then creates the internal representation to be used in the scenario run.

Student interface
The student interface launches the CSL compiler to build the internal representation. The scenario is then launched by moving to the first scene within the internal representation. It then handles the interaction between the student and the running scenario until the student exits from the scenario.

Data stores

Scenario
The scenario is a CSL text file that specifies the scenario using the scenes stored in the scene libraries.

Resources
Resources consist of the images, video clips, sound clips and documents used in the scenario which have to be installed on the disk drive available for use in the scenario.

Scene library
The scene library consists of the set of .lib files created by the scene librarian.

Internal representation
The internal representation is the data structure created by the CSL compiler from the information in the scenario and the appropriate scene libraries.

Example program

```
program itwalklb
scenelibrary\csl\demo\itoffice.lib
subtitlespeed 5
scene lindy1
        toperson lindy
        toquit
        toscene brian1
endscene
scene brian1
        toscene hod1
        toperson brian
        toback lindy1
endscene
scene hod1
        toscene hod2
        toback brian1
endscene
scene hod2
```

```
        toright rod1
        toback hod1
endscene
scene rod1
        todocument timetable
        toperson rod
        toleft hod2
        todocument invoice
endscene
person lindy
        speech video lindy1.avi lindy1.txt
endperson
person brian
        speech video brian1.avi brian1.txt
        speech sound brian2.wav brian2.txt
endperson
person rod
        speech stillvideo rod2.txt
                rod21.bmp 3
                rod22.bmp 4
                rod23.bmp 3
        endstillvideo
endperson
document timetable
        text timetab.txt
enddocument
document invoice
        image invoice.bmp
enddocument
```

Notes on the example
The first line identifies the program.

The keyword scenelibrary specifies a scene library file which contains scenes that can be referred to in the rest of the program. The keyword subtitlespeed is used to adjust the speed at which the subtitles are displayed.

The first scene is identified as *lindy1*. It has three hotspots. The first one matches the first hotspot in numerical order created in the scene librarian. It leads to the *person lindy*. The second, matching the second hotspot in numerical order, allows the user to quit. The third, matching the last hotspot in numerical order, leads to a scene named *brian1*.

Person lindy is defined below in the section beginning *person lindy*. This person consists of a speech implemented as a video clip to be shown when the corresponding hotspot in the scene is clicked. There is a corresponding subtitle file which shows subtitles as the video clip runs.

Notice that *person brian* has two speeches to make. The first is shown on the first click on the corresponding hotspot. The last is shown on all subsequent clicks on this hotspot. Generally, any number of speeches can be specified for a *person*. Each click causes the next speech in the sequence to be shown.

Speeches can be sound clips, video clips or stillvideo clips. A stillvideo clip is a speech, currently given as subtitles, which is illustrated by a sequence of images specified by name followed by a number indicating how many seconds that image is to remain on screen during the speech. An instance of a stillvideo speech specification is shown in the example for the *person rod*.

A document can be either text produced on a text editor and displayed in a text box. or an image in a picture file. In the example, timetable is an instance of the former while invoice is an instance of the latter.

As this scenario runs, the user clicks on hotspots, moving from scene to scene hearing speeches from the personalities and examining documents in the scenes. The following section details how the CSL was used to create a prototype version of an ICSS.

BUILDING AN INTERACTIVE CASE STUDY SIMULATION

The creation of an ICSS scenario may be separated into the following steps:

1. Choose a scenario.
2. Acquire raw materials.
    – actors
    – digital photographs and/or video clips
    – text, sound, and images.
3. Incorporate into the CSL.

To develop an ICSS, one must first choose a scenario that is to be simulated. For the prototype ICSS, an existing text-based scenario commonly used for our systems analysis course was adapted. In choosing a scenario, the characters within the scenarios (the employees of the company) and their respective roles must be identified. Once the general layout has been established, the multimedia material needed to reflect the system accurately must be produced. In other words, actors were needed to be filmed or photographed carrying out a number of tasks in a particular environment.

The CSL enables the incorporation of video clips, but due to insufficient hardware capabilities of the machines on which the pilot study was to be carried out, it was decided that stillvideos, in the form of digital photographs, would be used to portray the characters and their tasks in the ICSS. For this first pilot study, members from within our department were chosen to be photographed as characters in the case study. This was more difficult than may be first assumed. People were busy and not over-eager to be photographed. Once the photographs are taken, it is then necessary to transfer these to floppy disks, resized to meet the CSL specification, and incorporated into the ICSS environment. This is a time-consuming operation and may take a full day's work for each character within the scenario, with an average of 10-15 digital photographs to produce a stillvideo reflecting one task within a scenario.

It is only when the photographs are incorporated within the CSL that the quality can be judged and in some cases (especially for an inexperienced director) the photographs may be incomplete or of poor quality. Thus, more photographs need to be taken, by which time the relevant actor may have changed their clothing (as it may be the next day) or be unavailable. In addition, there was a lack of sets in which to photograph the actors. Finding rooms in which to photograph the actors was yet another time-consuming activity.

Sound clips were not used in the pilot study; again this was due to the insufficient hardware of the machines available for the pilot study. Hence, text files were used as subtitles for the characters describing their tasks and, as such, were easy to create, as were the image files used to depict documents within the simulation.

Once the raw material was developed to the required standard, it was possible to use the CSL mark-up language to create an ICSS. The mark-up language itself is commonsensical and therefore requires no previous programming experience, as can be seen in the example above. The CSL supports forward referencing and, as such, the addition of scenes, people and documents can be incorporated in a top-down fashion. For example, a scene containing a person and a number of documents may be added before the person or documents are defined. The addition of subtitle speed made aligning text and stillvideos straightforward.

The CSL is successful in its aim to be simple and generic for use by non-programmers. The greatest difficulty encountered while developing the prototype version was the lack of access to actors and sets. In addition, the general problem of artistic directorship was underestimated. A great deal of planning and organization are needed when creating a simulation; even simple case studies need a significant number of resources in the form of characters, text and image files.

RESULTS OF THE PILOT STUDY

Three pilot trials were carried out with small groups of student volunteers and a larger class of French students in June 1996. The students were asked to draw data flow diagrams (DFDs) while running an ICSS case study. The students then wrote down their comments and gave their reactions in a discussion immediately following the trials.

On examining the student DFDs, it was found that the students were generally successful in producing the required DFDs. In particular, personalities irrelevant to the flow of data were successfully ignored (which is not usually the case with paper-based case studies); valid assumptions about unexplained points were made and sink only/source only data stores were successfully spotted. No direct data store to data store data flows were used. All of these points cause difficulty for students using paper-based case studies.

The discussions and written comments showed that the students found ICSS an enjoyable experience. Personalities and visual context enhanced the case study and made it easier to make reasonable assumptions. The students also found it easier to spot discrepancies and omissions than is the case with paper-based case studies.

There were a number of criticisms. During the pilot studies, students were presented the case study without any initial guidance. Some found the student interface self-explanatory but others felt they would have been helped if they had been given instructions before starting. Navigation was fairly straightforward for most but some would have preferred to have a map available. Some wanted written summaries of the work of each department to be provided along with the ICSS! We pointed out that this was rarely available in the real world. The most important feature that the students would have liked to see was a mechanism for asking the personalities questions.

In conclusion, the results were promising in the overall aim of enhancing student learning experiences. However, it is recognized that more work needs to be done to obtain the full benefits of this innovative approach.

FUTURE DEVELOPMENT

Research continues at Liverpool Hope with the study of VR techniques to aid in the realism of the case studies, and the addition of a knowledge-based system to add 'intelligence' to the actors in the case study. Lecturers will be able to monitor student progress via a log of student decisions maintained by ICSS. Suggested future directions for ICSS involve the use of simulations via the Internet or CD-ROM for applications in distance learning.

ABOUT THE AUTHORS

Brian Farrimond, Sheila Lynch and Marti Harris are lecturers in Information Technology at Liverpool Hope University College. Brian received an MA in Physics at St Catherine's College, Oxford University and an MSc in Computer Science at Manchester University. Sheila undertook her BSc in Computer Science at Queen Mary College, University of London and is currently completing her doctorate in Knowledge Representation at the University of Liverpool. Marti received her BA from Mid-America Nazarene College (USA), an MLS in Library and Information Systems from Emporia State University (USA) and has completed all course work towards the PhD in instructional technology at the University of Oklahoma (USA).

Address for correspondence: Brian Farrimond, Sheila Lynch and Marti Harris, Liverpool Hope University College, Woolton Road, Liverpool, L16 8ND.

Chapter 15

Simulation-supported industrial training: A method for increasing the competence of people in companies

Jamie Villegas

ABSTRACT

The study conducted as part of a research project at Linköping University indicates that simulation games are useful tools for industrial training, and may probably be more effective for many purposes than other methods, particularly in complex areas such as production management. However, this research strongly indicates that the best results are achieved when simulation games are used in conjunction with other, traditional learning methods.

One of the contributions of this research project consists of the development and evaluation of a training method which helps participants to better understand their own problems at the company with the help of computer-based simulation games. The training method, SSIT – Simulation Supported Industrial Training – has the following main characteristics which make it unique:

- The simulation games are tailor-made to the participants' specific problems.
- The training is carried out directly at the work place.
- The training is based on the execution of a number of simulation games which successively illustrate the problems of the company.
- The training method combines the work on the simulation games with other traditional types of learning techniques such as theoretical instruction and group discussions.
- The training promotes not only the participants' individual learning, but also the organizational learning process.

This chapter presents the main ideas which have been used in the creation of the SSIT method and describes its main characteristics (for more detailed information see Villegas, 1996).

THE NEED FOR INDUSTRIAL TRAINING

As early as 1979, Warren (1979) made a strong statement in the preface to the first edition of his book: 'Training is no longer, like the house organ, nice to have if you can afford it. It is becoming a basic tool for increasing the effectiveness of the organisation… The organisation's problem becomes not whether to train but how'. This is supported by increasing evidence that firmly demonstrates that training has grown in importance and has become established as a vital activity in the company's life. The types of problems which companies face today are increasingly complex. The problems can vary in intensity and magnitude, but most of them can be classified in one of the following main groups:

- rapid changes in the market,
- strong competition,
- lack of qualified new employees with the necessary skills,
- constant development in the company requiring additional training of the company's staff,
- introduction of new products, and
- rapidly changing technologies.

According to recent reports, companies are not only trying to work out new policies which might allow them to increase productivity, the level of flexibility and their standards of quality, they are also attempting to empower the employees at the company. (This has been indicated as one of the most cost-effective alternatives; see for example, Churchill, 1990; Gross, 1993; Kofman and Senge, 1993; Toffler, 1985.) However, for employees at different levels in the company to be able to make the right decisions, they will require to be competent and undertake training. This conclusion in also reinforced by De Meyer's (1993) survey in 1992, which has indicated that among the ten most important future actions planned by European companies four of them were related to training aspects, namely: worker empowerment, interfunctional work teams, supervisor training and management training.

Consequently, what companies need today are good training tools and methods which help them to succeed with training projects. According to many recent academic and scientific reports, one of the ways companies are attempting to achieve this is by using computer-based simulation techniques as a support in their existing training projects (see Anderson, 1994; Fripp, 1993; Goldstein, 1992; Senge, 1990).

COMPUTER-BASED SIMULATION IN INDUSTRIAL TRAINING

Simulation has witnessed increasing development in recent years and has become widely recognized as a valuable means of learning and training in educational environments such as schools or universities and also in industrial companies.

The new trend of using computer-based simulation for industrial training purposes is mainly based on the idea of increasing trainee involvement in various activities of the simulation process. This has been possible due to the following basic reasons (Crookall et al., 1987; Forrester, 1995; Parzinger, 1992; Savén, 1995; Ståhl, 1988):

- New developments in simulation software have offered trainees the possibility of being more directly involved in the process of building simulation models.
- Increasing facilitation of the trainee's interaction with the simulation model.
- The creation of more specific simulation software in application areas such as

production. The new packages are richer in built-in functions and in the variety of output reports which enormously facilitate its use in concrete industrial applications and have greatly reduced the time consumed by the process of model building.

■ Simulation software can be run on PC computers. This has made the approach available to a larger number of users in almost all types of industries.

The main advantages of computer-based simulation in industrial training has been summarized by Webb and Hassell (1988) as follows:

1. Computer-based simulation aids understanding.
2. It makes abstract concepts more concrete and helps trainees to focus on important issues.
3. Better simulation support via animation and the user interface. These new features improve problem-solving ability and aid decision making.
4. Thinking logically is enhanced.
5. It allows greater testing and evaluation.
6. Simulating experiments may save time. The trainee can get a faster response to his or her actions.
7. It facilitates the process of generalizing knowledge and skills in new situations.
8. It encourages discussion and communication between trainees.
9. It improves the trainee's ability to assess outcomes, consequences and limitations of a certain action in a system.
10. It encourages trainees to actively participate in the training.
11. The trainee can plan and execute his or her own experiment plans.
12. It helps to link theory with reality.

THE SIMULATION GAMES

There is no clear definition of this type of computer-based simulation model. The concept can be simply defined as a traditional operative simulation model in the frame of a game. In other words this concept keeps the main characteristics of a traditional operative simulation model and puts them to work within an environment which appears as a game. A simulation game does not involve more than one trainee at a time and neither is the competition aspect exhibited in the business games.

According to Fripp (1993, p.23), 'The word "simulation" is sometimes considered too mechanistic for educational purposes... however, 'game' can imply time wasting, not taking things too seriously and engaging in an exercise designed purely for fun'. The concept of simulation game seems to offer the right combination and balance between both of these extremes. The main differences between these concepts can be summarized as follows:

1. In a traditional operative simulation model the objective is usually to find the best possible solution to a particular problem, while a simulation game always has educational purposes (see Fripp, 1993; Ståhl, 1988).
2. In order to stress the educational goals, rather than the entertainment nature of games, the users of simulation games are called 'participants' rather than

'players' (see Fripp, 1993) – and 'participant' is the term I use in this chapter.
3. Traditionally the experimental process in a simulation model has been expert driven. In a simulation game, participants can plan their own experiments, input parameters and follow what happens directly during the game (see Eriksson, 1988; Thatcher and Robinson, 1984).

Advantages

Senge (1990) has summarized the main advantages of simulation games as being:

- integration of the microworld and the real world;
- speeding up and slowing down time;
- compressing space;
- isolation of variables;
- experimental orientation;
- pauses for reflection;
- theory-based strategy and;
- institutional memory.

Some other characteristics and advantages of simulation games mentioned in the literature are:

- Simulation games increase the intuition and skills of participants.
- Simulation games are good at providing insight into the totality of a system.
- They can arouse the interest and motivation of participants.
- They promote communication and dialogue between participants in the training.
- Simulation games can make the training more effective by facilitating a trainee-centred orientation.
- Simulation games match fairly well the process of the individual's learning style in companies.
- The competition promoted by simulation games is not of the kind encouraged by other traditional games where players try to beat each other or try to compete against the computer.
- Oxford et al. (1987) have found that simulation games can also enhance learning by increasing the amount of the time that participants spend on the learning task. According to them the time spent on a task is closely associated with a better learning performance.

Even though considerable advantages of using games as a facilitator and support tool in training have been widely documented, there is not any concrete evidence that simulation games are superior or more effective than other techniques used in training. Nevertheless, as Fripp (1993) indicates, the evidence from all this experience suggests that simulation games are at least as good, and in many cases better than other methods. Fripp (1993) found in a survey in 1991 of 150 managers of companies in the UK that even though simulations can be time-consuming and expensive, 90 per cent of the users considered they were good value for money. Ahluwalia and Hsiao (1993) and Lierman (1994) have also found that simulation training, when combined with conventional training, can reduce total training time by 30 to 50 per cent. (For further discussion of these issues see Anderson and Lawton, 1990; Fripp, 1993; Goldstein, 1992; Headthman and Kleiner, 1991; Jaffe and Nebenzahl, 1990; Latham and Crandall, 1991; Ruohomäki, 1995; Simons, 1990; Whiteley and Faria, 1988.)

Simulation games are not widely used by companies in industrial training nor as well used as they might be. Part of the reason can be found in the lack of companies' expertise and knowledge of how to use computer simulation techniques. Another important reason postulated here is that there is a lack of appropriate training methods which could help companies in their implementation and use.

Disadvantages

The use of simulation games in industrial training also has some particular disadvantages. The most important of them are:

1. There is a risk that the focus will be on the technological aspects of the simulation game and not on its main educational purposes.
2. The demands in skills and practical experience on the developers of simulation games is quite high.
3. The training of participants using simulation games can be time-consuming.
4. If a simulation game is not properly designed, there is a risk that it will not produce the designed learning effects.
5. According to Watson and Blackstone (1989), games focus on more scored quantitative than qualitative factors.
6. The connection between the training results and real-world production issues, such as productivity, is hard to prove in most cases.

THE SSIT METHOD

The aim of this section is to describe the characteristics and the stages of the SSIT method. The method has been already used in four case studies and it is currently used in a larger training project at Saab Military Aircraft in Sweden.

Figure 15.1 presents the main stages of this training method and Table 15.1 provides a description of the training activities executed in each of the stages of the SSIT method.

The following sections describe in more detail each of the stages of SSIT method. (For a more detailed description of these stages, see Villegas, 1996.)

First stage: training framework definition

The goal of this stage is to set the boundaries of the training project and define its main initial characteristics. The information collected in this stage is quite simple, but it will have a relevance for the successful execution of the training. In this stage it is absolutely necessary to have support and help from other experts at the company.

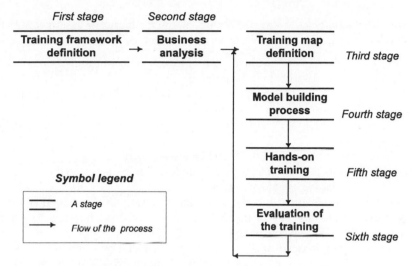

Figure 15.1 The main stages of the SSIT method

Table 15.1 The training activities of each of the stages of the SSIT method – third version

	Training stage	*Activities*
1	Training framework definition	• Selection of the participants in the training • Definition of the training domain • Definition of an estimated duration of the training • Definition of the type of problems • Definition of the training needs • Definition of the training resources
2	Business analysis	• Activity analysis • Problem analysis • Goal analysis
3	Training map definition	• Definition of the training blocks • The process of analysis and selection of the training aspect • Definition of the training map • Definition of the characteristics of the simulation games • Review of the training map
4	Model-building process	• Programming of the simulation game • Verification and validation of the simulation game
5	Hands-on training	• Theoretical instruction • Introduction of the game • Playing the game • Group discussions
6	Evaluation of the training	• Evaluation

The execution of this stage includes the definition of the following aspects of the training:

1. *The participants in the training*: the selection of participants is made with particular consideration to the following:
   - they might have different jobs and responsibilities in the company; this will enrich the discussion and the outcome of the training
   - it is an advantage if all participants have previous experience in the operation of computers
   - the number of participants should be around eight
   - participants must have a positive attitude and be receptive to the idea of the training and the use of simulation games.
2. *The training domain*: this is the definition of what part of production will be considered as a target of the training. It can be a production line, a department or an outline of the whole production cycle.
3. *The estimated duration of the training*: in consideration of the resources and aims for the training, the duration of the training project should be initially estimated. This information should give the training coordinator a fairly good picture of how to plan the execution of each of the stages of the training.
4. *The type of problems*: examples of this include production capacity planning and personnel planning. This information will facilitate the process of classification and analysis of problems during the business analysis.
5. *The training needs*: the aim of this activity is to provide a better idea of the main issues on which training should focus.
6. *Training resources*: it is very important to check what resources the company has available for the training, eg computers, printers and rooms. This might be an important motivation factor which could play a significant role in the participants' engagement in the training.

Second stage: the business analysis

The main aim of this stage is to provide support to the training method in the business analysis of the company. By doing this, the stage supports the development of the method and its later execution. The main goals of the business analysis are:

1. To analyse the problems of the company in a way that the results would help to define the training needs of the company and a training plan which might cope with these needs.
2. To gain a better understanding of the production activities of the company in such a way that this information facilitates the process of model-building for the simulation games.
3. To study the goals of the company in such a way that they would help to address the training needs in a proper way.

The execution of this stage is based on a method created at Linköping University, called Change Analysis, CA/SIMM (see Goldkuhl, 1993; Goldkuhl and Röstlinger,

1988, 1991, for more detailed discussion of the characteristics of this method and its strengths in the training context). From the number of components contained in the CA/SIMM method, three were selected as a support for the business analysis of the SSIT method; they were: activity analysis, problem analysis and goal analysis, described in more detail below.

The activity analysis
The purpose of the activity analysis is to describe the structure of the activities of the selected training domain in order to support the process of model-building for the simulation games. This description is mainly based on: execution order between activities, initiation of activities and conditional results.

The main characteristics of this type of analysis are:

- It uses activity diagrams which can include the description of information and material flow.
- The training domain can be described at any level of detail.
- The activity diagrams can greatly facilitate the model-building for the simulation games and help participants to understand the games or other problems discussed in the training.

Problem analysis
The problem analysis should provide answers to the following questions: which are the most important problems and what are the causes and effects of problems? For this purpose, the problem analysis includes three main activities:

1. Identification and formulation of problems with the help of a problem list.
2. Classification of problems by groups.
3. Analysis of the problem structure based on a problem graph.

It is highly recommended that the process of identification and formulation of problems should grow out of a brainstorming activity. The main aim is to create a picture of the problem situation which is as realistic as possible. Then, problems can be further analysed and discussed with participants and other experts in the company in order to select only those which will be addressed during the training.

The main aim of *classifying the problems by groups* is to make them easier to manage through the training process. The types of problems initially defined in the training framework might be a helpful guide in the formulation of these groups.

The analysis of problem structure aims to give the answers to the following questions: what are the relationships between the problems in the problem list? Which problems are causes of other problems and what are their effects? The analysis of cause-effect between the problems is carried out with the help of the problem graphs. They help determine which training aspects should be addressed in future training sessions and how problems have to be approached in the simulation games.

Goal analysis
The purpose of this type of analysis is to determine the current goals of the company and to try to connect these goals to the design and execution plans of the training project. This type of analysis should provide answers to the following questions: what

are the goals the company wants to achieve? What are the most important goals? What are the operative and strategic goals? In order to answer these questions, this analysis includes three main activities:

1. Identification and formulation of goals by help of a goal list.
2. Classification of goals.
3. Analysis of the goal structure based on a goal graph.

Third stage: training map definition

The main purpose of this stage is to create a training plan based on the execution of a number of training sessions which, step-by-step, lead participants from simple and operative problems in production to more complex and strategic problems in production. Each training session includes individual and group training activities with participants.

This approach is mainly inspired by the ideas of Gagné (1985) who suggests that there is a hierarchy of learning from very simple conditioned responses, to complex learning such as may be required in problem solving. He indicates that, for the learning process to be effective, the learner should start with simple rules and then progress and construct higher order rules. The more sophisticated these rules become, the more effective the learner will be in problem solving. Tannenbaun and Yukl (1992, p.404) have also addressed this issue:

> The instructional process should enhance trainee self-efficacy and trainee expectations that the training will be successful and lead to valued outcomes. For example, training should begin with simple behaviour that can be mastered easily, then progress to more complex behaviour as trainees become more confident.

Each training session includes the use of a simulation game which helps to demonstrate to participants the central problems found during the previous stage. If the training included the analysis of problems from different perspectives such as production control or personnel planning, the training sessions might mirror these. The level of difficulty of the training sessions in a new training block can be pitched according to what problems are analysed and what the goals of the training are. An outline of a training map is given in Figure 15.2. Creating a training map involves the following stages:

1. Definition of the training blocks.
2. Analysis and selection of training aspects which will be demonstrated in the training sessions.
3. Definition of the training sessions.
4. Definition of the characteristics of the simulation games.
5. Review of the training map.

The *definition of the training blocks* is based on the problem groups. The decision of how many training blocks should be included in the training, and in which order, will depend on the estimated duration of the training and the priority of these types of problems for the company.

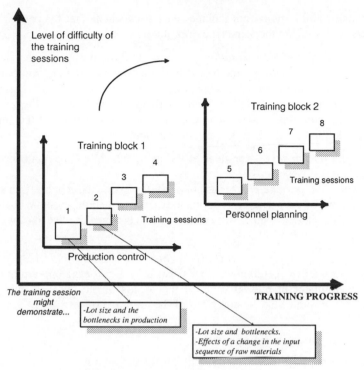

Figure 15.2 An example of a training map

The process of *analysis and selection of the training aspects* mainly consists of a study of the outcomes from the problem and goal analysis in order to select those issues which should be addressed during the training. The main idea is to determine what aspects have particular relevance for the participants and which might be worked out later by different training activities such as theoretical instruction, simulation games or group discussions.

The next step in the training map is the *definition of the training sessions*. Initially, only the first training session has to be fully defined; the rest of the training sessions can be temporarily outlined by a short description of what they will be about and what training aspects they will include. There are other important considerations as well in the definition of the training sessions; these are:

- Each new training session should be a natural continuation of the previous one.
- The training sessions should increase in level of difficulty as the training progresses.
- The first training session should be simple.
- Each training session can contain one or more training aspects.
- The training session must be documented by specifying its goals, the main topics of the theoretical instruction, the training aspects, what is the main problem the participant has to solve in the game and the estimated duration of it.

■ A training block should not include so many sessions that the participants get bored working with the same type of problems.

The *characteristics of the simulation games* are initially outlined at the end of this stage and later refined during the model-building process. The starting point is the documentation of the training sessions, then to define in detail the first simulation game. The remaining simulation games will be defined during the process of adaptation of the training after each iteration. The characteristics of the simulation games are defined using the following information:

■ *The input parameters* – variables in the game which will be controlled by the participants.
■ *The constant parameters* – variables of the game which are constant and well-known by the participants during the experimentation process with the game.
■ *Output information* – the results which will be produced by the execution of the game.

The final activity in this stage is the *discussion of the training map with participants and other experts in the company*. This can be a significant opportunity for the training coordinator to present some of the results of the business analysis, but especially to introduce the general plans of the training project.

Fourth stage: model-building process

The aim of this stage is the model-building of the simulation games which will support the execution of the training. There are two main stages: programming of the simulation games and verification and validation of the games.

Much of the success of this stage will depend on the experience and support that the programmer can get, not only from previous stages, but also from participants and other experts in the company. Today, there are a number of good simulation programs which help greatly in the model-building process, even for programmers with little experience. However, a proficient programmer of a simulation game is one who not only can produce a game according to the prerequisites of the training, but make it attractive for the participants and cost-effective. For this purpose, the creativity of the programmer is important in helping him or her to choose the right structure for the game, good game scenarios and relevant content in order to fit the learning ambitions of the training.

Once the simulation game is ready, it must be validated with the help of participants and other experts in the company. The main purpose of this validation is to check if the behaviour of the simulation game corresponds to the real system, ie, the flow of activities of the game are properly represented and its results correspond to those of reality.

The following list summarizes the main qualities that a simulation game should have in order to support the purposes of the SSIT method:

■ *It has to be realistic.* Participants have to be able to recognize the components and situations of the real system in the game.

- *It has to be simple.* The game should include only those details and components which could help participants to increase their understanding of particular problems.
- *It has to be interesting to play.* The game has to be able to generate interest and engagement, ie, the game will demonstrate problems which are close to the participants and they might find that the game could be useful and reliable for their own problem situation.
- *It has to be deterministic.* It is of absolute importance that the participant will be able to understand why a change in one parameter of the game could cause certain consequences in the results of the game. The type of relationships between components in any production system are already so complex that if in addition the game were to include stochastic events, the participants would not be able to understand the effects of their changes and the training would be meaningless. None of the case studies of the SSIT method has used stochastic games but this does not totally exclude the possibility of creating a game with some stochastic components and using it at the end of the training but not before all participants have demonstrated a proficient understanding of all the issues.
- *It has to challenge the participants.* The tasks that the participants have to solve in the game should be interesting and challenging, but not complex. Their tasks must stimulate participants' motivation and encourage their active participation in the training.
- *It has to be interactive.* A participant must have constant contact with the simulation game.
- *It should not be a time-consuming activity.* Participants must be able to follow the events of the game and fully execute it in under 15 minutes. According to our experience, this is approximately the time that a participant can keep his or her attention on what is happening in the game.

Fifth stage: hands-on training

The goal of this stage is to generate and control those training activities which will support the participants' learning process. It is in this stage where the direct work and the training of the participants takes place in the SSIT training method. The presentation of this stage is divided into three main components: the activities, the learning processes in a training session, and the control forms.

Activities

As explained in the training map definition, the training work with participants is organized by training sessions. Each training session includes the execution of all or some of the following activities: theoretical instruction; introduction to the game; playing the game; and group discussion. Figure 15.3 illustrates these activities and their possible order of execution.

The model of the training session is mainly based on the principles of learning by doing. The main purpose of these activities are:

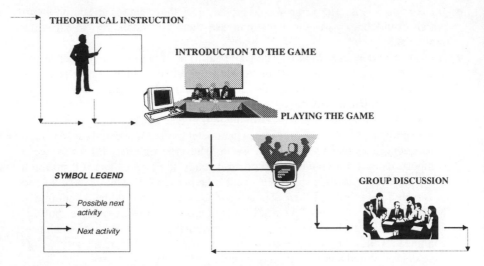

Figure 15.3 The activities carried out during the execution of a training session

- To prepare participants well at the beginning of the session in order to maximize the benefit they gain from the simulation game.
- To support the training at the individual as well as the organizational level.
- To provide participants with the opportunity to try out different ideas free of pressures or risks.
- To aid communication and discussion between participants.
- To ensure participants are not isolated from their real system and the training can be provided on-the-job.

Following is a description of the main characteristics of each of the activities of this stage.

Theoretical instruction
This is a formal meeting with all participants which follows approximately the same rules and procedures as an academic lecture where the teacher goes through certain relevant aspects of a theory and participants can intervene with questions and comments. The main purpose of this theoretical instruction is to call the participants' attention to certain relevant problems and production theories which they would probably be using during the experimentation with the games. This theory is presented and briefly demonstrated by the training coordinator or external cooperator in the training.

Introduction to the game
This activity is important and the training coordinator should not hesitate to make clear to all participants how to operate the computer and how to play the game. This activity includes the following:

- Instruction on how to operate the computer and how to start the simulation game.
- Detailed presentation and demonstration of each of the commands and menu alternatives of the game.
- Presenting and demonstrating the game to the participants.
- Handing over on paper, to the participants, instructions on how to play the game and the tasks they have to execute in the training session.
- Giving the participants the control form for that training session and discussing possible questions about them.
- Discussing with the participants the schedule for the training session.

Playing the game

This is the most practical part of the training session. During this activity participants get the opportunity to practise their knowledge and skills by changing different parameters of the game and reflecting on the possible consequences of these changes. So that the training keeps a positive atmosphere and the participants feel engaged, it is necessary to have permanent contact with them and to constantly keep the training project going. For example, participants could play a game for some days and then prepare themselves for a group discussion which might review part of the results of the game. The discussion might also help participants to understand better many of the issues demonstrated in the game. After this, participants could continue playing the same game for a number of additional days and prepare new results for a second group discussion. This process could be repeated several times until the training coordinator and the participants consider that they could go on to the next training session.

Group discussions

The main purpose of this activity is to give the opportunity to each of the participants to present and compare their results from the game with the results of others. Participants are encouraged to prepare their results and to present them to others during this meeting. The role of the training coordinator is important not only as a moderator of the discussions, but also as a recaller of other results from previous sessions and from the business analysis. He or she has to continually look for new ways of enriching the discussions and helping participants to find the connection between the game results and the real problems of the company. Before each group discussion, it is important that the training coordinator checks with each of the participants how much they managed to complete of the game and to provide them with valuable tips which could make the presentation more interesting and helpful for others. If important issues are discussed in a particular group, it might be possible for the discussions to be carried out over a number of meetings before the training goes on to the next training session. Before the new meeting participants will have the opportunity to complete even better experiments in the simulation game by incorporating those ideas they received from others in the discussions.

The quality of the group discussions plays a relevant role in the effects and results of the whole training. Particularly, it will affect the participants' transfer of knowledge and skills into the real system and will facilitate the consensus process.

The learning processes
This section summarizes the main types of learning invoked by the different activities of a training session; they are illustrated in Table 15.2.

Table 15.2 The main types of learning invoked during the training session

Activity of the training session	The learning process
1. Theoretical instruction	Instructional learning
2. Introduction to the game	Instructional learning
3. Playing the game	Learning by experience – Learning by doing – Learning by experience of others – Interpretation of acquired experience Single and double loop learning
4. Group discussion	Organizational learning Single and double loop learning

Instructional learning, also called verbal instruction, covers two main functions: to provide direction for learning in the training, and to aid the transfer of learning. The richest period of individual learning in the entire training sessions is likely to be the period in which the participants can experiment with the simulation game. In the previous section we reviewed how the whole learning cycle based in the Kolb's (1984) experiential learning is supported by the process of participant's interaction with a simulation game. We also discussed how this activity is mainly based on the principles of *learning by experience* which also includes the *learning by doing*. Additionally, in this interaction with the game the participant might experience the 'aha effects' which are indicators that they have corroborated their assumptions about the situation in the game or he has found something unexpected in the game. To correct this discrepancy so as to receive an acceptable answer the participant uses his or her present mental models, ie, single loop learning.

If the participant continues to perform more simulations in order to explain a specific problem situation, he or she may reach a better understanding of the problems exhibited in the game and consequently a better insight into the real system. During this process of trial and error the participant might change his or her mental models. This means that they change the way they explain a particular situation or realize how the real system works. They are improving their mental models and hence an individual double loop learning is taking place. Figure 15.4 provides an illustration of the individual single and double loop learning processes invoked in the participants' interaction with the game.

The group discussion is central to the individual and organizational learning process. Discussion will help participants confirm or correct their assumptions and will promote communication between participants in order to transfer the individual learning results to the organization level. The outcomes from the individual learning will only produce an impact on the company if the participants are able to discuss

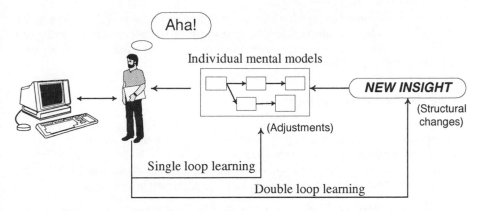

Figure 15.4 An individual's single and double loop learning based on experimentation with the game

the results of a game together and analyse the possible connections of those results with the real problems in production. This is the main role that the group discussions play in the execution of the training. The communication between participants during these meetings might help them to clarify many aspects of the problems demonstrated in the game and might lead to a consensus in the group of participants.

The contrast between the individual and group learning approach is one of the important characteristics of the SSIT method and the characteristics on which the success of the transfer of knowledge and skills from the training to the real system is based. This contrast can be seen as a continual reinforcement of the whole of Kolb's experiential learning model where the pace and the outcomes of the learning process can be even greater than just by the use of a simulation game, due to the extra impulse that participants might get from those training activities in the SSIT method.

The control forms
The use of the control forms in the SSIT method has two main purposes: to reinforce the learning process in the training by giving participants assignments that they have to solve with use of the simulation game, and to control the training progress.

The SSIT method considers the use of three main control forms. They are:

1. *The initial control form* – this is utilized at the beginning of the training and its main purpose is to check the participants' opinion and knowledge about different issues which will be covered by the training. This type of information might be relevant at the end of the training in order to evaluate how much participants have changed their behaviour during the training.
2. *The control session form* – this type of control form is used mainly as an internal control for each of the training sessions. It contains a number of assignments which have to be solved by participants with the use of the simulation game. To this end, the training coordinator can force participants to use different features of the game. This type of control might also enhance the participants' long-term retention of important issues raised during the game.

3. *The final control form* – this is mainly the final evaluation of the results of the training. This evaluation should be made from different perspectives and could include the training effects on participants and production and participant's attitudes toward the training.

Sixth stage: evaluation of the training

The main purpose of this stage is to make an assessment of the training progress and the present needs of the training in order to decide what the direction and characteristics of the next training session should be.

The evaluation of the training should be done in close cooperation with the participants. The following questions have to be answered in this stage:

- What should the next training session involve? The answer can be based on the present status of the training and the outline of the training map.
- How should these requirements be addressed in the next training sessions? What will be the changes in the simulation game? What aspects will be addressed in the theoretical instruction if there are any and what other material has to be handed out to the participants? One additional aspect of assessment for the training coordinator is the choice of activities to be executed in the next training session. The next training session could be introduced at the end of the group discussion and the participants could continue directly with the next simulation game after the meeting. This is the case where the next training session does not need any theoretical instruction.
- What difficulties did the participants encounter in the operation or understanding of the game? Knowing this will facilitate improvements in the game and will give a fairly good picture of any problems with the training. If the participants still have difficulties with the operation of the game, the training coordinator should make the necessary arrangements to provide extra support.

The evaluation of a training project includes an external and internal evaluation. The external evaluation covers three main points: effects on production and participants which includes understanding, system thinking, self-confidence, knowledge, skills, changed behaviour, communication and cost-effectiveness; participants' attitudes towards the SSIT method which includes interest, curiosity, motivation and challenge; and effects on problems included in the business analysis. The main purpose of the internal evaluation is to find out from participants what their view of the training was and how successful it had been in achieving its objectives. This evaluation consists of an assessment of the basic characteristics of the training method in relation to the simulation games used in the training and the combination of techniques such as instruction and group discussion.

EMPIRICAL RESULTS FROM THE CASE STUDIES

The following are some of the main empirical outcomes in the use of this training method.

The SSIT method has been implemented in four case studies, the main characteristics of which are illustrated in Table 15.3.

Table 15.3 The main characteristics of the SSIT method case studies

Case study	Number of participants	Total duration of the training project	Number of training sessions
1	5	53 weeks	8
2	11	28 weeks	5
3	8	16 weeks	3
4	8	16 weeks	2

Results from these case studies have provided evidence that the support to the participants' learning process was successful in different ways. The training impact on the participants and on production, however, had varying intensity in each of the case studies:

- *Understanding:* all case studies have reported better understanding on the part of the participants of the problems demonstrated in the games.
- *System thinking*: all case studies have reported that the training has contributed to the participants' ability to look at things from a 'system' perspective and has created a new way of thinking. Participants have demonstrated a better ability to examine the parts of a process in terms of the whole.
- *Self-confidence:* this was a difficult aspect to evaluate. It was mentioned, however, that participants have mainly corroborated their assumptions about the problems, and consequently acquired more confidence in their work.
- *Knowledge and skills:* the greatest impact was not on the participants' acquisition of knowledge and skills, but in the fact that participants could make their knowledge more precise and logical.
- *Communication:* our experience has shown that using SSIT enables participants to focus on understanding and communication in such a way that problems become more open for discussion.
- *Cost-effectiveness:* three of the case studies have presented an evaluation of the cost-effectiveness of the training. All of them concluded that the benefits to the company have been greater than the total cost of each training project. Table 15.4 summarizes the final training cost-per-hour in each case study and also presents for comparison the cost of other commercial production courses.

The case studies have also reported that the training has supported the participants' learning processes both at the individual and organizational level. At the individual level there was single and double loop learning. The first was mainly facilitated by the process of repetition and experimentation in the training which made it possible for participants to use their knowledge and practise their skills in production. The double loop learning was manifested in improvement of the participants' mental model; here, the group discussions and also the process of experimentation with the games have played a relevant role.

Table 15.4 The final training cost-per-hour in each case study

Case study/type of course		Training cost per hour (SEK-hour)
1.	1	747
2.	2	462
3.	3	595
4.	Average cost of a commercial production course*	547
5.	Minimum cost of a commercial production course	341
6.	Maximum cost of a commercial production course	1177

*This estimation is the result of a survey among Swedish companies; for more detail see Villegas, 1996.

The organizational learning process was promoted by the consensus generated in the group discussions. This has also facilitated a generalization of conclusions which has positively affected the transfer process of training results to the real system.

The participants' attitudes toward the SSIT method in the case studies have led to the following conclusions:

■ The training method has demonstrated special capabilities of awakening the interest and curiosity of participants.
■ The participants' engagement and active participation in the training was greatly disrupted by other activities in the company.
■ The simulation games have managed to challenge the participants. This has promoted their interest and participation in the training.

Other meaningful conclusions regarding the basic characteristics of the SSIT method are:

■ All the case studies have used deterministic simulation games. This quality has made it easier for participants to understand the problems demonstrated in the games.
■ The case studies have reported that the simulation programs provided helpful support for model-building for the simulation games. They have also concluded that the games should not be very sophisticated, and that model-building demands much creativity from the model developer, though he or she need not be an expert in simulation.
■ The combination of techniques in the training project was successful. Their main impacts were: better interest and motivation shown by participants; better support to the participants' individual and organizational learning process; more continuity in the training and consequently more support to the participants.

REFERENCES

Ahluwalia, M and Hsiao, J (1993) 'Process simulator-based systems are key to meeting training requirements', *Pub & Paper*, October, 111–14.

Anderson, G (1994) 'A proactive model for training needs analysis', *Journal of European Industrial Training*, **18**, 3, 23–8.

Anderson, Ph H and Lawton, L (1990) 'Perceptions of skill acquisition through cases and a general management simulation: a replication', in Belardo and Weinroth, op cit., pp 110–16.

Belardo, S and Weinroth, J (1990) 'Simulation in business and management', *Proceedings of the SCS Multiconference on Simulation in Business and Management*, 17–19 January, California, Vol 21, No 4, Simulation Computer Society, CA.

Churchill, J (1990) 'Complexity and strategy decision making', in Eden and Radford (eds) op cit.

Crookall, D *et al.* (eds) (1987) 'Simulation games in the late 1980s', *Proceedings of The International Simulation and Gaming Associations*, 17th International Conference, ISAGA, Université de Toulon et du Var, France, 1–4 July, Pergamon Press, Oxford.

De Meyer, A (1993) 'Creating the virtual factory', in *Management and New Production Systems. The 4th International Production Management Conference*, EIASM, London, April 5–6, pp.199–214, London Business School.

Eden, C and Radford, J (eds) (1990) *Tackling Problems. The role of group decision support*, Sage, London.

Eriksson, I (1988) 'Simulation for user training', Report Åboakademi, Department of Computer Science, Finland.

Forrester, J (1995) 'The look for simulation and gaming in management training' [online], available: http://www.neosoft.com/~pteragen/gamesim.html

Fripp, J (1993) *Learning Through Simulation. A guide to the design and use of simulation in business and education*, McGraw-Hill, Maidenhead.

Gagné, R E (1985) 'The conditions of learning and the theory of instruction', *Simulation*, Holt-Rinehart and Winston, New York.

Goldkuhl, G (1993) 'Contextual activity modelling of information systems', *Proceedings of 3rd Conference of Dynamic Modelling*, North-Holland, Amsterdam.

Goldkuhl, G and Röstlinger, A (1988) *Förändringsanalys. Aarbetsmetodik och förhållningssätt för goda förändringsbeslut*, Studentlitteratur, Lund.

Goldkuhl, G and Röstlinger, A (1991) 'Joint problem elicitation', *Proceedings IFIP 82*, Linköping University, Sweden.

Goldstein, I L (1992) *Training in Organizations. Needs assessment, development and evaluation*, 3rd edn, University of Maryland at College Park, Maryland.

Gross, J R (1993) 'Simulation-based training in support of law-inventory apparel production', *Production and Inventory Management*, 4, 72–7.

Headthman, D J and Kleiner, B H (1991) 'Training and technology: the future is now', *Training and Development*, September, 49–54.

Jaffe, E D and Nebenzahl, I D (1990) 'Group interaction and business game performance', *Simulation Gaming*, **21**, 2, 133–45.

Kofman, F and Senge, P (1993) 'Communities of commitment: the heart of learning organizations', *Organizational Dynamics*, **22**, 2, 5–23.

Kolb, D A (1984) *Experiential Learning*, Prentice Hall, Englewood Cliffs, NJ.

Latham, G P and Crandall, S R (1991) 'Organizational and social factors', in Morrison, op cit., pp.259–86.

Lierman, B (1994) 'How to develop a training simulation', *Training & Development*, February, 50–52.

Morrison, J E (ed.) (1991) *Training for Performance. Principles of applied human learning*, John Wiley, New York.

Oxford, R *et al.* (1987) 'Advances in the development of hand-held, computerized, game-based training devices. Simulation-gaming in the late 1980s', *Proceedings of the International and Gaming Association's 17th. International Conference*, Université de Toulon et du Var, France, 1–4 July, Pergamon Press, London.

Parzinger, T M (1992) 'A valuable training and development tool', *Bankers Magazine*, **175**, 3, 75–80.

Ruohomäki, V (1995) 'Viewpoints on learning and education with simulation games', in Riis, J O (ed.) *Design of Simulation Games*, Chapman & Hall, London, pp.13–25.

Savén, B (1995) 'Versamhetsmodeller för beslutstöd och lärande. En studies av diskret produktionssimulering vid Asea/ABB', 1968–1993. Linköping Universitet. Dissertation No. 371, Linköping, Sweden.

Senge, P M (1990) *The Fifth Discipline*. Doubleday, New York.

Simons, K L (1990) *New Technology in Simulation Games*, System Dynamics Group, Cambridge, MA.

Ståhl, I (1988) 'Using operational gaming', in Miser H J and Quade, E S (eds) *Handbook of Systems Analysis. Craft issues and procedural choices*, pp.121–71.

Tannenbaum, S I and Yukl, G (1992) 'Training and development organizations', in De Greene, K B (ed.) *Annual Review of Psychology*, Palo Alto, CA.

Thatcher, D C and Robinson, M J (1984) *Me the Slow Learner*, Solent Simulation, Hants.

Toffler, A (1985) *The Adaptive Corporation*, Gower, Aldershot.

Villegas, J (1996) 'Simulation supported industrial training from an organizational learning perspective – development and evaluation of the SSIT method', PhD thesis, Linköping University, Sweden.

Warren, M (1979) *Training for Results: A system approach to the development of human resources in industry*, 2nd edn, Addison-Wesley.

Watson, H J and Blackstone, J H jr (1989) *Computer Simulation*, 2nd edn, John Wiley, New York.

Webb, M and Hassell, D (1988) 'Opportunities for computer based modelling and simulation in secondary education', in Lovis, F and Taggs, E D (eds) *Computers in Education*, Elsevier, Amsterdam.

Whiteley, T R and Faria, A J (1988) 'A study of the relationship between student final exam performance and simulation game participation', in Klabbers *et al. Proceedings of the International Simulation and Gaming Association's 19th International Conference*, The Netherlands, 16–19 August.

ABOUT THE AUTHOR

Jaime Villegas is Assistant Professor at the Department of Computer and Information Science at Linköping University, Sweden. He has a PhD in computer simulation from Moscow University and a PhD in Economics from Linköping University. He is enrolled in the graduate student programme at the Department of Information and Computer Science at Linköping University. Jaime has participated in different simulation projects for Swedish companies and he is currently actively involved in various simulation projects in cooperation with university and industrial partners in Latvia.

Address for correspondence: Linköping University, 58 183, IDA-EIS, Linköping, Sweden. Tel: 013 282539; Fax: 013 282666; iVi@ida.liu.se For more information check http://www.ida.liu.se/labs/eis/people/jaivi.html

Chapter 16

Use of off-the-peg business games as a component of large-group learning

M F Warren, R J Soffe and R J Williams

ABSTRACT

During 1991 concerns about rising student numbers led to an experiment with a large first-year degree module in financial management, comprising students from a range of rural-based programmes, most of whom had no intrinsic interest in the topic. An off-the-peg game was used as the central means of learning, supported by lectures, computer-assisted learning, fortnightly tests, and surgeries. Annual evaluations of student perceptions, coupled with qualitative and quantitative outcomes of assessments, show the strategy to have been very successful, with a high quality of learning experienced by students despite numbers ranging from 130 to over 200 (40 companies). The fact that the game is based on a manufacturing business, rather than rural land-using, gave no difficulty. Staff enjoy being involved with a more highly-motivated student group, although reductions in formal contact time are balanced by other pressures.

A more complex game was subsequently used with third-year students in a module which had previously been based on 'live' case studies, allowing students to bring together various aspects of their managerial learning. Over 1,000 students have now taken this module, and reactions have been extremely positive – far more so than when real businesses were used. Future developments envisaged include incorporation of different types of game into other modules to create a 'game continuum' throughout the business pathway; involvement of teams from universities overseas; and development of learning support materials on a WWW server.

INTRODUCTION

This chapter recounts the experiences of 'lay' lecturers looking for a solution and finding it in the use of a business game, rather than business game experts seeking to apply a technique that they have previously devised. It has its roots in the push to modularize degree schemes in the early 1990s (giving rise to a wholesale review of learning processes, and increasing opportunities for combining groups of students from different study programmes), coupled with the dramatic increase in student numbers that we all faced at that time.

We were determined to respond positively to the pressure. We wanted students to learn more effectively and to enjoy the learning: we were pretty hard-pressed, like most of our colleagues, and wanted to reduce the pressure by working more efficiently. Moreover *we* wanted to enjoy the process: our department had in the past majored on participative learning and live case study work, and we could see a clear threat of this being replaced by more formal didactic methods which we regarded as less effective and more tedious. In what follows, we explain and analyse in turn how we approached two degree modules, one first-year and one third-year, and finally attempt to draw more general conclusions.

THE FIRST-YEAR MODULE (BMS 132: FINANCIAL MANAGEMENT 1)

The challenge

The pressure for change arose from three main influences: the size of student group, the diversity of interests within the group, and the difficulty for students in seeing the relevance of the topic studied.

When we redesigned this module in 1992, the module was taken by 140 students, rising to 206 in 1993, and steadying to around 180 a year average since. Up to 1992 the module had been taught by a senior member of staff using two or three hours of lectures per week, relying on sheaves of OHP acetates and reams of handouts It was a disaster. It was not possible to contemplate the use of tutorials, case studies or other more participative methods: we simply did not have the staff. The large numbers made it hard to identify those who were having problems, and even to know what the problems *were,* and it was difficult to provide adequate support once the problems were located. A further stimulus to change was the need for a 'trailblazer' module, demonstrating to others in the faculty that large groups need not mean more work and less effectiveness.

The module was shared by eight (later nine) first-year degree groups, all vocational courses. Some of the degree groups were based on rural land-using activities (eg, Rural Estate Management, Rural Resource Management, Agriculture and Countryside Management), some on food processing (Food Systems Management, Food Quality and Product Development, Food Production) and yet others on service industry (Tourism Management, Hospitality Management). At least 25 per cent were mature students, with different interests, experience and aspirations from those straight out of school. In the circumstances, one single form of teaching was unlikely to meet everyone's needs; one single pace of learning would leave some bored, others lost; and the use of industry-specific examples was difficult.

Nor was the relevance of the topic instantly apparent to first-year students. They all instinctively related strongly to their chosen major pathway, but were often baffled by the requirement to study business management. The fact that the latter was highly commended by past students of all programmes cut little ice with first-year students.

RESPONDING TO THE CHALLENGE

The essence of the new design was to use a mixture of media. Fortnightly lectures were used to stimulate and guide, but not to present all the facts or to develop skills. A recommended textbook provided factual information, including much that was not given in the lectures, and the opportunity to develop skills through activities and exercises. Computer-assisted learning was provided 'on tap' in the library: a largely text-based, low-cost system.

'Surgeries' were offered four afternoons every week for one-to-one consultation, in a seminar room, with attendance informal and voluntary. Fortnightly multiple-choice tests (six in all) provided regular formative and summative assessment, while a major end-of-module assignment comprised a business report analysing the performance of the business game company so far, and proposing an action plan for the future, supported by fully reconciled budgets for two further periods. Since each business was unique to four or five students, opportunities for plagiarism were severely limited.

Most importantly, a business 'game' was introduced – a computer-based simulation with students role-playing company management.

The game

After a period of intensive investigation, funded by an Enterprise in Higher Education scheme, the team chose to use BOSSCAT, produced by Harrison-Macey Ltd. BOSSCAT allows up to 12 companies per game, and so is better suited to large groups than many alternatives: we have tended to run four games ('markets') concurrently with ten companies each, creating 40 companies, each with four to five students. Student groups are selected at random from within the programme cohort. Companies produce two products (dolls), each using the same material and labour. One set of decisions is made per week over a period of 11 weeks. Communication of decisions and outcomes is via a post-in, post-out system, operated by a technical officer, who also presents some summary results graphically on notice-boards.

A relatively small number of decisions is made per period, concerning prices for products, orders for material, size and disposition of workforce, etc. No investment is possible, and the manufacturing process is one-stage – but at first-year level this does not seem to detract from the effectiveness of the game, and helps focus on financial management (rather than strategy, personnel management, and other issues). Comprehensive accounts are generated by the software, including a manufacturing account, profit and loss account, balance sheet and cash flow statement. Market information and a simplistic 'consultant's report' are available at a 'cost'.

The game was tested by use with a small group of postgraduate students before risking introduction to a big undergraduate group: an earlier experiment with another game had shown us the devastating effect of a combination of software bugs and staff inexperience.

The outcome

The first run of the new module, in 1992, went well considering the degree of innovation involved. Test results were reasonable after a shaky (and worrying) start, and sound understanding was generally shown in the company reports – some of these being extremely impressive. There was good informal feedback from students, and the availability of individual support on demand was reassuring to both students and lecturers. The lack of industrial relevance to students (a manufacturing business used as an exemplar for rural-oriented students) proved not to be the problem originally anticipated. In fact it was a positive benefit; no one group felt particularly disadvantaged compared to another.

Formal feedback, acquired through an end-of-module questionnaire focusing mostly on learning methods, was more variable. Tests, surgeries and the business game were highly valued, and most students found at least one method of learning that suited them. However, the book was loathed, some students regretted not having everything provided in lectures ('a good set of notes'), and better coordination was sought within the lecture series, and between business game and the rest of programme.

Staff reactions were similarly varied. Surgeries were not well enough attended some weeks. It proved exhausting preparing the first run – a continual treadmill of preparing lectures, exercises, (unambiguous) test questions, and keeping up with the business game. The process was not for someone without a sense of adventure and not fully committed; team-teaching was essential, giving mutual support, generating ideas, dealing with large numbers (especially marking assessments), manning surgeries (always three lecturers with some involvement). However, all were agreed that it was invigorating, challenging and fulfilling, bringing back some of the buzz into teaching.

Various improvements have been made since that early experience. Lectures quickly moved to a weekly basis, at the request of students. The group is now split into two and the lecture repeated (at the cost of SSR, but to the benefit of communication). A computer presentation package is used for lectures, which eases the burden of repetition and allows easy generation of note-form handouts. We changed the book again and again – we are now on the fourth so far, and still looking for the elusive perfect text: active-learning, comprehensive, gimmick-free, cheap – and *free of mistakes*. We have adopted a proactive approach to the first surgeries of the season, with students required to attend to 'register' their company and flag up potential problems in group working. Surgeries are held on neutral ground, in the refectory: now only three per week due to difficulties of finding times when reasonable numbers of students are free. The computer-assisted learning was abandoned after four years of attempting to improve its popularity: it made a dismal showing in the learning methods questionnaire. Optical mark reading was adopted for tests, allowing rapid feedback, excellent analysis of effectiveness of questions, and less work for support staff.

Reference is now made to the business game in every lecture, with each session beginning with a review of share price movements that week, and examples are drawn from the business game wherever possible. Students are exhorted to use the techniques and concepts learnt in their companies. Links are made across to IT learning – especially the use of spreadsheets. Again students are encouraged to use their skills in their companies. Virtually no change was needed to the operation of business game itself, however.

Future developments

Module feedback suggests a tailing-off in popularity of the business game as a learning method since 1994 (Tables 16.1 and 16.2 summarize some of the feedback statistics). We have made few changes in the running of the module during that time, so other factors must be at work. It may be due to variation within the group: cohorts do often vary from year to year. Moreover, in the last two years the proportion of Tourism Management and Hospitality Management students has increased; as a result the gender balance has changed, with a higher proportion of female students resulting. Could this be significant?

Table 16.1 Percentage of students rating different learning methods 'very good' or 'good' (5 and 4 on a 5-point scale)

	1992	1994	1996
Lectures	18	22	17
Surgeries	27	24	17
Computer-assisted learning (library)	10	12	n.a.
Business game	21	62	45
The programme of tests	49	57	54
Compulsory reading	51	47	26
Background reading	21	16	15
Informal discussions with others on course	26	34	41
Discussions with students on other courses	10	17	26
Mass media – TV, newspapers, etc	9	9	6
Other	15	20	14

Table 16.2 Percentage of students *not* using specific learning methods

	1992	1994	1996
Lectures	0	2	2
Surgeries	51	28	44
Computer-assisted learning (library)	48	53	0
Business game	2	0	1
The programme of tests	0	0	1
Compulsory reading	2	3	9
Background reading	42	23	33
Informal discussions with others on course	24	7	9
Discussions with students on other courses	44	34	26
Mass media – TV, newspapers, etc	59	27	43
Other	79	64	62

Another hint may be given by the rise in mentions of discussions with other students, on the same course or on other courses. There is informal evidence that students are using second- and third-year students for 'consultancy': in one sense this is a healthy development, and indeed at one time we considered building such peer support formally into the process. On the other hand, a consequence may be that the freshness and excitement is being dissipated – it is old hat, something to be just got through as a matter of routine. Is there a product life-cycle in operation here? Will we need constant innovation, and frequent changes of game, to keep the buzz?

We do not want to overreact, especially as there were marked differences in response rate to the questionnaire between years (70 per cent in 1994, 50 per cent in 1996). However, determining the cause of this trend and acting in time to avoid a similar phenomenon affecting the final-year game, are priorities for further developments.

THE FINAL-YEAR MODULE (BMS 332: INTEGRATING STUDIES)

The challenge

Designed as an 'integrating' module, this had traditionally been based on a 'live' case study business, within reasonable travelling distance of the campus. Small groups of students would then work on a prescribed range of objectives during the following weeks. Problems ranged from physical production and allocation of resources, to the improved marketing of current products or new lines. Towards the end of the module the business managers were invited to attend seminars where students presented their report. Normally the students would then submit a individual 'consultancy-type' report.

This approach (with a student:staff ratio of approximately 20:1) gave final year students the opportunity to confront real problems associated with the management of a business. The learning was deep and effective. However, as increased student numbers fed through from the earlier stages of the programmes it was clear that a 'live' visit would be impracticable. Inevitably fewer businesses would be willing or able to cope with 130 students (and rising), even if the department could cope with the costs of staffing and transport.

The challenge here was thus less to motivate students to study, than to provide a substitute learning experience that would achieve the module objectives without *reducing* motivation.

Responding to the challenge

When BOSSCAT was purchased, it came as part of a package with a more advanced version called WOODSTOCK. There are numerous similarities between the two games, which helps in many ways, since final year students are familiar with the format. They differ considerably in complexity and number of decisions, however: in WOODSTOCK there are four possible products, for instance; two manufacturing stages;

opportunities to substitute machines for labour and vice versa; and more flexibility for the game controller to alter conditions in the business environment. The game came complete with an extremely comprehensive set of exercises, case studies and OHP masters, as well as the usual manuals. Again, the game was pre-tested with a small group of postgraduate students.

Two lecturers run the module with occasional support from a demonstrator. A post-in, post-out system is used, and a technical officer is responsible for input of data and distribution of the output to students. With large numbers of students involved, excellent organization and communication are essential. A detailed time-table of events and assessments is provided to students at the start of the module, together with a comprehensive set of instructions.

Teams (self-selected in this case) are each given the same £400,000 capital to start their businesses from scratch, and make sufficient decisions to cover two production years (six sets of decisions per 'year'). Students are encouraged to regard the company as their own, thinking up an appropriate name, producing mission state-ments, aims and objectives (and logos) before the end of the first week. They are expected to attend a briefing each week ranging from 15 to 50 minutes depending on the state of the game. This session is vital to alert students to past common problems, brief students regarding related topics and to hint or state that a particular problem is imminent. Surgery sessions follow these briefings and are well received and well attended. Specific computer spreadsheet templates (for budgeting and marketing decisions, for instance) were made available for students on the computer network. Students who tutored themselves on these seemed to benefit throughout the game, but many groups failed to take the opportunity.

A number of variables are introduced during the game to encourage students to develop decision-making capability in the light of unpredictable events: they also allow cross-referencing to other modules, including marketing, business strategy and human resource management. Strikes, threatened strikes, even vague hints of unrest have been enough for urgent meetings to be called in all manner of places. Raw material supply interruptions caused by topical news events help to link the simula-tion with reality. Inflation rates and bank base rates also vary in line with the latest trends.

Following student evaluation (which confirmed our own feelings that in the initial years we were being over-zealous), we have cut the assessments down to two main elements. The first is a poster presentation produced by each student group analysing past performance and evaluating future prospects. Two regional bank managers join us to mark the posters and quiz the students. The quality of the presentation and comprehensiveness of information has risen each year. Each group has to complete a peer appraisal sheet and award marks for each member of the group, dependent on a range of criteria (including perceived effort and quality of each individual's work). These marks are combined with those awarded by the bank managers and lecturers to comprise 40 per cent of the module assessment marks.

The second assessment is based on an individual piece of work completed at the end of the simulation period. Students are asked to step back from the business and to act as a consultant to the group they have been part of. They are asked to criticize constructively the management of the business in all aspects, to draw conclusions from what they have found and to make firm recommendations, with budgets and other supporting information, for the next 12 months. The assessment performance of the individual is thus independent of the success or otherwise of the group's business. Industry standard data are supplied to each group before each assessment, based on the average results of the competing companies. Although this sounds similar to the first-year experience, far greater depth and breadth is required, with significantly more synthesis.

The outcome

The overwhelming reaction from students, sought through both informal and formal means, has been positive and enthusiastic. Perhaps not all the students are quite as ecstatic as the one who this year wrote: 'It's wonderful to have a module in the final year which is well taught, that you know is of practical use for the future; very worthwhile and enjoyable'. This is much nearer the norm, however than the one who wrote (among other things): 'I want to be an ecologist when I leave, why do I have to do a module on business management?' There will always be some whom we fail to convince... Enthusiasm is infectious; student feedback suggests that a buzz of excitement is created in week one and maintained throughout: apparently (and lamentably) a rare event in final-year studies.

Improvements made

Tutorials timetabled in the computer rooms during the early weeks of the module have been designed to encourage the use of the computer network, and particularly the simulation computer spreadsheets. These have proved extremely popular and effective, with additional spin-off in the form of increased use of computers for other sections of the module, particularly in presentation.

Surgery time, vital for both student and lecturers, started as an informal, ad hoc arrangement, but had to be formalized to cope with the large groups and large number of teams.

Feedback in the early years indicated that there were too many assessments on broadly similar topics. These were amended to give fewer but more detailed assessments.

Future developments

Feedback at the end of each module involves both written evaluation and a staff–student meeting to ask for constructive comments and suggestions for improvement. The most frequent comment this year – arising for the first time – was for more revision lectures on specific topics. We believe this reflects how we are pushing forward with the use of the simulation as an integrating medium, rather than any deficiencies in learning earlier in the course.

Students also asked for more 'action' earlier in the simulation, something we have resisted in the past as we wished teams to 'settle in' and build up their company. We have now revised the timing of industrial action.

The idea of integrating more completely with other study is attractive: for instance using the same game as the basis for other final-year business modules. Even if we could overcome the logistical (and human) problems involved, however, and the risk of depending so heavily on one simulation for so many modules, the very modularity of our degree scheme means that we cannot bank on all students being involved in every module.

We are also investigating the possibility of electronic means of data transmission, for input of decisions and output of results, exploiting the fact that all students have e-mail addresses.

CONCLUSION

We are not in the business of developing games, or of using games for their own sake. We had a problem, and the use of a business game was just one of the possible solutions. In the event, the results have far exceeded our expectations. Students and staff find the experience both enjoyable and educationally powerful, and in most respects better than the traditional live case study: 'It's a bit like a flight simulator, it packs a lifetime of experiences into one module'. Instead of just studying a process in cross-section, and second-hand, students are able to gain first-hand experience (albeit limited) over a period of time, during which they can monitor the effects of decision making in uncertainty, and take actions aimed at correcting or exploiting the results. They are in control.

Critical factors in the success of our use of business games include the following:

- reliable, tried and tested commercial products with excellent back-up (rarely used);
- simple system: post-in, post-out;
- actual mechanics of game handled by department support staff, and consequently success dependent on the quality of those staff. Although the administration becomes more routine with practice, the use of the game takes pressure off academic staff by putting it on support staff, and this needs to be fully recognized. Support staff must be treated as an integral part of the team;
- integration of the game in the learning, making it the central binding medium rather than an add-on extra. It maintains motivation, enhances learning;
- regular feedback to students;
- routine: decisions every week, same time, same place;
- surgeries to give informal support, and to compensate for large-group impersonality;
- low-cost, both in term of software and hardware needs.

The use of games is not a complete substitute for other learning methods. Although we would like to create a game continuum throughout all the stages of a degree, there is a danger that to make any more extensive use of them in this pathway would be overkill. The department has concurrently developed different but equally effective learning methods for other large-group modules, for instance 'training events' run by groups of students covering various issues in managing people, and groups of students acting as consultants to a large number of local companies. There are other ways of responding to the challenge of large groups.

Outside the confines of the degree programme, however, we have considered various other possible developments, including training for rural business owner/managers in the UK and Western Europe, helping fledgling managers adapt to growing market economies in Central and Eastern Europe, and running multinational games with students at overseas partner institutions (a sort of virtual mobility). Members of the department have obtained funding to allow development of learning support materials for Continuing Vocational Education on our World Wide Web server: it would be a simple matter to develop associated support services for players of the games, whether in-house or at a distance. A complementary development would be the generation of interactive multimedia support on CD-ROM, but the cost implications are substantial, and careful pilot testing would be required to ensure that there would be a substantial benefit for users.

Whether we can achieve any or all of these without a specialist game for land-using industries remains to be seen, and of course some involve substantial extra costs, such as international licences or purchase of multiple copies of software. In the meantime we remain delighted with our experience of 'off-the-peg' business games. We heartily commend the technique to others facing the challenge of teaching people what they may desperately need for the future, but are reluctant to learn here and now.

ABOUT THE AUTHORS

Martyn Warren is Head of Land Use and Rural Management Department in the University of Plymouth, and Richard Soffe and Robert Williams are both Senior Lecturers in the same department. Despite being known primarily as agricultural management specialists, they share an interest in rural business management in the widest sense, coupled with a determination to make learning both effective and fun.

Address for correspondence: Seale-Hayne Faculty of Agriculture, Food and Land Use, University of Plymouth, Newton Abbot, Devon, TQ12 6NQ. Tel: 01626 325673; Fax: 01626 325657; e-mail: mwarren@plymouth.ac.uk; WWW: http://141.163.121.36/

Chapter 17

'Are you who I think you are?' Making friends and playing games in cyberspace

Tina Wilson and Denise Whitelock

ABSTRACT

The adoption of fun environments in computer-mediated communication (CMC) is being considered by many institutions worldwide to overcome the problems of isolation associated with distance education and training courses. M205–STILE (Students' and Teachers' Integrated Learning Environment) is one such project that used a CMC environment with 110 distance learning students and nine tutors throughout the UK and Europe. The participants were online with conferencing and WWW facilities for a period of 10 months from February to November 1995. The provision of these online facilities put the students in touch with other students and their tutor. In order to find out what essential characteristics make a CMC enjoyable, we monitored the students' online activities and reactions within the environment. The data includes a case study.

This chapter reports on how remote and urban students used the online conferencing system to make friends and find like-minded colleagues to work with. Our results suggest that having fun and conveying a sense of humour are important factors in the formation of peer groups for online learning and therefore they are important factors in the design of interactive online environments for conferencing and WWW.

INTRODUCTION

Course developers worldwide are beginning to realize the benefits of making electronic media for education and training fun. Projects investigating how tutors facilitate learning and how students enjoy learning, in such online environments, are becoming of increasing interest to designers and educationalists alike. One project which was piloted at the Open University, and used modems, e-mail, conferencing and World Wide Web (WWW), was M205–STILE (Students' and Teachers' Integrated Learning Environment). The participants, nine tutors and 110 distance learning computer science students were based throughout the UK and Europe. The main aim of this project was to improve the presentation of the course by providing structured access to interactive online facilities. The students were hooked into the environment with the opportunity to make new friends in cyberspace, the chance to use new technologies to improve their learning, and the promise of extra teaching materials not provided elsewhere. This chapter reports on how the tutors enticed the students into the conferencing environment, and how the participants made friends and had fun while teaching and learning.

M205–STILE was the Open University implementation of the STILE project which included three other universities: Leicester, Loughborough and De Montfort. These latter sites used a system based on the WWW, to provide extra course materials to students working on campus. The Open University in addition to supplying online resources was providing students with online access to their tutors and other students. Access to the Web was given through the Netscape browser (©1994, Netscape Communications Corporation) and Trumpet software (©1993, 1994, Peter R Tatum and Trumpet Software International Pty Ltd). However the Web did not support conferencing suitably enough for our needs in 1995 and we also supplied the FirstClass conferencing and e-mail system (©1994, Softarc Inc.).

STUDENT FAMILIARITY WITH COMPUTER GAMES

The subjects were based throughout the UK and Europe. The course which the students followed was Fundamentals of Computing (M205) which catered for students from a variety of backgrounds, some without previous experience with conferencing, e-mail, WWW and modems (see Wilson and Whitelock, 1997a). The majority, some 78 per cent, were male students which is a typical percentage for students following a computer science course at the Open University. We obtained figures about subjects' computer usage at work using a questionnaire (see Wilson and Whitelock, 1997a). We also asked them about their home usage of a computer, as this might influence how they responded to the online facilities. For example, if they played computer games, would this affect their approach to the environment, which could in turn affect the learning dynamics in the system? We sent questionnaires out in March 1995, one month after the course started, to the 94 students who were online. We received a 66 per cent response rate. All of the students reported that they used their computer at home at some time. They were asked what activities they used it for and although these students were following a computer science course, 95 per cent said their main activity was use of word-processing and graphics applications. Running games packages was the second highest category and programming in one or various languages came third.

It was interesting to find that 66 per cent of these students did use games applications and we wondered therefore how much they would find the online facilities fun, and hence an aid to the learning process.

THE ENVIRONMENT AND HOW IT WAS STRUCTURED

We wanted to see how we could lure the students into the environment. We offered them the opportunity to meet their tutor and other students online to reduce their isolation; new technologies to support their learning; and extra materials to help with their study. The environment was set up with these in mind. The students and tutors did not meet before the project started and it was therefore important to have a facilitator whom everyone knew as a point of contact. We elected to have an independent person, whom we called the Interactive Media Facilitator or IMF, who would take overall responsibility for the online part of the course. Although the tutors were the facilitators as far as the course work was concerned, the IMF was the lynchpin who coordinated the whole activity from designing the online environment and the instructional materials, to keeping the discussion going throughout the project. The FirstClass online facilities were made available to the participants for the duration of the course, ie from February through to November 1995. Access to the Web facilities was delayed until July 1995 when the students had sufficient experience to install and set up the more complicated software necessary. (For more information on the role of the IMF and the design of the environments, see Wilson and Whitelock, 1996; 1997a; 1997b.)

RESULTS

This chapter presents a range of empirical findings which were chosen to address the following questions:

1. Did the environment make the students feel less isolated?
2. Did subjects find like-minded colleagues to work with?
3. Was a sense of fun conveyed during the learning process?
4. How can designers and tutors entice students to use these environments?

A variety of evaluation techniques were used to answer these questions. These included monitoring (i) the students choice of user name; (ii) online questionnaires completed by both the students and tutors; (iii) students' use of the facilities to find friends; and (iv) how subjects conveyed a sense of fun. The latter two were found by reading conference messages and using the FirstClass search facility. They include a case study.

Early enthusiasm for the online facilities

Initially the students were very enthusiastic participants. In fact 42 per cent of the students logged into FirstClass in the first five days of access. This indicates perhaps that students found it relatively easy to install and set up the FirstClass software. They had been sent their loan modem, software and comprehensive instructions approximately two weeks before their course started. The students had not met face-to-face before using FirstClass. As this system did not provide the facilities to allow aural or visual feedback, participants' names were one of the few early indicators of colleagues' personalities. The students were first registered on the system with their initials and surname but we offered them the opportunity to change from their initials to their preferred first name. Many students availed themselves of this option. In fact 89 per cent of the subjects participating requested the use of their first or preferred name instead of their initials. This high percentage of those prepared to reveal their first name and thus their gender, is perhaps an indication of their confidence with the system. As Kinkoph (1995) proposes, 'the gender you choose as your ID or handle plays an important part in how you're treated on-line'. Kinkoph (1995) also mentions that 'people even go so far as to make up on-line personas... no one will ever really know if you are who you say you are in cyberspace'. This raised important points about how we perceive ourselves and others in an online environment and how we convey our personality in such circumstances. One student described her perception of herself online as follows:

> I am surprised to find myself a bit shy and paranoid in fact.
> (Not being particularly so in real life)
> Although it's true that I never provoke interactions with strangers (City life?)

To other people this student was a real live wire online, constantly trying to cajole her colleagues into participating more.

Lessening isolation for remote students
Many Open University students work in isolation due to the large distance involved in travelling to meet tutors or fellow students whether at tutorials, self-help groups or just socially. Students in remote areas such as the Highlands and Islands of Scotland and Europe are even more isolated as in most cases they do not meet face-to-face at all. The provision of the online facilities enabled these students to get in touch with each other. Comments from students suggest that this communication lessened their sense of isolation. The following two examples from a European student illustrate this point:

> 1. Thanks for the messages. It's great I am feeling less isolated already.
> 2. Isn't it nice though to get through. Makes you feel the continent is no longer an island!

Getting in touch with like-minded colleagues
Although the students did not know each other before the course started, they very quickly started taking social risks online. They introduced themselves, shared personal details about their family, surroundings and hobbies, etc. Many students' initial messages were directed at finding online playmates:

> 1. Hello to anyone else who reads this message, my first name is Ade, and I look forward to conferencing with you.
> 2. Hello to all my fellow students on the M205 course.
> Apologies to anyone I haven't replied to that I was supposed to. I'm not being rude it's that I'm still finding my way around. Looking forward to using the STILE project to its fullest. Don't know about you but boy! Do I miss my spell-checker! By the way, am I the only Welshman taking part in this experiment?

As time progressed some students felt comfortable enough in this environment to convey more information about their cultural background. They started writing some of their messages in their chosen language, some in Welsh and some in French. Once students found like-minded colleagues they were enthusiastic to go online to keep in touch with them:

> I am sat here just after midnight also a little bored but feel free to chat I find I can stay online at this time of night much easier. I am not quite sure what all this is about just yet but it is good fun so I keep logging on to talk to you again.

This student saw the conferencing system as communication, as talking. He did not feel limited by the fact that they could only use text.

Students who could also attend face-to-face tutorials were keen to meet their tutor and fellow students in the flesh after meeting them online:

> Hello Sheila! I've just managed to find you! Still a bit confused with all this! However am looking forward to meeting everyone at the first tutorial.

Even though they were able to attend face-to-face tutorials, students still used the system to find like-minded peers online. This meant that they were not restricted to working with the students in their own tutorial group and they could set up self-help groups online which spanned the UK and Europe. More importantly the remote students were also able to make use of the facilities to find colleagues. One student who was indeed remote – she lived in the Highlands and Islands – said, 'Thanks for putting me on your list. I've already chatted with someone in Cumbria. This is great!'

Students activities

The students were given access to the facilities approximately two weeks before their course started. The IMF urged them to undertake various activities when they first came online, many of which encouraged them to socialize among themselves (see above, and Wilson and Whitelock, 1996). The activities included:

- sending an e-mail message,
- replying to an e-mail message,
- sending a message to a conference,
- replying to a conference message,
- working offline,
- downloading a file,
- attaching a file to an e-mail message,
- and introducing themselves to others with a resume.

Their ingenuity while undertaking these tasks was fascinating, whether it was conveying a sense of humour in their messages, or initiating games.

Conveying a sense of humour

It has been suggested by Nixon and Salmon (1995) that it is difficult to convey 'emotion and responses such as humour or anger... in computer conferencing'. We found however that many of the early messages from students conveyed a sense of humour through their use of language, punctuation and use of expressions sometimes called emoticons, such as 'grin'. One student commented, 'It was just fun getting to know other students by reading their postings – which were quite often humorous'. Bales' (1970) analysis of people's group behaviour draws attention to the use of jokes in articulating group structure and positive emotional support. The following two examples show how even though the students have encountered problems they can still laugh about it, on the very system that has caused the problem:

1. Hello. I'm still terrified of using FirstClass. It's akin to someone handing you a clarinet and saying 'play it'.

2. Well I've made it at last, even though I had to send one of the kids under the floor to pull a cable through, no doubt now I'll have lot's of fun exploring these facilities or maybe that's not what you want to hear.

Another student who knew they would use the system a lot because they felt very comfortable with it commented, 'Love the system, but no doubt will get to hate the bills <grin>'.

Having fun online
The students did have fun online; they also continued to have jokes with one another and some started to take more risks. Others however were more reticent but when they gained confidence they posted messages in what they felt was a safe environment. For example one student moved outside their tutorial conference (into the wider M205–STILE arena), for the first time on 4 June, some five months after the project started: 'I've not got around to leaving a message outside of the tutorial conference yet and thought it was about time I did...'. Many students also found the FirstClass system itself fun to use. One student mentioned how they had downloaded an online manual, but said: 'It's more fun using trial and error'. Another student enjoyed using FirstClass so much that she had a letter from France Telecom, asking if they had 'the funds to pay for the outrageous phone bill, they were running up'.

The students' sense of fun was also conveyed by their use of smiley or frowning expressions. Angell and Heslop (1994) suggest that 'too often the lack of inflection or facial expression can cause a typed phrase in an email message to be interpreted incorrectly' and infer that for this reason these types of expression 'emerged to help the reader decipher the writer's original intent'. The use of this type of notation in M205–STILE was probably inspired by a message entitled 'greetings', which was posted in the first month by one of the students. He said:

The normal BBS conventions of <grin> or:-> work well. There are thousands of variations as I am sure you know, some not printable here either:-<

Throughout the period from February to November a number of different forms of expression emerged. Punctuation such as parenthesis and exclamations marks were used a lot for emphasis. The most popular happy face was :-) while the most popular sad face was :(There were variations on smiley faces and grimaces; we even have one with a tear.

The conference which commanded the most expressions was the Meeting Place conference, which was a social area for all participants. The conferences which displayed few or no facial expressions were the Staffroom and the Student self-help conference. These conferences could be described as quite serious areas. However the M205–Help and Tutorial conferences had quite high proportions of smiley and sad faces even though these areas were focused more on work-related issues. Sad faces were used in messages where students had difficulty and were asking for help.

Although the system is icon- and text-based, the students were only able to manipulate the text, not the icons. Some students were very inventive and exploited the textual aspects of the conferencing system to the fullest, as the following two examples show.

> But it's because I am off on holiday that I'll be Off-Line:)
> ///// I \\\\\
> ||| ~ ~ |||| \I/   Bye for now
> ||[* I *]||| I   Helen
> ||| ~ |||| I
> ||| I I ||||| I

This picture is quite inventive and not found in texts on the subject. The person who initiated the trend for smiley and sad faces also challenged himself. It was interesting that his choice (but not the additional comment) can be found in some texts (Kinkoph, 1995):

> How about this then
> @>->— Normally sent to a member of the opposite gender when one wants to convey affection
> Answer A rose

This type of expression was not immediately understood by onlookers; even with the explanation, they did not realize that it should be viewed from a different perspective.

Playing games

Nixon and Salmon (1995) mention that 'without the usual non-verbal and face to face cues of speech, problems may arise over keeping the discussion going'. We found in M205–STILE, that the students themselves initiated various activities online such as offering each other the latest screen saver and offering the latest computer peripherals for sale. However one of the most interesting ploys used by one particular student to liven up group interaction is discussed below. This case study is a good example of playful behaviour online. This students' games drew other students in to give more cohesion to the group in this new environment. A typical example of the games she would play follows. In the Students Common Room she put a message headed TMA 8 (i) (Tutor Marked Assignment), on 10 July 1995. This TMA was not due in for marking until 3 October 1995. Many students were still working on TMA 6 which had a deadline of 1 August. Needless to say this message must have caused some consternation among students and provoked many to open the message. When the students opened the message they were greeted with:

> Ha!!!! that made you look.
> I haven't actually got anything to say.
> Just wanted to do that for the hell of it.
> Sorry, Helen.

The students did not realize before they opened the message what game was being played on them and many reacted differently. The first response was, 'Well you had me fooled. I was going to leave a rude message, but there's no need now:('. This student was disappointed that they could not respond to the message heading in a similar way when the contents of the message diffused their initial fervour. Helen, reading their responding message, showed no remorse and kept the game going:

> Ha! It worked, I am glad that I succumbed to my silliness then.
> I suppose others might see our messages and say...
> 'My god there's two of them on TMA 8!'
> It got what I wanted anyway...
> I actually found a message to read in here.
> It was one of Lizzie's messages that inspired me by the way!
> > Speak to you soon,
> > Helen.

A second student was enticed by Helen's playfulness to read the message. They admitted they were fooled by the message heading: 'You were right Helen... another one fished in!!!-:)'. A third student conveyed their sense of panic by saying:

> OK OK... you got me too!
> Numerous obscenities were heard in the room when I saw the subject header
> Nice one Helen!

A fourth student took this sense of outrage a step further: 'If there was a summer school you would be prime candidate for going for a swim in the nearest lake ;-) another one sucked in'.

Helen's response to these messages held no shame and even a further tease:

> I have no regrets!!!
> I have unearthed strange, until now unseen names.
> I have even communicated with some of these unknowns.
> I actually know of someone...
> who is finishing off his M205 TMAs, plus the TMAs for his other half credit,
> before going on holiday!!!!!!
> I'd better not reveal his identity though.
> By the way, about TMA 7 Q4(ii)!

By engaging in this activity, Helen has lured some of the students in from the sidelines. Not long after this flurry of activity, the Students Common room went a little quiet when many students were away on holiday. Not satisfied with this, Helen on her return from holiday on 31 August posted the following message to try again to stimulate participation

> I am back!!!
> I notice that I didn't miss much,
> I know it was a dramatic exit for a holiday that didn't even last a week, but..
> I historied my message, and saw all those nice familiar names.
> It's nice to open a forum/conference and find something, isn't it?
> So make my day
> Go on... even if you don't know me, put a flag in my box.
> (Sorry I've been on the Calvados!)
> So we've got till October 30th before we get robbed for this, so...
> Let's go for it...

The response on 2 September indicates that some students were also busy at this time setting up their Netscape software:

> A flag in your mailbox, as requested!
> If I'm typical of all the others, it's been quiet because I've been busy investigating the Internet software (now might be a good time to buy shares in BT).
> Perhaps we should make a lot more use of this set-up from now til 30 Oct – then we might really convince the OU to give us continuing access. How about some conferences for (perhaps the most popular) courses which members of our group are doing next year? Not necessarily involving tutors, if this causes problems: I was thinking more in the line of peer group type teaching.
> Glad you enjoyed your holiday: the UK was certainly hot this summer but we're back to the usual weather now (ie rain and dull skies!)
> Lizzie:-)

These messages also indicate that these students see this medium as a forum that they should make the most of, in the time they have left, to make sure they don't lose it for follow-on years.

Hooking the students into the environment

In addition to making friends online, the students also had online tutorial conferences where they could contact their tutor and other students in their tutorial group. Some tutorials were more active than others. One enthusiastic tutor tried to lure the students into his tutorial conference, saying:

> I am glad that many of you have got connected to the Tutorial conference. I am sure that some of you are reading the messages and haven't yet posted any messages. Reading messages without letting others know you are in there is known as 'lurking'. There is nothing wrong with lurking but I would encourage you all to take part in the conference. Please do post, even just a short message to say hi.

This message did encourage some of the quieter students to post messages.

The students were also offered the opportunity to download and use additional material not provided elsewhere. The FirstClass material for blocks 1 to 4 was in the form of questions with follow-up answers. The Web material for block 5 was in more of a tutorial style. (See Wilson and Whitelock, 1997b, for students' reactions to the presentation of the extra material and which interface they preferred.) The tutor who prepared the Block 5 material for the Web suggested at a meeting at the end of the project that the extra material was a way of enticing the students in. He commented:

> I think it's a way of luring people in if they think there is something they are missing out on that might be helpful, they're going to get in there and start exploring. The act of doing that means that they realise what is there, it is hard to describe cyberspace, that whole culture to someone in words but if you get in there and start putting things in, you realise what it is about and it is quite useful. You've got to give people a lure to start using it, and one way is to say there is some quite interesting teaching material, they might not read it but at least it has got them in.

SUMMARY

One interesting outcome related to the culture of the online group was the absence of any outbursts of 'flaming', or harassment in any of the conferences and none was reported to the IMF. Angell and Heslop (1994) propose that 'the email medium has inherent characteristics that make it a tinderbox for explosive, emotional email exchanges'. Kinkoph (1995) suggests that anonymity means that 'on-line flaming can be more aggressive than in real life'. The conferencing environment could be similarly characteristic, where the numbers of participants can ensure that a 'flame war' can ensue over many messages in a short period of time. In order to overcome such situations, Nixon and Salmon (1995) suggest that participants need to be supplied with information called 'netiquette'. In M205 – STILE the IMF took steps to avoid the occurrence of flaming.

The documentation that was sent to tutors and students before they came online included a section on 'protocols and netiquette' from Selinger (1994). In addition the IMF allocated message approval status to the tutors to enable them to monitor student messages in the tutorial conferences before the messages were available to all students. The IMF who was responsible for all social conferences similarly monitored the student-only conference at the start of the course. This activity enabled the IMF to quickly stop and counsel one student who did not realize that their comments about national traits, etc could be misunderstood and cause an upset to other students. This action, where no one except the IMF could see the message initially, possibly prevented a 'flaming session' and saved this student from embarrassment.

Once this student and others realized what was acceptable behaviour, the IMF removed message approval. The downside of introducing message approval is the possibility of stilting message flows in the early days of the conferences, unless the IMF or tutors are online enough to quickly approve messages. There is perhaps a payoff, however, for having message approval and the influence of the IMF and tutors in the early days to create a comfortable and safe environment for all participants. One of Minsky's (1984) theories suggests that 'humour evolved in a social context. Its forms include graciously disarming ways to instruct others about appropriate behaviour and faulty reasoning'. The key perhaps is to find a balance between using a sense of humour, and over-policing to prevent activities such as flaming. We would recommend that message approval be used for at least the first two weeks or until acceptable behaviour has been established. This will require the IMF and tutors to be online more often when the conference is first opened.

We suggest that three of the main variables in maintaining the dynamics of the group in our environment are: participation which can be either passive or dominant; having fun; and avoiding 'flaming'. The IMF has an important role to play in addressing this balance. We found that students exploited the textual nature of the medium to convey their personality, including their sense of humour. They looked for friends to lessen their sense of isolation, and for like-minded colleagues to work with, in the UK and Europe. They had fun and played games.

Although the extra material did lure some students into the environment and we did include some of the motivating factors necessary for this environment (see below), we need to consider the following issues. In terms of Malone and Lepper's (1987) task challenges, the students did experience feelings of self-esteem because the different tasks set alleviated feelings of an uncertain outcome. However, though the goals should have been clear, the tutors did not realize that their intentions were not communicated to the students. The tutors may not have given enough performance feedback to students, and need to be instructed in how to give the students indications of progress in this environment.

One influential notion from epistemologists such as Piaget (1970) is that people actively construct their own knowledge. How they do this and interact with others in this process is illustrated by the playfulness and humour described or shown on the system. One such example is that of Helen whose actions illustrate how knowledge is socially constructed and her dialogue could be thought of as scaffolding others, when viewed from Vygotsky's (1988) perspective.

FUTURE WORK

This chapter perhaps raises more questions than it provides answers, and future research agendas should address the issues of how students choose peer groups online. How do they decide who they are going to work with, given the limitations of the system, ie just text, smiley faces, names and punctuation, and what conditions help students find a play mate or a peer group, however transient? One tutor's heart-felt plea at the end of the project was: 'how do you get the students familiar with the culture before they actually start using it in earnest?' Because we loaned modems to students we were limited to engaging the students in the environment just two weeks before their course started. In future we would recommend that the IMF took an active role in establishing a comfortable environment for students at least two months in advance of the course start date.

ACKNOWLEDGEMENTS

The research described in this chapter was undertaken in the Computing Department, Faculty of Mathematics and Computing, at the Open University as part of the STILE project. The project was supported by a grant from the Teaching and Learning Technology Programme which is jointly funded by the four higher education funding bodies, HEFCE, HEFCW, SHEFC and DENI.

We would like to thank all nine tutors involved in M205–STILE, especially those who designed the extra material for FirstClass: Diana Worster, Gerry Hayden, Tony Dickinson, Elizabeth Broumley, and George McLeod who prepared the extra material for the Web.

REFERENCES

Angell, D and Heslop, B (1994) *The Elements of E-mail Style*, Addison Wesley, Wokingham.
Bales, F R (1970) *Personality and Interpersonal Behaviour*, Holt, Rinehart & Winston, London.

Kinkoph, S (1995) *The Complete Idiot's Guide to Sex, Lies and Online Chat*, QUE Corporation, Indianapolis, IN.

Malone, T and Lepper, M R (1987) 'Making learning fun', in Snow, R and Farr, M (eds) *Aptitude, Learning and Instruction: Cognitive and affective process analyses*, Lawrence Erlbaum, Hove.

Minsky, M (1984) 'Jokes and the logic of the cognitive unconscious', in Viana, L and Hintikka, J (eds) *Cognitive Constraints on Communication*, Reidel Publishing, Holland.

Nixon, T and Salmon, G (1995) 'Spinning your Web', paper presented to the Society for Research Into Higher Education Annual Conference, Edinburgh.

Piaget, J (1970) *Psychology and Epistemology: Towards a theory of* knowledge, Penguin, Harmondsworth.

Selinger, M (1994) *FirstClass Handbook for the Postgraduate Diploma in Education*, School of Education, Open University, Milton Keynes.

Wilson, T and Whitelock, D (1996) 'Piloting a new approach; Making use of new technology to present a distance learning computer science course', *Association for Learning Technology Journal*, **4**, 1.

Wilson, T and Whitelock, D (1997a) 'Facilitating electronic communication; Evaluating computer science tutors' and students' interaction using computer mediated communication at a distance learning university', in press for the 3rd edition of a report to ICEM entitled: 'An International Survey of Distance Education and Training for Organisations: From Smoke Signals to Satellite III'.

Wilson, T and Whitelock, D (1997b) 'Opening up horizons: providing online course material in cyberspace', in press, special issue of *Displays on multimedia*.

Vygotsky, L (1988) *Thought and Language*, The Massachusetts Institute of Technology, Boston, MA.

ABOUT THE AUTHORS

Tina Wilson is a software designer in the Centre for Educational Software at the Open University, UK. Her research interests include the educational use of conferencing, e-mail and the Internet to teach computer science to distance learners and the dynamic nature of student interaction in this process.

Denise Whitelock is a lecturer in Information Technology in the Institute of Educational Technology at the Open University. Her research interests include the role of new technologies in the teaching of formal knowledge systems, such as science and computer science, to distance learners.

Addresses for correspondence: Tina Wilson, Centre for Educational Software, The Open University, Walton Hall, Milton Keynes MK7 6AA. Tel: 01908 654026; e-mail M.E.Wilson@open.ac.uk
Denise Whitelock, Institute of Educational Technology, The Open University, Walton Hall, Milton Keynes MK7 6AA; e-mail D.M.Whitelock@open.ac.uk

Chapter 18

TERRITORY: **A simulation in biology**

Claude Bourlès

ABSTRACT

The game TERRITORY is designed for use with students following introductory courses in areas of biology such as animal behaviour, ecology, evolution and population genetics. It uses packs of ordinary playing cards and game counters. Groups of up to 60 students can play.

INTRODUCTION

The game TERRITORY was first designed to introduce the question of territoriality in animal behaviour. It appeared that the game was also useful in teaching ecology, Darwinism, evolution and population genetics. The game was used with students in psychology and in ecology. The use of a game, through intensive interaction, enhances the interest of students in the subject. Another effect of the game, through creating a friendly atmosphere, is to act as an icebreaker.

PRESENTATION

Number of players: 12 to 60.
Material required: several standard 52 card packs (one pack for every 20 players). Up to 40 counters of four different colours (red, yellow, green, blue) and two shapes (a circle, and square or rectangle).
Duration: one hour; more if the variations are used.
Where to play: in any room large enough for the group to fit and move around. The game can even be played outdoors. This is not a game for sitting or resting.
Objective: to make a group of people familiar with the notions of territory, sexual selection and populations genetics through a game using inexpensive materials.
General idea: standard playing cards are used to represent the resources of the

environment and the features of live beings. The four suits (hearts, clubs, diamonds and spades) are used. The values of the cards are taken into account from one to ten; king, queen and jack are worth one.

Preliminaries: for a 12 to 20 player group, allow a 52 card pack and a box of counters from different colours and shapes (three to five colours; square or rectangle counters will represent males, circular counters will represent females). Sort the cards by suit. Prepare six copies of the territory sheets on which << TERRITORY, RESOURCES, MALE'S DOMINANCE and MATE'S FERTILITY>> are written; see Figure 18.1.

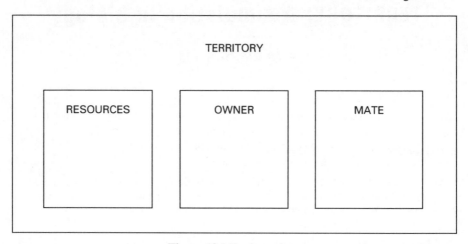

Figure 18.1 Territory sheet

Setting up: arrange the territory sheets on separate tables, but not too far from each other.

Instructions to players: 'You are live beings of the same species, maybe birds, rodents or any other animals. An important feature of your species is your Territoriality: every one needs a territory to live, survive and reproduce. Players will be parted into two groups of about the same size: the "males" and the "females". Only those who will get a territory will be able to find a mate and (maybe) reproduce. In order to control a territory, you will need a high level of dominance'.

The club cards represent the resources of the territories, which may change each turn.

The animal's dominance is represented by heart cards for the males and diamond cards for the females. Spade cards represent female fertility. The cards will be dealt each turn.

RULES OF THE GAME

0. Initial census

It is better to start the game with 16 animals: four categories (red, yellow, green, blue), four animals in each category (two males and two females). Whatever the starting number, it is necessary to write down this number on a flipchart or blackboard. For the sake of the demonstration, it is better if the four categories begin with equal numbers.

1. Resources of the environment

On each territory, the facilitator puts down or has a player put down a club card which will represent the food resources of the territory; with the remaining cards, the resources of territories which are poor (value one) can be improved by adding a card (only one). Obviously some territories are more interesting than others.

2. Males' dominance

The facilitator gives a coloured counter to each 'male' player. As far as possible, these should be equal counters of each colour – if there are eight male players, give two red, two yellow, two green and two blue ones. Hand out four heart cards to each red player; the player will keep the card with the highest value and return the others to the facilitator. Then the yellow players are given three of the remaining cards in the same way. Then it is the turn of the green players with two cards, and last the blue players are dealt with one card. This process is meant to simulate interindividual variability.

3. Females' features

The facilitator gives a coloured counter to each 'female' player. An equal number of counters of each colour is given; if there are eight female players, give two red, two yellow, two green and two blue ones.

Females' dominance
Hand out four diamond cards to each red player; the players will keep the card with the highest value and return the others to the facilitator. Then the yellow players are given three of the remaining cards in the same way. Then it is the turn of the green players with two cards, and last the blue players with one card. As before, this process is meant to simulate interindividual variability.

Females' fertility
Hand out a spade card taken at random to each female player. Do not allow the player to see the value of the card. Don't use the remaining cards. The dominance feature is not linked to the fertility feature.

4. Territory appropriation

The males seize the territories, starting with those who get the highest dominance. Once a territory is occupied, no one can challenge the owner.

5. Mates' selection

The females come and find the males. They can show their diamond cards, but must not show their spade card. Two procedures are possible:

1. Starting with the highest dominance, the female players select the males who own the territories with the highest resource level. The female player puts their counter beside the male counter on the territory.
2. All females are looking for a mate, and when two of them are in competition the most dominant stays. The female player puts their counter beside the male counter on the territory.

6. Reproduction

Examine the female fertility card and the territory resource card. The fertility card indicates the number of children the female can breed and raise to adult age. The territory resource card indicates the number of offspring the territory can feed up to adult age; it is a restricting factor of the environment. Keep the lowest value; it represents the number of offspring which will survive. Put down on the territory a number of counters equal to this value. The offspring counter colour is chosen according to the colour of the parents:

– if the parents have the same colour, this will be the colour of the children;
– if the parents have different colours, half of the counters will be of the father's colour and the other half will be of the mother's colour. In the case of an odd number of children, the supernumerary individual will be of the most dominant possible colour.

Put aside the parental counters. This will help the census at the end of the turn.

Notice that the high values of the spade cards are the most interesting. Notice that males cannot know the level of fertility of the female they select.

7. Evaluation of the reproductive success (census)

Count the number of counters of each colour. Discuss the effects of limiting factors upon reproduction.

8. Pick up all the cards while keeping the different suits separated for the following turn. During several successive runs, observe the variation of colours. One colour or more may disappear.

If after several turns, counters are of the same colour, deal again counters of the four colours in equal quantity and try the following variations:

Variation 1: The males will know the fecundity of the females. During phase 5, the female players must show their spade fecundity card.
Variation 1.1: Like variation 1, but the female's dominance and fecundity characters are linked; high dominance linked to high fertility.
Variation 1.2: Like variation 1, but the female's dominance and fecundity characters

are inversely linked; high dominance linked to low fertility.

Variation 2: Alternative determination of offspring number: divide the resource value of territory by the fecundity of female. Round down the result. This result will represent the number of offspring which will survive. Put aside the parental counters. Notice that low values of spade cards are the most interesting now.

Variation 3: Alternative territory appropriation: everybody tries to seize a territory, and when there is a conflict, the most dominant male occupies the territory. In case of equality, the following and decreasing hierarchy apply: ten down to ace, king, queen, jack. The player puts his counter on the territory paper to mark his possession. It may happen that a player with a higher dominance appears and turns out a player already settled. Write down the number of individuals owning a territory (and who will be able to reproduce in principle) and the number of individuals without territory.

Variation 3.1: Dominance genetically dominant. When the counters of the children are put on the territory, keep the most dominant colour, so, for instance, when a parent is red and the other yellow, use red counters for the offspring.

Variation 3.2: Dominance genetically recessive. When the counters of the children are put on the territory, keep the least dominant colour, so, for instance, when a parent is red and the other yellow, use yellow counters for the offspring.

Variation 4: Influence of predation. Give two players the joker cards from the card pack. They become the predators. The predators are allowed to pick up a counter every minute during the game. What happens if the predators select one colour – the red counters, for example?

DEBRIEFING

Can we find examples of animals behaving like those of the model?
After several turns, have the proportions (nearly equal at the beginning) changed?
Which factors make for reproductive success?
How is selection operating?
Between which limits is the number of offspring evolving?
What is the influence of human activities?
What is the influence of predation?

SUGGESTED READING

Books about animal behaviour

Brooks, F (1992) *Animal Behaviour*, Usborne Science & Nature, London.
Stidworthy, J (1992) *Animal Behaviour*, Prentice Hall, Hemel Hempstead.
Owen, J (1980) *Feeding Strategy*, The University of Chicago Press, Chicago, IL.
Halliday, T (1980) *Sexual Strategy*, The University of Chicago Press, Chicago, IL.

Articles

Pfenning, D and Sherman, P (1995) 'La reconnaissance parentale', *Pour la Science*, 214, 40–46.
Nowak, M, May, R and Sigmund, K (1995) 'L'arithmétique de l'entr'aide', *Pour la Science*, 214, 56–61.

Games using playing cards

Cudworth, A and Loveluck, C (1993) 'OPTIMIZE', in *The Simulation and Gaming Yearbook*, Kogan Page, London.
Corbeil, P (1995) 'SCRUTIN', in *Entreprendre par le jeu*, Editions Transcontinental Inc, Canada.
Thiagarajan, R and Thiagarajan, S (1995) 'INDUCT: a game of scientific induction', in *Simulation and Gaming*, **26**, 4, 518–23.

Games for teaching evolution

EXTINCTION, the game of ecology (1978) Carolina Biological Supply Company, Burlington, NC.

ABOUT THE AUTHOR

Claude Bourlès has been a member of SAGSET (Society for Active Learning) and ISAGA (International Simulation and Learning Association) since 1989. He has taught biology and animal behaviour since 1970 to students in psychology at IPSA (Institut de Psychologie et Sociologie Appliquées d'Angers). Recently, he began to teach ecology to the students of IEA (Institut d'Ecologie Appliquée). He is developing games in biology and in other areas such as economy and contemporary problems.

Address for correspondence: GERSAFE-IPSA-UCO, BP 808, 49008, F 49008 Angers Cedex 01, France.

Chapter 19

Tough choices: The Prisoner's Dilemma in the classroom

Steve Davis

ABSTRACT

In this chapter I show how participants in a series of activities can explore for themselves the strategies they employ when they have to solve complex problems. The vehicle for these problems is the well-known Prisoner's Dilemma – a scenario that examines, in detail, the intractable nature of interpersonal relationships, and the complications attendant on the choice between self-interest and the common good. The problem simulations that I derive from the Prisoner's Dilemma are content-free, are very easy to explain and operate, and can be handled by individuals at their own level of analysis and complexity. This allows them to be used with a wide range of age groups and ability levels. I have used them in this way on many occasions and I comment on the sort of outcomes that can be expected from them, and the sorts of discussion that can be engendered. I also endeavour to set the exercises in context, with suggestions about lead-in and follow-up work. The whole provides a course of study that allows an in-depth, hands-on consideration of tough choices.

The activities themselves, which are described in detail, are all designed to occupy class sizes, and are of two main types. First there are small group activities – bead games – where the class is divided into a series of individual contests. Second, there are whole-class activities, where everyone participates in one large decision-making contest. The beauty of using the Prisoner's Dilemma as a teaching ploy is that its matrix representation easily allows the development of further simulations. The ways that these, and other non-zero-sum matrix games, can be used as teaching devices is discussed at the end of the chapter.

I have found the whole set of activities rewarding and enjoyable for both myself and my students. This chapter gives me the opportunity to present my findings, and convey my enthusiasm for this flexible, simple, yet all-embracing approach to problem-solving.

THE PROBLEM OF COLLECTIVE ACTION

I once saw an episode of the *Twilight Zone* called *The Shelter*. It tells of a group of comfortably-off American families who are suddenly faced with a nuclear alert. Only one family, the doctor's, has a fallout shelter, which he has spent a good deal of time constructing. The family enters the shelter and close the door. As the episode unfolds, other families arrive and ask to be let into the shelter. Unfortunately, the air filter in the shelter will only support the doctor, his wife and their young son. Eventually the mob outside the shelter becomes uncontrolled and they end up smashing in the door, thereby ruining the shelter for everyone. At that moment, a *deus ex machina* in the form of a stand-down announcement on the radio ends the action: everyone is safe. A suitable moral pronouncement about civilized people acting in a civilized manner terminates the programme. By describing such a scenario to my classes, I am able to pose two questions which are essential to an understanding of the prisoner's dilemma. The second is asked after responses have been taken to the first:

1. Did the doctor have the right to lock his own family in the shelter and refuse some others the right to survive instead?

The invariable response to this question is 'Yes'. The doctor was in the right and the rest of his neighbours were in the wrong to make demands of him. After all, the programme itself, through the doctor, makes the point that he spent a long time in building his shelter while the others were enjoying themselves. The doctor has earned the right to survive and the rest should have acted more responsibly.

2. If the doctor has the right to ensure the survival of his family, don't the neighbours also have this right?

This is a perplexing question, and classes have difficulty answering. This is not surprising, because it is the crux of the Prisoner's Dilemma. If the doctor has the right, then presumably so have the others. The doctor cannot really expect to be the only one to act selfishly while the others act altruistically. The work he has already done is irrelevant. Whether you plan for safety in a nuclear war over five years or over the last five minutes does not deny an individual's right to try to survive: death should not be the penalty for lack of foresight. If, however, we allow the right of survival to all, then the film shows clearly the consequence: the destruction of the one amenity which could save lives. So everyone dies. Where a resource is scarce, therefore, some should perhaps forego their right of survival so that others might live. But who should survive and who should die? Certainly there are not only problems for rational choice here, but also deep moral issues to be considered.

THE PRISONER'S DILEMMA

The Prisoner's Dilemma is a paradigmatic case of the group decision being at variance with, indeed undermining, the individual rationale. The resultant group ethos may present the individuals in a poor light even though, individually, they are doing their best to cope with the want to–ought to polarity. The dilemma, generally attributed to A W Tucker of the Rand Corporation, is named after two fictional prisoners. They are held for a minor crime, but are suspected of a major one. They are separately offered a deal, which they are not allowed to discuss with each other. If one is prepared to confess to the major crime, and the other doesn't, then the confession will help convict the other who will be severely punished. In return for his help, the first prisoner will be freed. If both confess to the major crime, then they will be punished but with some leniency because they confessed. If neither confesses, they will simply serve the sentence for the minor crime. The payoff Prisoner I receives in relation to Prisoner II's strategies is shown in Figure 19.1.

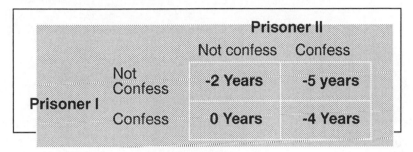

Figure 19.1

This matrix shows that if I doesn't confess and II does, then I gets five years. If they both don't confess they get two years. If they both confess, they get four years. If I confesses and II doesn't, I serves no sentence. The figures are given in negative amounts to represent the amount of liberty that Prisoner I loses. Conventionally, however, games in the strategic form tend to be represented in a positive way: the amount a player gains rather than loses. This can be achieved quite easily by adding a positive number to each payoff. The result for Prisoner I's payoff is shown in Figure 19.2.

	Prisoner II	
	Not confess	Confess
Not Confess	3	0
Confess	5	1

Figure 19.2

Here five has been added to each payoff and the now meaningless 'years' dispensed with. If liberty is of utmost importance to the prisoners, then the numbers are a weighted value of how much Prisoner I prefers each outcome. In other words, he or she would prefer the scenario where he or she confesses almost twice as much as the one where neither confesses. This matrix can be said, therefore, to express *utility* values: that is, the weighting that is given by each prisoner to each choice.

Further additions can be made to the matrix. First, it only shows payoffs for Prisoner I. Again by convention, Prisoner II's payoffs are shown to the right of Prisoner I's; see Figure 19.3.

		Prisoner II	
		Not confess	Confess
Prisoner I	Not Confess	3,3	0,5
	Confess	5,0	1,1

Figure 19.3

A second variation is to represent preferences simply in their order and not their strength. For both prisoners, the preferred order of strategy combinations, from greatest to least is:

I confess, other doesn't	4
Neither of us confesses	3
Both of us confess	2
I don't confess, other does	1

For each prisoner, the numbers represent the order of preferences, the highest being the most preferred. These numbers are shown next to the strategy combinations. The matrix shown in Figure 19.4 results.

		Prisoner II	
		Not confess	Confess
Prisoner I	Not Confess	3,3	1,4
	Confess	4,1	2,2

Figure 19.4

Both styles of representation, the utility and the ordinal, have their uses. Utility matrices are used to model actual scenarios, and can be manipulated to investigate the thresholds of behaviour. Ordinal matrices can be used to model the general preference structures, and so make comparison with other combinations of preferences possible. In particular, the use of ordinal matrices makes the generation of new models a relatively easy job. (I will investigate this application below, where the use of such matrices in the classroom is described.) The type of representation to be used, therefore, varies according to the nature of the activity under consideration.

It can be easily seen why this type of game is called a non-zero-sum game. Games, commonly, are taken to mean those of the parlour variety: bridge, chess, Monopoly and so on. In this type of game, whatever one player wins the other loses. The total of losses and gains is, therefore, zero. These games are called zero-sum games, and are games of pure conflict. In a game such as the prisoner's dilemma , both players can win. For example, the strategy combination 'Don't confess – Don't confess' allows both to benefit. The total of their gains and losses, therefore, is not zero. As we will see, the games still involve a measure of conflict, but the ability for both players to benefit enables an element of cooperation. I shall have more to say on this issue later.

Since non-zero-sum games model a complex mix of cooperation and conflict, they provide a tough challenge for decision makers. I intend in the rest of this chapter to describe a series of such games, games which pose increasingly intractable problems, leading to the spontaneous development by the players of an extensive array of strategies based on combinations of cooperation and defections from cooperation.

TACIT AGREEMENT AND INFORMAL RULES

The first activity to be described consists of a series of contests played in groups of three players. Two play each time and the third acts as scorer and umpire. Three games are played in a set, so each player plays every other. The games are based on choices from matrices, in the way that the prisoner's dilemma are represented. However a matrix representation is not used. Instead the matrices are turned into separable games, a device which is described in Guyer *et al.* (1973). These are much simpler to play. For example, the first game uses the matrix shown in Figure 19.5.

		Player II	
		Choice A	Choice B
Player 1	Choice A	2,2	1,2
	Choice B	2,1	1,1

Figure 19.5

This game is not a Prisoner's Dilemma, but is generally referred to as the assurance game. The urge to defect from cooperating in this game lies not in a gain in points over what can be gained by cooperation, but by a gain in points over the other player. This game would be represented in separable form by the following rule:

Choose a counter (Green = 2 – choice A; Red = 1 – choice B). Give the score you choose to the other player.

An analysis of the different combinations which can be played will reveal that it generates exactly the payoffs shown in the matrix.

A second game has this rule:

Choose a counter (Red = 1; Green = 2). Give the score to the other player, except if you both pick red. In this case you get 0.

This rule generates a similar matrix to the first, except that a mutual B choice yields no score. This is a more risky form of the assurance game, in that defection might lead to a very low payoff if defection becomes mutual. The only excuse for defection is a desire to score more points than your opponent. It's risky nature makes it more of a Game of Chicken.

A third rule is:

> Choose a counter (Red = 1; Green = 2). If you pick red you keep the score. If you pick green you give the score to the other player.

An inspection of the payoffs from all combinations of choices here reveals that the resultant matrix is the prisoner's dilemma. If the actions are reversed (give the red score and keep the green score), then we have the altruist's dilemma, where the player selecting green gains even more if the other selflessly picks red. Both suffer if they both act selflessly, however.

A final rule is:

> Choose a counter. If you choose green, score 1 for yourself and give 2 to the other player. If you choose red do nothing.

This again produces a form of the assurance game, where the only incentive to defect lies in gaining a better score than the other player, even though a mutual choice of green gives the best score of all. A choice of red in this game is particularly negative, in that it contributes nothing in any circumstances. A mutual choice of red could well lead to a Chicken Game again, as each tries to force the other to pick green and at least gain something.

By using separable games therefore, many games can be easily played and their outcomes analysed and discussed.

The lesson employs the first two games described. Eventually all groups learn to cooperate, but the manner by which they learn is exceptionally interesting. First, it is necessary to emphasize that although cooperation is not specifically requested, it is fully enabled by the way in which the games are presented. At no times are rival players referred to as 'opponents'. More importantly, success at the games requires players to score higher than a target score. It is emphasized that beating the other player's score does not count, simply beating the target score. It is possible, therefore, for all players in the room to win. Finally, it is emphasized that talking with the other player and discussing the game is entirely acceptable.

The players, although they are playing in groups of three, all broadly follow the same strategies and styles of play. Every group begins by selecting the counters at random, effectively turning it into a game of chance. Discussion and cooperation simply involve devising sensible or effective ways of doing this. Some choose their own counters, others offer closed hands to be selected by the other player. While the target score is low (for example, to score 12 over ten choices each), there is no incentive to change this randomizing approach. Only with a rise in the target (to 17 and finally 20, the maximum that can be scored), do groups begin to think of other approaches. First one group begins to pick green every time, then others, until the idea spreads throughout the class. Most interestingly, the groups who develop this strategy are accused of cheating. Discussion with classes reveals complex thinking about social mores. Although it is pointed out that the rules do not preclude choosing a particular colour every time, most people are adamant that this is cheating. This view seems to be based on the following arguments which individuals arrive at independently but which become a view held by all in the group:

- This is a game, and my experience of games like Snakes and Ladders is that they are a matter of luck. Therefore, to succeed at these games involves luck – picking at random.
- The aim of a game is to score more than the other person.
- Games are fun. To play in other ways would be boring.
- Look after myself. In other words, the players do not understand that giving away points, if done mutually, is the equivalent of gaining points.

So overlaying the formal rules of the game are a set of informal rules. Just because they are informal, they are no less valid or valued than formal rules. They are quickly formed, universal, binding and long-lasting. Anyone who contravenes them is as much a cheat as if he or she contravened the formal ones. Groups that break these rules are reviled. Interestingly, although players showed little inclination to cooperate in playing the game, the players as individuals quickly reached an informal tacit agreement over what constituted fair play and what didn't. My support of the 'cheats' reduced the resentment they suffered, but it is a moot point as to whether they actually acted rationally by defecting from the group consensus on rules. Certainly, in the scores they obtained they acted rationally to a game theoretician. In the scorn they called down upon themselves, they certainly did not act in their best interests.

TACIT AGREEMENT AND THE PRISONER'S DILEMMA

The activities described so far demonstrate that, in the vast majority of cases, groups function well because an individual's choice is reflected, in aggregation, by the group choice. In this way, tacit agreement develops and a set of informal rules emerge. Problems arise, however, when the individual is forced to make a choice which is contrary to that of the group. The following activity, which is based on games described in the seminal work on agreement and conflict, *The Strategy of Conflict* by Thomas Schelling (1960), shows how easily tacit agreement can fall apart. During these activities discussion is not allowed, since the aim is demonstrate the spontaneous growth of tacit agreement.

> 1. Think of a playing card and write it down. You win if you pick the card that most others in the group pick.

The majority of players select the ace of spades. In Schelling's terms, this is an obvious choice which, without other information, the group will opt for. If the activity is repeated, even more choose the ace of spades, because the first game has made it even more obvious. Other choices can be devised which produce similar outcomes: pick a time you would arrange to meet someone, then a place, and so on. The playing card activity is particularly effective, however, since members of the group are amazed by the extent to which their one out of 52 choice is mirrored by others.

2. Write a number between one and ten. You gain the number of points you write down.

This is almost trivial, and produces a tacit agreement of ten.

3. Write a number between one and ten. You obtain those many points providing no one in the class writes a lower.

The minor rewording from activity 2 leads to a completely different problem, and a rapid breakdown of tacit agreement. This activity is the Prisoner's Dilemma in another form. Cooperation within the class would lead to a high score for everyone. Invariably, however, several players defect from this strategy, select the number one, and so obtain a certain but meagre payoff. If the rules are relaxed to allow any number to be written and to allow group discussion beforehand, stranger results obtain. Even though individuals urge the group to write a given high number so everyone wins, players still persist in writing low numbers. Most perversely, every time I have played this game, players have actually written negative numbers, effectively losing points! So great is the urge to win, players will actually handicap themselves in order to do so. The principal problem still seems to be that players view these games as parlour games, where defeating the other players is of paramount importance, even at the expense of a personal loss.

ZERO-SUM GAMES AND NON-ZERO-SUM GAMES

The next lesson consists of a multi-person game based on selections from a prisoner's dilemma matrix. The technique used was suggested by Douglas Hofstadter in his article on the Prisoner's Dilemma in *Scientific American*, later reprinted in his *Metamagical Themas* (Hofstadter, 1985). Simply, using a standard prisoners dilemma matrix, each player chooses from a row and scores the payoff from the matrix multiplied by the numbers making each choice in the column. The matrix in Figure 19.6, for example, could be used.

	Choice A	Choice B
Choice A	3	0
Choice B	5	1

Figure 19.6

Suppose that six players pick A and seven players pick B, then those picking A will receive 6 x 3 + 7 x 0 = 18, while those picking B will receive 6 x 5 + 7 x 1 = 37.

Therefore, as with all prisoner's dilemma games, the highest scores are made by a few defectors free-riding on a large number of cooperators. Large-scale defection leads to scores lower than can be made from large-scale cooperation. But the move to large-scale cooperation again paves the way for free-riding by a few defectors.

As with the individual-player games described earlier, an external target is set, the achieving of which is deemed a win. Again, therefore, there is no value gained from simply beating an opponent or obtaining the highest score in the group. The payoffs obviously vary with the numbers in the group, and the balance of cooperation – defection choices. For example, and using the above matrix, payoffs for a group of 15, for each round of choices would be those shown in Figure 19.7.

Cooperators	15	14	13	12	11	10	9	8	7	6	5	4	3	2	1	0
Payoff	45	42	39	36	33	30	27	24	21	18	15	12	9	6	3	-
Defectors	0	1	2	3	4	5	6	7	8	9	10	11	12	13	14	15
Payoff	-	71	67	63	59	55	51	47	43	39	35	31	27	23	19	15

Figure 19.7

The game is played over 20 choices, and the target is calculated so that up to three defections could consistently occur and still allow the cooperators to gain sufficient points to win. In the above game, therefore, a target of 36 x 20 = 720 would be set. This was an arrangement I had to introduce since all groups, even before the game started, indicated certain players who would never cooperate. These nearly all proved to be consistent defectors, but so did several others, including, in many cases, the accusers! This observation tends to support the intuitive contention that people with a predisposition to defect will often see this trait in others. To win in numbers, therefore, a group had to remain cohesive and committed to cooperation. As each set of choices was made, a running total was kept on a score sheet, showing the numbers of cooperators and defectors in each round, and the scores they achieved. So although the players were not shown a full table of payoffs, they were soon able to work it out. Further, they were able to work out the total points of someone who had, for example, defected in every round. In this way, they learned about the difficulties implicit in the game as they went along, difficulties which were not evident in the simple two-by-two matrix.

My role was to expedite this learning process. This meant I often seemed to act as devil's advocate, much to the chagrin of the players. Where cooperation occurred, for example, I would point out the advantage to be gained from defection. Where defection occurred, I would point out that it was scoring less well than full coopera-tion. In the payoff table above, for instance, it can be seen that eight defectors fare less well than full cooperation. This point was most upsetting, since all groups began the game with full or nearly full cooperation which began to degenerate over time. I would also point out the rewards that certain consistent defectors were gaining on the backs of cooperators. This often led, paradoxically, to classes cooperating in defection, to reduce the payoff of the consistent defectors. At all times full discussion was encouraged. Periodically I would stop the game to summarize scores, and request questions or comments. Often individual players would stand up to make impassioned pleas for cooperation, or propose complex rounds of cooperation and defection in order to maximize everyone's payoff. Suggestions were invariably ignored. At this time, players become rapidly frustrated with their own inability to influence the group. This is not just an inability to influence by the weight of their particular choice, although this is certainly evident. More obviously, they were unable to influence others by word, action or debate. The passion generated in the activity was largely produced by individuals being unable to make others see what they thought was obvious and sensible.

In a series of eight games with eight different classes, only two classes produced individuals who achieved the target. This was the case even though winners were offered a Mars bar as a prize. Invariably, groups started with good intentions, but the urge to defect on the part of some players gradually became overwhelming. This urge was partly based on the game, which provided a points incentive for defection. Also, I believe that several players just wanted to act against the crowd. One or two of these inveterate defectors in fact began to cooperate once everyone else defected. As later rounds of the game arrived and most players had lost any chance of winning, they simply aimed to spoil the chances of those that might. Generally, the session ended with a plea for me to restore order. Given anarchy, bad faith and disappointment, the result seems to be a recourse to coercion and externally enforced rules. Of the two classes that did produce winners, only one produced a total cooperative choice from first to last. This class had fared particularly poorly in the counters game, a fact I was not slow to point out. I suspect, therefore, that they were out to beat me in this game. In other words, they treated this game as a straight zero-sum game between them and myself. And it cost me 24 Mars bars to realize that they were playing a different game to the one I intended. I think it is all too easy to assume that games and simulations are perceived by the recipients in the same light as we, the designers, offer them. I have tried to show in this whole section on gaming that this is often not the case. Especially with abstract games which have no context with which to interpret them, the players often bring their own context to bear. Players, consequently, play with several different agendas, and each expects different outcomes from the game.

Discussion after the game is centred on two issues. First, the distinction is drawn between the zero-sum game, where if one player wins the other loses, and the non-zero-sum games, where everyone can win or everyone can lose. A good example of a non-zero-sum 'game' is an exam with a pass mark. In most exams, if one person passes, this doesn't mean another does not. Provided they both achieve the pass mark, then they both pass. In fact, non-zero-sum games are much more reflective of the situations one meets in life than zero-sum games. Unfortunately, just as everyone can succeed, so everyone can fail, and non-zero-sum games can tend to generate Prisoner's Dilemma-type situations. The second issue considered is the problems that games of this type can cause. The lesson itself provides ample material for discussion, and parallels to real-world situations can be drawn.

OTHER GAMES

An interesting feature of non-zero-sum games in the matrix form is that they can be easily manipulated to produce new games. Although the production of new games with meaning is difficult, since it is hard to perceive the dilemmas they will produce without playing them, pupils can be invited to invent their own. A particularly interesting activity is to ask pupils to devise a game that will not cause a problem. A popular answer is to take the prisoner's dilemma and swap the two left-hand numbers of the matrix. Figure 19.8 shows the result shown in ordinal form.

	Choice A	Choice B
Choice A	3	0
Choice B	2	1

Figure 19.8

A reference to the previous section reveals that this in fact is the assurance game. It will be remembered that here everyone benefits most from cooperation. Isolated defections do not fare well. Played as a multi-player game using this matrix, however, if more than four players defect, they actually do better than the cooperators. Nevertheless, as with all the dilemma games we are considering, defection in terms of points scored does worse than cooperation. Like the prisoner's dilemma, the assurance game becomes a problem when individuals try to score more points than others, rather than being content with the same score as others, which cooperation achieves. The Chicken Game also obtains of modelling by the previously described matrix, and I have also used this with classes (no pupil as yet has generated it him or herself); see Figure 19.9.

	Choice A	Choice B
Choice A	2	1
Choice B	3	- 5

Figure 19.9

Here, a choice of defection has disastrous consequences. The advantage for a few defectors, however, is great. These defectors are playing chicken with the rest of the class, and basing their defection on the fact that others will not dare to defect also. the altruist's dilemma can be modelled differently to the way described earlier to make it work as a group game. Figure 19.10 encapsulates the altruist's dilemma.

	Choice A	Choice B
Choice A	1	0
Choice B	3	2

Figure 19.10

It can be seen that the best payoff is obtained for a defection and indeed for the whole group if everyone but one cooperates. Cooperation, however, has a meagre reward. Therefore, acts of cooperation to ensure the profit of others are, in this game, altruistic.

Again, the games are played to a specified target figure over a predetermined series of goes. As with the prisoner's dilemma, great difficulty is encountered in trying to play them successfully, since the desire to do better than others, or not let others do better than oneself, seems to predominate. In discussion, pupils continuously return to this need to outdo or not to be outdone. The idea of general improvement by cooperation, rather than on the basis of one's rugged individual strengths, seems an alien one indeed. Cooperation can be induced by reward, but this cooperation also has at the back of it overt threats from dominant members of the group who want the reward. Appealing to people's better nature, therefore, may be a barren strategy.

REFERENCES

Guyer, M, Fox, J and Hamburger, H (1973) 'Format effects in the prisoner's dilemma game', *Journal of Conflict Resolution*, **17**, 4.
Hofstadter, D R (1985) *Metamagical Themas*, Penguin, Harmondsworth.
Schelling, T (1960) *The Strategy of Conflict*, Harvard University Press, Cambridge, MA.

ABOUT THE AUTHOR

Steve Davis is a senior manager in a large Hull comprehensive. For several years he has used games and simulation as the basis for the development of thinking skills. The work on the prisoner's dilemma was drawn from his PhD thesis, which considered the paradoxical nature of decision making.

Address for correspondence: Sydney Smith School, First Lane, Anlaby, Hull HU10 6UU. Tel: 01482 652622; Fax: 01482 651690.

Chapter 20

'Sweet nothings' as a demonstration of sampling distributions of the mean

Marte Fallshore

ABSTRACT

In order to demonstrate the difficult concept of sampling distributions and the logic of hypothesis testing, I begin each term with students taking samples (five samples with n = 5 and five samples with n = 10) from a population of scores. They are told that the scores constitute a population of 'sweet nothing' scores (scores on how skilled a particular population is at whispering sweet nothings in their sweetheart's ear).

They actually work with the samples in various exercises throughout the term, but the most impressive demonstration comes when we speak of sampling distributions. At this point, I have them compute the mean and standard deviation of the means of each sample; this gives them hands-on experience at what we mean by 'mean of means' and 'standard deviation of means'.

In class we discuss which samples have less variance (ie, the samples with n = 10) and why, and what the shape of the distributions of hundreds of samples of n = 5 and n = 10 would look like. Finally, I show them what the population looks like (skew = 0.83) and what the sampling distributions of the mean for 460 samples of n = 5 (skew = 0.485) and n = 10 (skew = 0.331) look like. I have actually received 'oohs' and 'ahhs' for this demonstration!

Beginning statistics students have great difficulty understanding many of the concepts discussed in a typical introductory statistics class. In fact, even graduate students have difficulty with many fundamental concepts necessary for full understanding of statistics ideas (Mendez and Pellegrino, 1990). There are many areas of misunderstanding in statistics (eg, Kissane, 1991; Smith, 1977) which would take a whole book to address sufficiently. In this chapter, I will discuss an approach I take when addressing one critical area: sampling distributions and the logic that underlies hypothesis testing. That is, why can we use just one sample to make inferences about a population? What are the basic assumptions that allow us to make inferences? How are the basic assumptions related to each other in order to allow us to make probability statements? What are probability statements in the first place? The answers to these questions are important because they underlie all of inferential statistics, and inferential statistics is a powerful tool in most, if not all, sciences. It therefore behoves students to understand inferential statistics in order to critically assess their own and others' work.

Inferential statistics involves many different, yet intricately interconnected concepts. Because of this interrelatedness, it is difficult to determine just where an explanation of the logic of hypothesis testing begins. That is, does it begin with the first lecture that introduces sampling distributions? Or does it begin with probability? Or perhaps with the very definition of data? Part of the problem of where to begin also comes from the terminology itself. Some names for concepts have common usage so students are familiar with the words and possibly some aspects of their definitions, but not the specific meaning used with regard to statistics, eg, population, sample, average, or probability. Other concepts are highly theoretical and abstract and so are difficult for beginning students to find real-world connections to, eg, standard normal curve, standard deviation and variance, probability distribution. In addition, statistics also involves concepts and viewpoints rarely, if ever, previously encountered by students (eg, probability statements, arbitrary cutoffs (∞), double negatives (reject the hypothesis that there is no effect, so conclude that there is an effect), indirect proof, theoretical distributions, and recursive calculations, eg, means of means.

In my view, an explanation of hypothesis testing begins on the first day of class and continues to mid-term. It begins on the first day because, if the students do not understand what descriptive statistics are, for example, they certainly will not understand inferential statistics. In this chapter, I will first explain what I mean by understanding the logic of hypothesis testing; I will then detail the demonstration of sampling distributions of the mean I use.

WHAT STUDENTS ARE EXPECTED TO KNOW

By the end of the introduction to hypothesis testing, I expect students to be able to not only define terms and symbols (eg, μ, δ, s, etc) but to be able to apply the information conceptually as well as procedurally. That is, I expect students to be able to move freely from symbols to English and back and to be able to interpret conceptually what the symbols mean. For example, they should know that $\overline{X}$ is the symbol for a sample mean and that the mean is the sum of all the scores divided by the number of scores. Furthermore, they should know that the mean is one of three measures of central tendency we discuss, or a measure of a point that all the scores tend to centre around. They should also be able to draw a graphic representation of a given situation (eg, a positively skewed distribution or a representation of the upper 10 per cent of a normal distribution). Underlying all these ideas are the terms used to explain them – sampling, sampling distributions, variance, standard deviation, n, probability, etc. Without a good procedural and conceptual understanding of the underlying information, the highly abstract ideas of the central limit theorem and hypothesis testing will be lost. To that end, the demonstration is designed to try to increase students' understanding of the underlying concepts before we get to the central limit theorem or the logic of hypothesis testing.

THE DEMONSTRATION

Data collection

The demonstration begins with Day 1 and a discussion of sample, population and data. Following the introduction, I begin by involving students in working with a known population (N = 131) of 'sweet nothing' scores – the scores come from a hypothetical population that was tested in their ability to whisper sweet nothings in their sweetheart's ear. The population 'lives' in a bag and consists of laminated cards with one score per card (see Table 20.1 for a list of all scores in the population). A high score indicates extraordinary ability, while low scores indicate little or no ability. The students take ten samples from the population: five with n = 5 and five with n = 10. The samples are taken in clusters of five or ten with replacement following each sample. This gives the students hands-on experience with taking samples from a known population and it gives us something concrete to refer to in illustrating critical concepts. These samples are referred to throughout the term, and throughout this chapter.

Table 20.1 The population of 'sweet nothing' scores used in this chapter

1	2	2	2	2	3	3	3	3	4	4	4
4	4	5	5	5	6	6	6	6	6	6	6
7	7	7	7	8	8	8	8	8	8	8	8
8	9	9	9	9	9	9	10	10	10	10	10
10	11	11	12	12	12	12	12	12	12	12	12
12	13	14	14	14	14	15	15	15	15	16	16
16	16	16	16	18	18	18	18	18	18	20	20
20	20	20	21	21	21	21	22	22	24	24	24
24	24	24	24	24	24	24	26	27	27	27	28
28	28	28	30	30	32	32	32	33	33	36	36
36	36	36	39	40	40	40	44	44	48	52	

In addition to taking the samples, they answer some questions regarding samples, populations, and sampling in general. These questions (with samples of actual student answers) are provided in Table 20.2. We have not discussed these issues in class, beyond defining population and sample, but nevertheless, as can be seen in the table, the students' intuitions are quite accurate.

Table 20.2 Questions and sample responses for the sampling exercise given to students at the beginning of the term

---

1. What is a sample? *A subgroup of a population.*

2. What is a population? *All members of a group of individuals who are alike on at least one specified characteristic.*

3. Why do you think I had you do this exercise?
   (a) *To be able to distinguish between a population and a sample.*
   (b) *To see how accurately the sample represents the population.*

4. Why do you think I had you select samples of two different sizes? *To show that the larger the sample, the more representative it is of the entire population.*

5. Why do you think I had you choose more than one sample of each size? That is, why not just one sample of n = 5 and one of n = 10?
   (a) *To see how many of the same cards were pulled out of the bag.*
   (b) *To see that no two samples are the same.*

6. Do you think the size of the samples makes any difference?
   (a) *Yes, see 4 above.*
   (b) *The larger the sample, the less variable the data are within a given sample.*

7. Do you think it is important that you never had more than one sample out of the bag at a time? Why or why not?
   (a) *Yes, because a population consists of all members – if we chose a sample while another sample was out of the bag, then we wouldn't be drawing from the same population.*
   (b) *Yes, because if you took out more than one sample, there would be no chance for the cards in Sample 1 to be in Sample 2 and so on, and that would affect the results.*

Descriptive statistics

To ease grading, a single student's data were copied and distributed to the class to be used in homework and class discussion. This single data set will be referred to as the 'summary data', and the data are presented in Table 20.3. The students first use this summary data in a homework assignment to compute descriptive statistics on the pooled data. That is, they pool the n = 5 data so they have 25 data points and they pool the n = 10 data so they have 50 data points. This gives them two samples of pooled data, one with n = 25, the other with n = 50. (I have them pool the data primarily to ease their work. When I first started using this method, I had the students compute means, etc, on the ten individual data sets, but this seemed unwarranted and cruel.) They compute means, variances, and standard deviations on these pooled data. They then answer conceptual questions regarding the results. For example, the students are asked to talk about the differences in the standard deviations depending upon the sample size and which set they think best represents the population parameters and why. Through the use of these discussion questions, they get their first introduction to the law of large numbers and one aspect of the central limit theorem (reduced variance with larger sample sizes) without explicitly mentioning either concept at this point. On the day the homework is due, these questions are discussed in class with only guidance from me. That is, I might ask which sample had greater variability, n = 25 or n = 50 and why. The students usually have good intuitions regarding *why*, but if they are far off the mark, I guide them back. Other than this, my only input comes in summarizing main points. Following this section, we have an introduction to probability, with an emphasis on probability distributions and conditional probability.

Table 20.3 The data used by students to complete specific homework assignments related to the teaching method

	Summary 'sweet nothing' data The following are five samples each with n = 5				
	Sample 1	Sample 2	Sample 3	Sample 4	Sample 5
	21	52	22	4	3
	44	10	6	8	12
SCORES	16	24	8	9	15
	18	10	11	15	36
	21	27	24	27	32
	The following are five samples each with n = 10				
	Sample 1	Sample 2	Sample 3	Sample 4	Sample 5
	27	28	7	7	10
	24	12	4	24	15
	24	11	2	28	9
	18	9	36	16	8
SCORES	18	6	33	14	5
	20	6	21	14	11
	30	24	18	8	8
	20	12	16	36	16
	4	28	44	12	10
	8	48	22	6	10

Sampling distribution exercises

Getting to sampling distributions is the heart of learning inferential statistics, and also the heart of learning in uncharted territory for most students. In order to introduce the idea of sampling distributions, we begin by noting that when a sample is taken from a population, you expect the sample mean to be different from the population mean by chance alone. We refer to the summary data (and to their original data) to illustrate that point. We know for a fact that all the sample came from the same population, yet all of the sample means are different. Differences in samples statistics are further illustrated using the usual small population ($n = 6$ in my case) so that all possible samples of size two and three can be drawn and all means, means of means, and standard deviations of means can be computed. This procedure is used not only as an explicit example of a sampling distribution of the mean, but also to introduce new terminology (eg, standard error of the mean), to make explicit what is meant by 'all samples of size n', and the information provided by the central limit theorem.

The students are then given a homework assignment, again using the summary data, that further attempts to drive home these points. In this homework, the students compute means for all five samples with $n = 5$ and $n = 10$. That is, they end up with ten different means, five for the $n = 5$ data and five for the $n = 10$ data. They then compute the mean of the means and standard deviation of the means for the two groups, separately. This gives them hands-on calculation experience with means of means and standard deviations of means, difficult concepts by themselves. The homework includes discussion questions on the difference between the standard deviations of the two sets of means with regard to the central limit theorem. That is, it asks them to describe which standard deviation of means is smaller and why, and which mean would best represent the population and why. Through these questions, this exercise addresses the three main ideas of the central limit theorem: shape, mean, and standard deviation of the sampling distribution of the mean. It also allows them to have first-hand experience with the central limit theorem. The students are asked to further elaborate these ideas with regard to their expectations of the shape, mean, and standard deviation of several hundred class samples combined. The exact questions are provided in Table 20.4.

Following completion of the homework, during a class discussion, the students are given a histogram of the distribution of scores for the population along with histograms for 460 samples of size five and 460 samples of size ten, thus making explicit that even with a skewed population (as this population is), the sampling distribution of the mean tends to be normal and the larger the sample size, the more normal the sampling distribution of the mean. These graphs are provided in Figures 20.1 to 20.3, respectively. The class is visibly impressed with this graphic example of the central limit theorem, based on verbalizations and movement among the students when the graphs are distributed and displayed.

Table 20.4 Homework questions for the central limit theorem using the summary data to compute means of means and standard deviations of means

Using the means of the 5 samples of size 5 (and the same for samples of size 10), compute the mean of the means and the standard deviation of the means.

1. Which has a lower standard error of the mean? Would you have predicted this? Why?

2. I'm going create a histogram of 460 similar sweet nothing sample means (ie, means of 460 samples of n = 5 and means of 460 samples of n = 10) from previous collections from the sweet nothing data. I will create one graph for the n = 5 means and one for the n = 10 means and compute the means of the means and the standard deviation of the means.

   (a) Which set of data (n = 5 or n = 10) do you think will be more normally distributed? Why?
   (b) Which set of data (n = 5 or n = 10) will have the smallest variability of means? Why?
   (c) Can you say anything about which set of data (n = 5 or n = 10) will have a mean of means closest to the population mean? Why?

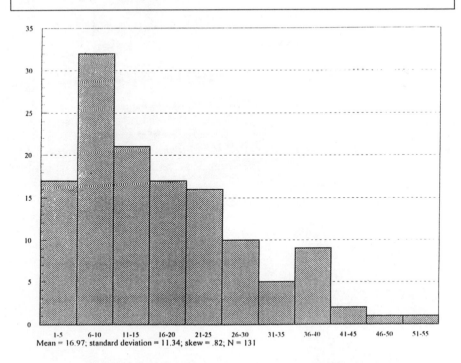

Mean = 16.97; standard deviation = 11.34; skew = .82; N = 131

Figure 20.1 Distribution of population of sweet nothing scores

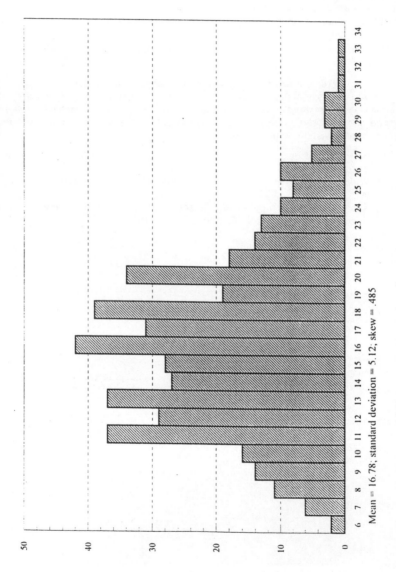

Mean = 16.78; standard deviation = 5.12; skew = .485

Figure 20.2 Distribution of means for 460 samples of n = 5

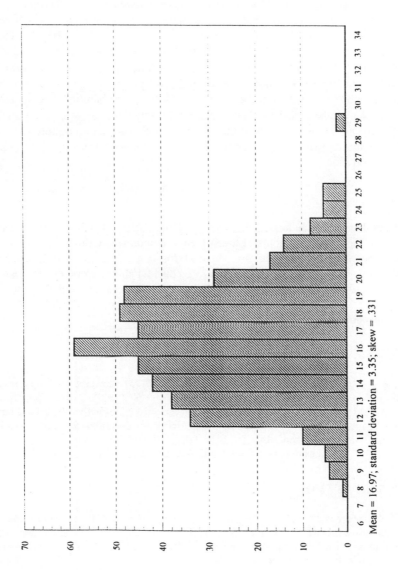

Figure 20.3 Distribution of means of means for 460 samples of n = 10

Hypothesis-testing exercises

Following this discussion of sampling distributions and the central limit theorem, we are ready to begin discussing the logic of hypothesis testing. To facilitate this discussion, we begin with a hypothetical situation where they have a new, improved teaching method and the students need to convince the 'powers that be' that they should implement this new method throughout the school system. The students design the test of the teaching method, select their criterion (∞), etc. This discussion format allows the introduction of new terms and concepts in an interactive environment. During this exchange, concepts such as conditional probability statements in the context of hypothesis testing, null and alternative hypotheses, ∞, etc are introduced. Following this less formal discussion of hypothesis testing, a more formal, structured lecture is given. This lecture reiterates the concepts discussed in the more free-form discussion.

DISCUSSION

I have been developing and using this method since I started teaching statistics six years ago. Subjective judgements of the students' reactions and direct reports from students give me confidence in this method for conveying these difficult and counter-intuitive concepts. Therefore, while I consider this a work in progress, I believe it is ready to be shared with others in the field who are faced with the arduous task of teaching statistics to reluctant (and sometimes openly hostile) students. Further suggestions are invited.

REFERENCES

Kissane, B V (1991) 'Activities in inferential statistics', *NCTM Yearbook: Teaching probability and statistics*, NCTM, Reston, VA, 182–93.
Mendez, H and Pellegrino, J (1990) 'Understanding and misunderstanding the central limit theorem', paper presented at session 29.45 of the American Educational Research Association Annual Meeting, Boston, MA.
Smith, S G (1977) 'Demonstrating the central limit theorem', *Mathematics Teacher*, **70**, 542–4

ABOUT THE AUTHOR

Marte Fallshore received her PhD in Cognitive Psychology from the University of Pittsburgh in 1994 and has been teaching at Utah Valley State College since that time. She is dedicated to student involvement via simulations in all her classes and is constantly reworking her lectures to include them. She welcomes any and all feedback!

Address correspondence: Marte Fallshore, Behavioral Science Dept, Utah Valley State College, Orem, UT 84058; e-mail: fallshma@uvsc.edu

Chapter 21

Entertaining Hamming coding with four-letter word mutations

David Sharp

ABSTRACT

This chapter describes a game I used to help teach Hamming coding to second-year networks and communications students on the Imperial College BEng and MEng degrees in computing. The game gives the students practice in encoding and decoding messages using Hamming codes.

When computers communicate with each other over a network, text is usually sent using a unique seven-bit binary code for each letter of the alphabet. For example, the letter A is sent as the binary sequence 100001 and the letter C is sent as the binary sequence 100011. As a result of noise on the communication link it is possible for one or more bits to be corrupted during transmission. For example, if an A was sent and the second bit from the right-hand side was corrupted from 0 to 1 the A would be received as a C by mistake. This sort of error is common on teletext pages in areas of poor television reception.

Hamming coding is a method of adding extra bits to each letter so that if a one bit error occurs the extra bits can indicate which bit is in error. The error can then be corrected by inverting the affected bit.

To practise Hamming coding, teams of four students are invited to send Hamming-coded four-letter words to each other, with one student coding each letter. The students choose which bits of their word get corrupted during transmission. The corruption of course results in another four-letter word being received. For example, the word LEGO can be corrupted to the word DUCK by introducing appropriate one-bit errors in the code for each of the letters.

By sending extra Hamming-encoded error-correction bits with each letter, it becomes possible for the receiving team to deduce that although they received the word DUCK, it should in fact have been the word LEGO. With an appropriate list of how errors in each of the bits affect the letter that is sent, many entertaining four-letter word mutations are possible.

Students have found the exercise to be a highly entertaining and useful way of practising Hamming coding. A prize is awarded for the best four-letter mutation that is correctly sent and received.

A team-pack showing how to play the game is reproduced below.

Team pack for team _____.
There should be four people in a team

This pack contains:

1 x Instructions (this page), 1 x Message form, 1 x ASCII sheet.
4 x Receive form, 4 x Sending form.

Team instructions

1. Choose a team leader who will read you these instructions.
2. Decide on a four-letter word that can be corrupted to another four-letter word by changing up to one bit in each letter (eg, PITS becomes PIPS by changing one bit in the third letter and changing no bits in the other letters). Use the ASCII sheet to help do this. (A prize is available for the best four-letter word mutation.)
3. Each of the four team members should fill in a sending form – one form for each letter. The sending form guides you through Hamming encoding one of the letters and corrupting the appropriate message or check bit.
4. The team leader should fill in the message form using the information from the sending forms. Having checked that all the message forms are correct and that the sending form is correct, find another team and swap your message form with theirs.
5. Each of the four team members should now fill in a receiving form – one form for each letter received from the other team.
6. Check with the other team that you successfully decoded their message and that they successfully decoded your message.
7. What is the efficiency and redundancy of the code that you sent?
8. Fill in the team summary below.

We corrupted the word

to the word

We received the corrupted word

and corrected it to

Message Form sent from team [ ] **to team** [ ]

First Letter:

m7	m6	m5	c3	m4	m3	m2	c2	m1	c1	c0

Second Letter:

m7	m6	m5	c3	m4	m3	m2	c2	m1	c1	c0

Third Letter:

m7	m6	m5	c3	m4	m3	m2	c2	m1	c1	c0

Fourth Letter:

m7	m6	m5	c3	m4	m3	m2	c2	m1	c1	c0

ASCII sheet for team

Effect of a One-bit Error on ASCII Letters

A	→	Q	I	E	C	@
B	→	R	J	F	@	C
C	→	S	K	G	A	B
D	→	T	L	@	F	E
E	→	U	M	A	G	D
F	→	V	N	B	D	G
G	→	W	O	C	E	F
H	→	X	@	L	J	I
I	→	Y	A	M	K	H
J	→	Z	B	N	H	K
K	→	[	C	O	I	J
L	→	\	D	H	N	M
M	→	]	E	I	O	L
N	→	^	F	J	L	O
O	→	_	G	K	M	N
P	→	@̄	X	T	R	Q
Q	→	A	Y	U	S	P
R	→	B	Z	V	P	S
S	→	C	[	W	Q	R
T	→	D	\	P	V	U
U	→	E	]	Q	W	T
V	→	F	^	R	T	W
W	→	G	_	S	U	V
X	→	H	P̄	\	Z	Y
Y	→	I	Q	]	[	X
Z	→	J	R	^	X	[

ASCII Codes for the Capital Letters

A	1	0	0	0	0	0	1
B	1	0	0	0	0	1	0
C	1	0	0	0	0	1	1
D	1	0	0	0	1	0	0
E	1	0	0	0	1	0	1
F	1	0	0	0	1	1	0
G	1	0	0	0	1	1	1
H	1	0	0	1	0	0	0
I	1	0	0	1	0	0	1
J	1	0	0	1	0	1	0
K	1	0	0	1	0	1	1
L	1	0	0	1	1	0	0
M	1	0	0	1	1	0	1
N	1	0	0	1	1	1	0
O	1	0	0	1	1	1	1
P	1	0	1	0	0	0	0
Q	1	0	1	0	0	0	1
R	1	0	1	0	0	1	0
S	1	0	1	0	0	1	1
T	1	0	1	0	1	0	0
U	1	0	1	0	1	0	1
V	1	0	1	0	1	1	0
W	1	0	1	0	1	1	1
X	1	0	1	1	0	0	0
Y	1	0	1	1	0	0	1
Z	1	0	1	1	0	1	0

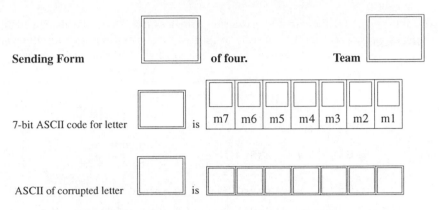

Sending Form [ ] **of four.** Team [ ]

7-bit ASCII code for letter [ ] is | m7 | m6 | m5 | m4 | m3 | m2 | m1 |

ASCII of corrupted letter [ ] is | | | | | | | |

(Note: if you are going to corrupt a check bit the letter will stay the same.)

Now work out the Hamming code using even parity (the additions below are modulo 2.)

c3	c2	c1	c0			
0	0	0	0	-		
0	0	0	1	c0	[ ]	= m1 + m2 + m4 + m5 + m7
0	0	1	0	c1	[ ]	= m1 + m3 + m4 + m6 + m7
0	0	1	1	m1	[ ]	
0	1	0	0	c2	[ ]	= m2 + m3 + m4
0	1	0	1	m2	[ ]	
0	1	1	0	m3	[ ]	
0	1	1	1	m4	[ ]	
1	0	0	0	c3	[ ]	= m5 + m6 + m7
1	0	0	1	m5	[ ]	
1	0	1	0	m6	[ ]	
1	0	1	1	m7	[ ]	

Now corrupt the appropriate message or check bit and fill in the bits to be sent:

m7	m6	m5	c3	m4	m3	m2	c2	m1	c1	c0

Receiving Form ☐ **of four.**   **Team** ☐

Incoming message: | m7 | m6 | m5 | c3 | m4 | m3 | m2 | c2 | m1 | c1 | c0 |

bit 11   bit 1

Corrupted (?) ASCII code | m7 | m6 | m5 | m4 | m3 | m2 | m1 | is the letter ☐

Recalculate the even-parity Hamming checks, this time including the received check bits in the calculation. The new checks c1', c2', c3', c4' tell us where the bit error has occurred.

c3	c2	c1	c0

c3	c2	c1	c0			
0	0	0	0	-		
0	0	0	1	c0	☐	$c0' = c0 + m1 + m2 + m4 + m5 + m7 =$ ☐
0	0	1	0	c1	☐	$c1' = c1 + m1 + m3 + m4 + m6 + m7 =$ ☐
0	0	1	1	m1	☐	
0	1	0	0	c2	☐	$c2' = c2 + m2 + m3 + m4 =$ ☐
0	1	0	1	m2	☐	
0	1	1	0	m3	☐	
0	1	1	1	m4	☐	
1	0	0	0	c3	☐	$c3' = c3 + m5 + m6 + m7 =$ ☐
1	0	0	1	m5	☐	
1	0	1	0	m6	☐	
1	0	1	1	m7	☐	

There is therefore a bit error in position | c3' | c2' | c1' | c0' | , ie we must flip bit ☐

Correct 7-bit ASCII code: | m7 | m6 | m5 | m4 | m3 | m2 | m1 | is the letter ☐

ABOUT THE AUTHOR

Dr David Sharp is a lecturer in the Department of Computing, Imperial College, London. He teaches undergraduate and MSc courses in communications and networks, multimedia systems and microprocessor interfacing.

Dept of Computing, Imperial College, 180 Queen's Gate, London SW7 2BZ. Tel: 0171 594 8335; Fax: 0171 581 8024; e-mail: dwns@doc.ic.ac.uk

Chapter 22

Using the case approach to teach negotiation skills: The potential for a management game

Peter Trim

ABSTRACT

Negotiation is a complex subject which hardly ever features in a postgraduate business school programme. This is surprising when one takes into account the importance of face-to-face discussions and the fact that in a global market, characterized by a shrinking supplier base, longer lead times and reduced product life-cycles, the need for business combination arrangements becomes both obvious and in some cases essential if an organization is to survive in an ever-turbulent business environment.

This chapter addresses a number of issues, mainly: how the case method can be used to produce reasonably complex teaching material to be used for teaching negotiation and what factors designers of games should take into account when turning a negotiation case exercise into a management game.

INTRODUCTION

Negotiation as a subject of study is likely to receive attention in the future as European companies become hybrid in organizational form and management style, and trans-mute into unrecognizable organizational structures and forms, as a result of the process of globalization. One can expect that European integration will accelerate the need for negotiation to become a subject worthy of academic study as it allows students to better understand the cultural context in which international business decisions are made and how people manipulate or are manipulated by others through communicative processes.

The case study method is an acceptable vehicle through which theory can be translated into practice, as it represents a simulation. The case method can require the student to undertake data collection, but its main strengths from an educational perspective are analysis, interpretation and the implementation of a theoretically derived solution. A negotiation case allows a student (either working independently or in a group) to take responsibility for their learning and to develop their project management and interpersonal skills.

In order that the subject of negotiation is placed within an educational context, it is important for the teacher/instructor to adopt a structured approach to teaching the subject and to have a formal method of establishing what the student has learned from the process. A course on negotiation (a separate module or part of a course such as purchasing management) should, to be accepted by academics as academically credible, be taught over a period of time (five to eleven weeks) and the lectures should be reinforced with selected readings from academic journals and textbooks. A course on negotiation should cover the following: introduction to negotiation; the process of negotiation; negotiating tactics and strategy; negotiating styles; and negotiation and cultural issues (Trim, 1994a, pp.33–4).

For those who have not taught the subject of negotiation before, it is important to think in terms of a three-hour session each week, composed of a formal lecture followed by a seminar/group work. This will provide the students with enough time to develop their knowledge of the subject and read the background material and, if necessary, collect relevant background information. By adopting a rigorous and structured approach to teaching negotiation it is hoped that all of the teaching objectives, however defined, will be met.

It is useful to think in terms of introducing some sort of role play into the negotiation course, and this is acceptable. However, I do not consider this necessary, although it could reinforce the content with respect to the educational objectives. I have experience of conducting negotiation exercises in The Netherlands; France and the UK and have taught both young and mature adults, mostly from Europe and the Far East. The comments made in this chapter are, therefore, partly derived from practitioner research carried out over a number of years.

THE CASE METHOD AND FACTORS GAME DESIGNERS SHOULD BE AWARE OF WHEN DEVELOPING A MANAGEMENT GAME

The case study method, as used by academics in business and management schools, has been likened to a simulation. Why is this? The most immediate answer is that a case study analysis can be regarded as a form of management game. Larreche (1989) has put this into perspective by stating, 'A game is a tool that allows individuals to use and develop their decision-making skills in a fictitious competitive environment' (p.347). Kibbee et al. (1961) have added some weight to the idea by suggesting:

> The term 'simulation' means trial-and-error experimentation with a model, whether for research, problem solving, or training purposes. The term 'management game' is used to refer primarily to those simulations in which groups of human beings are engaged in making decisions, usually for training purposes. (p.13)

According to Birnbaum (1982), a simulation can be used to explain organizational and administrative issues and can be based on a specific 'conceptual orientation that provides a unifying structure to the experience' (p.8). It has been suggested that simulations allow individuals to be assigned duties and responsibilities; role plays allow an individual to act out a certain part; games allow an individual to play out a part as a player; and exercises allow an individual to be a problem solver and decision maker (Jones, 1995, p.18).

As regards game orientation, one needs to take into account whether there is to be a total enterprise as opposed to a functional game approach, and whether a general as opposed to specific industry game approach is to be adopted (Greenlaw *et al.*, 1962, pp.16-23). The case study example referred to here relates to a generalized and hypothetical company, and is based on a high-speed rail link and a large construction project, information upon which was collected from desk research (library work) and relates to a real-world example. The case can also be classified as competitively interactive (Greenlaw *et al.*, 1962, p.23) as the proceedings can be influenced extensively by one group (the most informed/persuasive group), but it should be stated that students participating in such an exercise should view the process from a 'win/win' and not from a 'win/lose' position. The case research method is academically sound as it can generate information and understanding about a specific situation, and once the case material is developed into a teaching case it will have strengthened the case study method as a means of illustrating established theory (Smith, 1989, p.3). A case study can therefore be used to:

- reinforce a company's business strategy (link between theory and practice);
- encourage group work and class participation (students are divided into groups);
- test an individual student's intellectual ability (formal examination); and
- enhance group decision-making skills (peer group accountability).

The decision making that goes into the case study method can be classified as convergent, which has been defined by Morrison *et al.* (1992) as 'the group... attempting to narrow down information into a manageable unit' (p.94). Case studies and simulations have been used to reinforce lectures and seminars and can be considered action-oriented (Larreche, 1989, p.348). The main emphasis is on quality and speed of decision making, motivation and learning via feedback (Larreche, 1989, p.347).

Videos can be used to enhance teaching. Basically, a specific video programme can be shown at a particular stage in the educational programme (the start or middle of the course), and videos can be used to highlight certain events and/or convey images. Videos can be custom made (a specifically designed training video) or general (business programme/documentary), depending upon the teaching objectives set and the relevance of the material.

It may also be useful to video the proceedings of a class negotiation exercise (one-to-one or group work) and to replay the content of the tape at a later date. The feedback will allow individual students to pay attention to areas of self-improvement (communicative skills and general presentation, for example). One could also suggest that in an extreme case, the objective of the exercise would be to encourage a personality change (a person can be groomed to develop a more assertive stance, for example).

The objective of a negotiation case exercise is to get people to work as a team and not for any individual (except the leader) to pursue his or her own personal objectives.

Informational factors are important. For example, Hamburger (1979, p.179) has stipulated that communication is the 'passage of information from one party to another'. Although the case is given to all the group members (in advance of the first negotiation session), separate and classified information is given to each group (both groups are taken aside by the teacher/instructor and are provided with facts which are privy to that group only). Another aspect of structure which is important is rules (Hamburger, 1979, pp.179–80). Rules determine who can do what and when and in what form it can be undertaken (the leader of each group delegates responsibility and formulates a game plan).

Management games are designed so that the players can learn about management decision making and as a consequence develop their skill base prior to participating in decision making in the real world. Games or simulations, as they are often referred to, are composed of a number of stages (Kibbee et al., 1961, pp.4–6): briefing participants; group (team) meetings to discuss strategy and objectives; various game periods (day, week, month, quarter or year) during which the players' contribution and overall effectiveness are monitored by an independent observer, appointed by the teacher/instructor at the start of the negotiation exercise, so that individual performance is monitored; and end-of-game discussions and a feedback session (critique with respect to individual performance). In the case of a two-group negotiation exercise, it is important that the observer is briefed as to the purpose, scope and mechanics of the game (Kibbee et al., 1961, p.82). Feedback must be fair and delivered from an impartial stance and, if criticism is necessary, it should be constructive not destructive.

Games can be incorporated into a course and used in association with role playing or the case study method (Kibbee et al., 1961, p.56). Other factors which may be important as regards the outcome of a negotiation exercise are: frequency of interaction; the amount of information shared by the parties; the affective tone used during the negotiation sessions; and the reciprocity of exchange (Valley et al., 1992, p.118). Network analysis can be used to model the interaction among and between those participating in the negotiation exercise (Valley et al., 1992, pp.120–21) and correlations can be made between the process and the outcome variables (Valley et al., 1992, pp.129-34).

Tape-recording the negotiation exercise may assist with respect to content analysis and feedback (Valley et al., 1992, pp.133–4). From a learning perspective, the teacher/instructor may decide that tape recorders are not to be used, as each individual participant is expected to make written and mental notes.

As regards group play, a number of rules should be observed by the teacher/instructor (Greenlaw et al., 1962, p.30): the individual group members organize and distribute the work among themselves; (some) individual group members are assigned roles (this is normally limited to the leader and the recorder); the groups are required to undertake a number of assignments; and, each group is provided with a specific task (stated in the form of written objectives). Since individuals can become tired and frustrated, this may enhance the risk of conflict especially if one side is following a delaying strategy for no obvious reason (this could result if the group members have not undertaken adequate preparation).

Messages can be misinterpreted and this can cause misunderstandings and distrust. Putnam and Roloff (1992, pp.3–4) are of the opinion that:

> Communication in bargaining entails multiple factors, including verbal messages, non-verbal cues, vocal overtones, information exchange, language, communication media, symbols, and meaning. Strategies and tactics of negotiating, for example: threats, demands, and offers; are expressed through verbal messages, gestures and vocal overtones. Bargainers rely on both the content and the function of the messages to provide information about proposals as well as reveal clues about their opponents' preferences and interests.

The case entitled: 'The Northern Europe Complex' (Trim, 1995) is written (from published sources) as a negotiation exercise to be undertaken by postgraduate business/management students. It features a hypothetical situation, mainly the building of a high-speed railway line from Amsterdam in The Netherlands to Moscow in Russia. The project is the brainchild of Dr Max Bender, chairman of The International Power and Electric Company which represents a pan-European company. The project also includes the building of the Northern Europe Complex which is composed of a skydome, a 200-room luxury hotel, a number of industrial factory units and housing. Two working groups from within the same company are formed; one group is required to research into the prospect of siting the Northern Europe Complex in Groningen, the other working group concentrates on Oldenburg as a location. The two groups are required to undertake some research and to negotiate a solution. The individuals are required to write a proposal indicating the size and location of the project and the financing package; draw up a plan of priorities with dates; and develop a public relations strategy. Students are divided into two groups of equal size; a student/graduate assistant is appointed as the official observer and works closely with the course teacher/instructor. The observer is required to monitor the contribution of each student both during the informal group meetings and during the formal face-to-face negotiation sessions. Each group has a leader and a recorder appointed and it is the group leader's task to delegate the work load (basic data collection and area of specialization, for example). Having been given the case in advance of the negotiation session, each group is required to make a 20-minute presentation at the start of the first negotiation session which outlines their objectives; this is immediately followed by the first formal, face-to-face meeting.

The objectives of such an exercise are to:

- ensure that students who have followed a management course are capable of working in a team on a related project;
- ensure that team work is put before individualism; and
- ensure that students develop an appropriate mindset, ie move away from the win-lose approach otherwise known as 'zero-sum thinking' as expressed by Brooks and Odiorne (1984, p.33).

It could be argued that students participating in a negotiation session gain experience, are able to develop their interpersonal skills (with the members of their own group and their counterparts) and, if class participation carries marks, receive an individual or group mark related to their contribution. Brams (1990, pp.29–63) has looked at bargaining from a quantitative angle and suggested that participants can be rewarded (bonus procedure) if they arrive at a satisfactory deal. In two-person bargaining games a third party who is independent can act as a referee and administer the rewards, but only if a fair exchange takes place. The criterion that establishes whether the parties are entitled to a reward is that individuals are honest and sincerely want a good deal, hence when a deal is struck it results in mutual benefit.

Each group that participates in a negotiation session is required to keep to the basic rules as defined by Fowler (1986, p.49): define the issues; probe the other party's case; strengthen their own case; use adjournments; and search for common ground and work towards an agreement. One must also assume that the groups participating in the negotiation exercise are 'not in conflict for the sake of it' (Rojot, 1991, p. 57).

Marimon and McGrattan (1993, p.36) have focused on adaptive learning in strategic form games and this provides a useful insight into developing a new framework for studying models and their construction. To design a successful game, the game designer needs a reasonable knowledge of the gaming process and game construction. A successful game is developed from a narrowly defined brief which highlights the objectives (game outcome) and the teaching needs as they relate to the curriculum. As long as the students know what the rules are and how they will be enforced if the need arises, then the game should be played out according to set criteria. The game designer must decide for him or herself what is the most important learning factor: individual participation (process related – gathering information, screening information and actively participating in the decision-making process) or learning to apply a tool/technique. Management games come under the generic title of 'operational gaming simulation' and are used to show students how to make interdependent business decisions, to evaluate material and present new ideas, and to introduce and apply decision-making techniques (Thierauf *et al.*, 1985, pp.347–8).

It is possible to award marks for each individual student's contribution to a case study solution and to establish what an individual has learned via a written examination. However, large cases such as those made available through the European Case Clearing House at Cranfield, the Harvard Business School, the Western Business School at the University of Western Ontario in London, Canada and the Darden Graduate School of Business Administration at Virginia University, can be classified as substantial and relatively complicated as far as the average student is concerned. Hence it is important for university teachers to allow students enough time to adequately undertake the work required (Wolfe, 1993b, p.468).

The objectives outlined herewith which relate to turning a negotiation case into a management game can be classified as role-specific simulation in the sense that the roles adopted by the players of the game 'correspond to a specific real-world equivalent' (Lester and Stoil, 1979, p.168). The data the students are required to collect reinforce the preparatory information provided to each group, allow the individuals in the group to broaden their understanding of the subject matter and better appreciate the consequences of their decision making. It can be stated, therefore, that one element built into the game should be the collection of additional information (secondary data) as this can reinforce the learning objectives. A number of additional factors can be cited (Trim, 1994c, pp.14–15):

- Incentives can be used as a form of extrinsic motivation (Tafoya, 1979, p.405).
- Players of games should be proud of their achievements (Law-Yone, 1982, p.60).
- The learning process can be reinforced by learning by doing (Robinson, 1978, p.4).
- Games and simulations can encourage communication between and among participants (Lederman and Ruben, 1978, p.268).
- Games and simulations can be used to enhance student performance with respect to decision-making skills (van Sickle, 1978, p.414; Lucas, 1979, pp.61–74).
- The content and structure of the game can be extended by introducing new content, therefore, a new game can be produced (Thiagarajan and Stolovitch, 1979, p.289).
- Games can be used to assess a cultural meaning system and to establish how individuals from different cultures relate to one another (Noesjirwan and Freestone, 1979, p.190). This means that cross-cultural contact can be studied from two perspectives: the individual and group work (Noesjirwan and Freestone, 1979, p.196; Smith and Stander, 1981, pp.346–7).
- Ruben and Lederman (1982) have highlighted the term 'construct validity', which is of interest as it allows the educator to establish if the game has introduced the 'learner to an intended set of skills and/or concepts' (p.238).
- The educator can use game play as a means to study group size and sex roles (Smith and Stander, 1981, pp.345–60).
- The approach can be used to study 'in-group bias' (Harrod, 1983, p.310).

Locatis and Atkinson (1981) have stated that with respect to training: 'Short, intensive training experiences in workshop formats with a high degree of involvement are most effective' (p.341). Bredemeier and Greenblat (1981, pp.307–32) have paid attention to group size, group dynamics, group performance and motivation for example. Gentry (1980) has looked at group size and has indicated that one person might be the key to group performance, but is of the opinion that:

> smaller groups (two or three members) work better than four-member groups in a simulation game in terms of minimising group dissension. However, group size has no effect on the relative performances. Counterbalancing the greater group dissension experienced by the larger groups were the findings that performance was better explained by the group leaders' class performance than by the group mean, and that the larger the group, the more likely it was to have a more talented group member (pp.458–9).

Rosen (1981) has made a valid point when stipulating that:

> the greatest value from the simulation is realised in conjunction with other courses. Students who had taken a number of related courses before the simulation generally were able to apply the theories they had studied to the situations in which they found themselves. Alternatively, students without prior substantive background emerged from the simulation with questions they could bring to subsequent courses (p.24).

Van Oosten and Laseur (1980) have stipulated that: 'the quality of the decision-making process is a function of the interpersonal relationships that develop in the course of the game between the management team members' (p.430). They have also indicated (p.433) that a game designed for one cultural group may not be suitable for another, owing to different cultural perspectives; and Kringen (1980, pp.140–41) has suggested that gaming can help members of an organization to improve communication, test real-world situations and improve judgement.

When designing a game, the educator must take into account four distinct phases (Yefimov and Komarov, 1982, pp.150–54):

1. the concept phase (formulation of the game and the requirements imposed on its functional subsystems);
2. the definition phase (procedures aimed at identifying solution alternatives);
3. the development phase (documents relating to the simulation itself and computer programs);
4. the operational phase (game materials, the manageability of the game and the feedback mechanism).

Duke (1980, p.27) has outlined nine steps associated with game design:

■ Develop written specifications for game design.
■ Develop a comprehensive schematic representation of the problem.
■ Select components of the problem to be gamed.
■ Plan the game with the Systems Component/Game Element Matrix.
■ Describe the content of each cell in writing.
■ Search your 'Repertoire of Games' for ideas to represent each cell.
■ Build the game.
■ Game evaluation (against the criteria of step 1).
■ Field use and modification.

Computer packages have advanced enormously over the past 20 years and programs exist which make writing computer programs quicker and less costly. Computers have two main advantages over manually-operated games (Kibbee et al., 1961, pp.136–7): they are speedy (able to undertake many computations simultaneously) and are extremely accurate (oddities can be highlighted to the operator). Computer packages can interpret information and provide alternative courses of action (expert systems). The advantage of using computer packages is that students are required to interact with technology and at the same time develop new skills. Computers possess additional advantages (Wolfe, 1993a, p.451): they allow impartial judging and algorithmic validity.

Klabbers et al. (1980, pp.65–7) have produced a valuable insight into how a computer simulation model can be developed and two distinct phases (conceptualization and formalization) have been given special attention. As regards conceptualization, the following steps should be borne in mind (Klabbers et al., 1980, p.65):

■ Identify problem.
■ Formulate the problem.
■ Define the time horizon.
■ Choose system boundaries.
■ Choose level of aggregation.
■ Define the elements of the system.

■ Define matrix of cause-effect relationships or draw a flow diagram of causal relationships.
■ Make a verbal description of processes indicated by step 7.
■ Verify this (qualitative) model.

As regards formalization, Klabbers *et al.* (1980, pp.65–6) have suggested:

■ Map causal network into mathematical system (allocate elements of the qualitative model to system variables).
■ Define system equations.
■ Choose appropriate programming language and program mathematical system.
■ Estimate parameters.
■ Perform sensitivity analysis.
■ Carry out scenario analysis.
■ Compare the results of the analysis with available knowledge about the actual system.
■ Draw consequences.

With respect to interactive simulation, a number of steps can be identified (Klabbers *et al.*, 1980, pp.66–7):

■ Define the purpose of the interactive simulation.
■ Select computer hardware and software.
■ Define the decision structure.
■ Select the mode of interaction between humans and computer.
■ Specify the dialogue program.
■ Couple the language program with the simulation program.
■ Use the interactive simulation.

The interactive simulation can next be developed into a game via a number of steps (Klabbers *et al.*, 1980, pp.70–71):

■ Specify the purpose of the game.
■ Define the role(s) of the players in relation to the decision structure.
■ Define the steps during the game.
■ Make role descriptions.
■ Test and adjust the game.
■ Run the game.

Klabbers *et al.* (1980, p.79) have also identified a number of steps associated with a game:

■ Preparation phase.
■ Actual gaming phase.
■ Evaluation of game sessions.

Model building is a valid approach as it allows real-world events to be interpreted from a scientific perspective (Easterly, 1978, p.24). Analytic models have clearly defined payoff functions and each group is aware of what the other group is trying to achieve (Brewer, 1978, p.314). In the case of behaviourally oriented models, the goals may change through time owing to the fact that the game is played over a long period (a few days or weeks) (Brewer, 1978, p.314).

Pratt *et al.* (1980, p.338) have stipulated:

> The ability to predict those students who will learn from simulation-type exercises in the classroom and those who will not, would greatly improve the instructional strategies of any teacher, and these studies indicate that further research into the relationship of personality characteristics and various instructional strategies might prove useful.

Norris and Niebuhr (1980, p.304) have stipulated:

> Whether highly cohesive groups are also high performers appears to depend upon the norms adopted by the group. Only if norms of high production were chosen would we expect strong cohesion to increase group performance.

As regards the broader issues associated with the design of management games, Rohn (1994) has suggested that it is important to consider the qualitative (behavioural) aspects as well as the quantitative aspects; this view has been reinforced by Siebecke (1994). Muller (1994) is of the opinion that both the pedagogical and methodological aspects should be kept in mind, and Fripp (1994) has indicated that game designers and developers should consider the current and future needs of gamesters. Braun and Oldenburg (1994) have outlined the fact that attention should be given to the subject of negotiation; this point has been reiterated by Trim (1994b), Wolff (1994), Schuit (1994) and von Furstenberg (1994). Pfeiffer (1994) has highlighted the fact that negotiation is a subject which can help gamesters to develop their intercultural competence. Greenblat (1980, pp.40–57) has looked at a number of issues relating to the harmful consequences of gaming and in particular the negative consequences associated with game design for individual participants. Parasuraman (1981, pp.191 and 199) has stressed the need for proper evaluation of simulation gaming methods, especially from the point of inputs (time and money) and outputs (practical benefits to students).

CONCLUSION

There is no doubt that the subject of negotiation is of general interest from both an educational and social anthropological point of view, and an opportunity exists to exploit the link between various academic disciplines. The skills of negotiation can be taught using the case study method, and teaching objectives can be reinforced by various aids such as videos. A formal approach to game design should make it easier for the game designer/developer to have his or her work translated into computer software and marketed in the form of a computer package. One can extend the boundary of the negotiation exercise by arranging for groups in different geographical locations to interact via a computer terminal and, if appropriate, participate in video/computer conferencing.

REFERENCES

Birnbaum, R (1982) 'Games and simulations in higher education', *Simulation & Games*, **13**, 1, 3–11.

Brams, S J (1990) *Negotiation Games: Applying game theory to bargaining and arbitration*, Routledge, London.

Braun, G and Oldenburg, S (1994) 'Management game and assessment centre as a combined instrument for management development: a project study', paper presented at the 10th European Forum on System Simulation and Management Gaming Conference, 14–16 November, Deutsche Planspiel-Zentrale, Bad Neuenahr.

Bredemeier, M E and Greenblat, C S (1981) 'The educational effectiveness of simulation games', *Simulation & Games*, **12**, 3, 307–32.

Brewer, G D (1978) 'Scientific gaming: the development and use of free-form scenarios', *Simulation & Games*, **9**, 3, 309–38.

Brooks, E and Odiorne, G S (1984) *Managing by Negotiations*, Van Nostrand Reinhold, New York.

Duke, R D (1980) 'Format for the game – logic or intuition?', *Simulation & Games*, **11**, 1, 27–34.

Easterly, J L (1978) 'Simulation game design – a philosophic dilemma', *Simulation & Games*, **9**, 1, 23–8.

Fowler, A (1986) *Effective Negotiation*, Institute of Personnel Management, London.

Fripp, J (1994) 'Business simulation at Ashridge Management College: past, present and future', paper presented at the 10th European Forum on System Simulation and Management Gaming Conference, 14–16 November, Deutsche Planspiel-Zentrale, Bad Neuenahr.

Gentry, J W (1980) 'Group size and attitudes toward the simulation experience', *Simulation & Games*, **11**, 4, 451–60.

Greenblat, C S (1980) 'Group dynamics and game design', *Simulation & Games*, **11**, 1, 35–58.

Greenlaw, P S, Herron, L W and Rawdon, R H (1962) *Business Simulation in Industrial and University Education*, Prentice Hall, Hemel Hempstead.

Hamburger, H (1979) *Games as Models of Social Phenomena*, W H Freeman, San Francisco, CA.

Harrod, W J (1983) 'In-group bias in the minimal organizational setting', *Simulation & Games*, **14**, 3, 309–16.

Jones, K (1995) *Simulations: A handbook for teachers and trainers*, Kogan Page, London.

Kibbee, J M, Craft, C J and Nanus, B (1961) *Management Games: A new technique for executive development*, Reinhold Publishing, New York.

Klabbers, J, Hoefnagels, K, Truin, G J and Hijden, P van der (1980) 'Development of an interactive simulation/game', *Simulation & Games*, **11**, 1, 59–86.

Kringen, J A (1980) 'Utility of political gaming', *Simulation & Games*, **11**, 2, 139–48.

Larreche, J-C (1989) 'On simulations in business education and research', in Cook, V J, Larreche, J-E and Strong, E C (eds) *Readings In Marketing Strategy*, The Scientific Press, New York, pp. 347–54.

Law-Yone, H (1982) 'Games for citizen participation', *Simulation & Games*, **13**, 1, 51–62.

Lederman, L C and Ruben, B D (1978) 'Construct validity in instructional communication simulations', *Simulation & Games*, **9**, 3, 259–74.

Lester, J P and Stoil, M J (1979) 'Evaluating a role-specific simulation', *Simulation & Games*, **10**, 2, 167–88.

Locatis, C N and Atkinson, F D (1981) 'Designing instructional simulations: heuristics for training college and university faculty', *Simulation & Games*, **12**, 3, 333–44.

Lucas, H C (1979) 'Performance in a complex management game', *Simulation & Games*, **10**, 1, 61–74.

Marimon, R and McGrattan, E (1993) *On Adaptive Learning in Strategic Games. Economic Theory Discussion Paper Number 190*, (January), Judge Institute of Management Studies, University of Cambridge, Cambridge, 1–50.

Morrison, J, Morrison, M and Vogel, D (1992) 'Software to support business teams', *Group Decision and Negotiation*, **1**, 2, 91–115.

Muller, H (1994) 'Simulation and games of another type', paper presented at the 10th European Forum on System Simulation and Management Gaming Conference, 14–16 November, Deutsche Planspiel-Zentrale, Bad Neuenahr.

Noesjirwan, J and Freestone, C (1979) 'The culture shock: a simulation of culture shock', *Simulation & Games*, **10**, 2, 189–206.

Norris, D R and Niebuhr, R E (1980) 'Group variables and gaming success', *Simulation & Games*, **11**, 3, 301–12.

Parasuraman, A (1981) 'Assessing the worth of business simulation games', *Simulation & Games*, **12**, 2, 189–200.

Pfeiffer, R (1994) 'The internationalisation of business games', paper presented at the 10th European Forum on System Simulation and Management Gaming Conference, 14–16 November, Deutsche Planspiel-Zentrale, Bad Neuenahr.

Pratt, L K, Uhl, N P and Little, E R (1980) 'Evaluation of games as a function of personality type', *Simulation & Games*, **11**, 3, 336–46.

Putnam, L L and Roloff, M E (1992) 'Communication perspectives on negotiation', in Putnam, L L and Roloff, M E (eds) *Communication and Negotiation*, Sage, Newbury Park, pp.1–17.

Robinson, J N (1978) 'Are economic games and simulations useful? Some evidence from an experimental game', *Simulation & Games*, **9**, 1, 3–22.

Rohn, W E (1994) Chairman's concluding remarks, at the 10th European Forum on System Simulation and Management Gaming Conference, 14–16 November, Deutsche Planspiel-Zentrale, Bad Neuenahr.

Rojot, J (1991) *Negotiation: From theory to practice,* Macmillan, Basingstoke.

Rosen, D J (1981) 'Metro-Apex as a course', *Simulation & Games*, **12**, 1, 15–27.

Ruben, B D and Lederman, L C (1982) 'Instructional simulation gaming: validity, reliability and utility', *Simulation & Games*, **13**, 2, 233–44.

Schuit, W (1994) 'Design deliberations for a management game: a case study', paper presented at the 10th European Forum on System Simulation and Management Gaming Conference, 14–16 November, Deutsche Planspiel-Zentrale, Bad Neuenahr.

Siebecke, R (1994) 'Future perspectives and potentialities of gaming', paper presented at the 10th European Forum on System Simulation and Management Gaming Conference, 14–16 November, Deutsche Planspiel-Zentrale, Bad Neuenahr.

Smith, C L and Stander, J M (1981) 'Human interaction with computer simulation: sex roles and group size', *Simulation & Games*, **12**, 3, 345–60.

Smith, N C (1989) *The Case Study: A vital yet misunderstood research method for management, Working Paper SWP 4/89*, Cranfield University Management School, Cranfield, pp. 1–23.

Tafoya, D W (1979) 'The motivation game', *Simulation & Games*, **10**, 4, 403–18.

Thiagarajan, S and Stolovitch, H D (1979) 'Frame games: an evaluation', *Simulation & Games*, **10**, 3, 287–314.

Thierauf, R J, Klekamp, R C and Ruwe, M L (1985) *Management Science: A model formulation approach with computer applications*, Charles E Merrill Publishing, Columbus, OH.

Trim, P (1994a) 'Negotiation and the business school curriculum', *Journal of European Business Education*, **3**, 2, 29–38.

Trim, P (1994b) 'Negotiation and intercultural skills: enhanced by various teaching methods', paper presented at the 10th European Forum on System Simulation and Management Gaming Conference, 14–16 November, Deutsche Planspiel-Zentrale, Bad Neuenahr.

Trim, P (1994c) *Games, Simulation And Negotiation, Canterbury Business School Working Paper Number 26*, December, University of Kent, Canterbury.

Trim, P (1995) *The Northern Europe Complex Case Number 390-010-1*, European Case Clearing House, Cranfield University, Cranfield, pp. 1–22.

Valley, K L, White, S B and Iacobucci, D (1992) 'The process of assisted negotiations: a network analysis', *Group Decision and Negotiation*, **1**, 2, 117–35.

van Oosten, R C H and Laseur, W (1980) 'The management games at the University of Groningen, The Netherlands', *Simulation & Games*, **11**, 4, 423–39.

van Sickle, R L (1978) 'Designing simulation games to teach decision-making skills', *Simulation & Games*, **9**, 4, 413–28.

von Furstenberg, G (1994) 'Conflict solution using simulation gaming', paper presented at the 10th European Forum on System Simulation and Management Gaming Conference, 14–16 November, Deutsche Planspiel-Zentrale, Bad Neuenahr.

Wolfe, J (1993a) 'A history of business teaching games in English-speaking and post-socialist countries: the origination and diffusion of a management education and development technology', *Simulation & Games*, **24**, 4, 446–63.

Wolfe, J (1993b) 'Successful student case analysis strategies', *Simulation & Gaming*, **24**, 4, 464–75.

Wolff, U (1994) 'Project planning and control with a simulation game', paper presented at the 10th European Forum on System Simulation and Management Gaming Conference, 14–16 November, Deutsche Planspiel-Zentrale, Bad Neuenahr.

Yefimov, V M and Komarov, V F (1982) 'Developing management simulation games', *Simulation & Games*, **13**, 2, 145–63.

ABOUT THE AUTHOR

Peter Trim is a Lecturer in Management at Birkbeck College, University of London. He has held appointments at the Universities of Groningen and Kent, and has been a visiting academic at the European Institute of Purchasing Management in France. He is currently undertaking research into partnership arrangements between institutions in both further and higher education.

Address for correspondence: Department of Management and Business Studies, Birkbeck College, University of London, 7–15 Gresse Street, London W1P 2LL.

Chapter 23

References to recent articles on research and practice in simulation and gaming

Mike McDonagh

ABSTRACT

The following references have been kindly made available by the ERIC Clearinghouse. They provide the listing of ERIC journal articles and documents dealing with games and simulations. All articles are in English unless otherwise stated. The help of ERIC/CHESS is gratefully acknowledged as is that of DIALOG Information Services Inc.

GENERAL

Exploring Prejudice in Young Adult Literature through Drama and Role Play.
Bontempo, Barbara T
ALAN Review, 22 (3) 31–3 Spr 1995

An Ethnomethodological Study of Concerted and Biographical Work Performed by Elderly Persons during Game Playing
Mangrum, Faye Gothard; Mangrum, C W
Educational Gerontology, 21 (3) 231–46 Apr–May 1995

Authoring for Simulation-based Learning
Hensgens, Jan *et al.*
Instructional Science, 23 (4) 269–96 Jul 1995

Simulated Environments for the Exercising of Critical Decision Makers: Utilizing Networked Multimedia
Crego, Jonathan; Powell, James
Journal of Instruction Delivery Systems, 9 (2) 35–9 Spr 1995

Constructive Lessons: Building and Playing Simulation Games.
Gussin, Lawrence
CD-ROM Professional, 8 40–42, 44, 46, 48, 50 May 1995

Games that Teach
Hequet, Marc
Training, 32 (7) 53–8 Jul 1995

Traveling in the Snite Museum: A Gallery Game for Families and Young Children
Matthias, Diana C J; Grey, Richard
Notre Dame University, IN. Snite Museum of Art, Jun 1994, 15pp

Using Simulations to Develop Cultural Sensitivity in Preservice Teachers: The Heelotia Experience
Hoelscher, Karen
Multicultural Education, 3 (3) 39–43 Spr 1996

Epistemic Forms and Epistemic Games
Sherry, Lorraine; Trigg, Maggie
Educational Technology, 36 (3) 38–44 May–Jun 1996

Using Computer Simulations to Enhance Conceptual Change: The Roles of Constructivist Instruction and Student Epistemological Beliefs
Windschitl, Mark; Andre, Thomas
Paper presented at the Annual Conference of the American Educational Research Association, New York, April 8–12 1996, 6pp

Ten Steps to Better Simulations
Adkins, Carol
Science Scope, 19 (7) 28–9 Apr 1996

Testing-the-Limits and Experimental Simulation: Two Methods to Explicate the Role of Learning in Development
Lindenberger, Ulman; Bates, Paul B
Human Development, 38 (6) 349–60 Nov–Dec 1995

Everyone Can Play : Adapting the Candy Land Board Game
Raschke, Donna B *et al.*
Teaching Exceptional Children, 28 (4) 28–33 Sum 1996

Effects of Coaching on the Validity of the SAT: A Simulation Study
Baydar, Nazli
Educational Testing Service, Princeton, NJ, Apr 1990, 70pp

Instructional Applications of Computer Games
Dempsey, John V, *et al.*
Paper presented at the Annual Meeting of the American Educational Research
Association, New York, April 8–12, 1996, 13pp

Creating Simulations: Expressing Life-Situated Relationships in Terms of
Algebraic Equations
Verzoni, Kathryn A
Paper presented at the Annual Meeting of the Northeastern Educational Research
Association, Ellenville, NY, October 26 1995, 13pp

The Effect of Cooperative Gaming Techniques on Teacher Confidence toward
At-risk Students
Barrington, Kyle D
Journal of Experiential Education, 18 (3) 138–44 Dec 1995

Assessment of a Peer-helping Game Program on Children's Development
Garaigordobil, Maite; Echebarria, Agustin
Journal of Research in Childhood Education, 10 (1) 63–9 Fall–Win 1995

Animation as Feedback in a Computer-based Simulation: Representation Matters
Rieber, Lloyd P
Educational Technology Research and Development, 24 (2) 195–205 1996

An Investigation in Evaluation Issues for a Simulation Training Programme
Saunders, Danny; Gaston, Karen
British Journal of Educational Technology, 27 (1) 15–24 Jan 1996

Computer Games: Increase Learning in an Interactive Multidisciplinary
Environment
Betz, Joseph A
Journal of Educational Technology Systems, 24 (2) 195–205 1996

Problem Framing through Gaming: A Rebuttal to Law-Yone
Klabbers, Jan H G
Simulation and Gaming; 27 (1) 98–102 Mar 1996

Problem Framing through Gaming_and Problematic Games: A Response to
Klabbers
Law-Yone, Hubert
Simulation & Gaming, 27 (1) 93–7 Mar 1996

Problem Framing through Gaming: Learning to Manage Complexity, Uncertainty,
and Value Adjustment
Klabbers, Jan H G
Simulation and Gaming, 27 (1) 74–92 Mar 1996

Team Cohesion, Player Attitude, and Performance Expectations in Simulation
Wellington, William J; Faria, A J
Simulation & Gaming, 27 (1) 23–40 Mar 1996

Straws in the Wind: Some Perceptions and Attitudes Toward Simulation and
Gaming in the United Kingdom
Cherrington, Ruth; van Ments, Morry
Simulation & Gaming, 27 (1) 5–22 Mar 1996

Creating Opportunities for Prospective Elementary and Early Childhood Teacher
Reflection, Simulations, Teaching Cases, Portfolios, and More
Dana, Nancy Fichtman; Westcott, Laurie
Paper presented at the Annual Meeting of the Association of Teacher Educators,
St Louis, MO, February 1996, 25pp

Harnessing Simulations in the Service of Education: The Interact Simulation
Environment
Thomas, Ruth; Neilson, Irene
Computers & Education, 25 (1–2) 21–9 Sep 1995

A Hierarchical Simulation Model to Study Educational Interventions
Bosker, R J; Guldemond, H
Groningen University (The Netherlands); Twente University, Enschede (The
Netherlands), Centre for Applied Research in Education, Nov 1994 70pp

Affects of Age and GPA on Learning Electronics via Computer Simulation-based
and Traditional Instruction
Nejad, Mahmoud Arshadi
Paper presented at the Annual Conference of the Mid-south Educational Research
Association, 24th, Biloxi, MS, November 8–10 1995, 19pp

Locus of Control, Self-esteem, Achievement Motivation, and Problem-solving
Ability: Logo Writer and Simulations in the Fifth-grade Classroom
Tyler, Doris Kennedy; Vasu, Ellen Storey
Journal of Research on Computing in Education, 28 (1) 98–120 Fall 1995

A Framework for Simulating Computer-based Individual and Work-group
Communication
Amini, Minoo S
Journal of Education for Business, 71 (1) 49–53 Sep–Oct 1995

Games and Icebreakers
National Energy Education Development Project, Reston, VA
1994 25pp

Do You Use Developmentally Appropriate Games?
Conkell, Carol S.; Pearson, Huey
Strategies; 9 (1) 37–42 Fall–Win 1992

Making Game Artifacts to Facilitate Rich and Meaningful Learning
Kafai, Yasmin
Paper presented at the Annual Meeting of the American Educational Research
Association, San Francisco, CA, April 1995, 20pp

Children's Independent Exploration of a Natural Phenomenon by using a Pictorial
Computer-based Simulation.
Kangassalo, Marjatta
In: *Educational Multimedia and Hypermedia*, 1994, Proceedings of ED-Media 94
– World Conference on Educational Multimedia and Hypermedia, Vancouver, BC
Canada, June 25–30, 1994, 7pp

Assessing the Impact of a Proposed Expert System Via Simulation
Croy, Marvin J *et al.*
Journal of Educational Computing Research, 13 (1) 1–15 1995

The Early Days of 'Simulation & Games': A Personal Reflection.
Stasz, Clarice Stoll
Simulation & Gaming, 26 (4) 511–17 Dec 1995

The Story of 'The Guide to Simulations/Games for Education and Training'
Horn, Robert E
Simulation & Gaming, 26 (4) 471–80 Dec 1995

Recollections About the Inter-Nation Simulation (INS) and Some Derivatives in
Global Modeling
Guetzkow, Harrold
Simulation & Gaming, 26 (4) 453–70 Dec 1995

Thirty-five Years in Gaming
Feldt, Allan G
Simulation & Gaming, 26 (4) 448–52 Dec 1995

Gaming: An Emergent Discipline
Duke, Richard D
Simulation & Gaming, 26 (4) 426–39 Dec 1995

Tugboats and Tennis Games: Preservice Conceptions of Teaching and Learning
Revealed through Metaphors
Gurney, Bruce
Journal of Research in Science Teaching, 32 (6) 569–83 Aug 1995

Hands-on and Computer Simulations
Hasson, Brian; Bug, Amy L R
Physics Teacher, 33 (4) 230–36 Apr 1995

The Hakayak's Last Odyssey: A Computer Game with a Difference
Bauza, Guillem Bou; Gelabert, Miguel Essomba
Educational Media International, 32 (2) 97–101 Jun 1995

Word Problems: Game or Reality? Studies of Children's Beliefs about the Role of
Real-world Knowledge in Mathematical Modeling.
De Corte, Erik *et al.*
Paper presented at the Annual Meeting of the American Educational Research
Association, San Francisco, CA, April 18–22 1995, 27pp

So You Want to Deliver a Simulation
Lynch, Patricia L
Paper presented at the Annual Meeting of the Central States Communication
Association, Indianapolis, IN, April 19–23 1995, 15pp

Using Games to Understand Children's Understanding
Dominick, Ann; Clark, Faye B
Childhood Education, 72 (5) 286–8 1996

The Cognitive Impact of Multimedia Simulations on 14 Year Old Students.
Yildiz, Rauf; Atkins, Madeleine
British Journal of Educational Technology, 27 (2) 106–15 May 1996

Seriously Considering Play: Designing Interactive Learning Environments Based
on the Blending of Microworlds, Simulations and Games
Rjeber, Lloyd P
Educational Technology Research and Development, 44 (2) 43–58 1996

BIOSCIENCES

Demonstrating Biological Classification Using a Simulation of Natural Taxa
Vogt, Kenneth D
American Biology Teacher, 57 (5) 282–3 May 1995

Global Responses to Potential Climate Change: A Simulation
Williams, Mary Louise; Mowry, George
Project Crossroads, Sante Fe, NM Dec 1995, 73pp

IMMUNOSCENARIOS: A Game for the Immune System
Taylor, Mark F.; Jackson, Sally W
American Biology Teacher, 58 (5) 288–95 May 1996

DNA Sequencing Simulation
Contolini, Nancy
Science Teacher, 63 (4) 26–9 Apr 1996

Role Playing and Mind Mapping Issues on Nitrate Contamination
Pan, W L
Journal of Natural Resources and Life Sciences Education, 25 (1) 37–42 Spr 1996

A Germanation Simulation
Hershey, David R
Science Teacher 62 (9) 40–43 Dec 1995

A Simulation Game for the Study of Enzyme Kinetics and Inhibition.
Chayoth, Reuben; Cohen, Annette
American Biology Teacher, 58 (3) 175–7 Mar 1996

A Candy Gene Game for Teaching Genetics
Burns, Roxanne H
American Biology Teacher, 58 (3) 163–5 Mar 1996

Understanding Our Environment: Challenge. Clear Water Challenge: A Role Play
Activity
Lieblich, Suzanne (ed.)
National Science Teachers Association, Arlington, VA, 1995, 38pp

Training Quantitative Thinkers by Using spreadsheets as Simulation Drivers for
Biology Classes: Selective Predation Effect on Prey Gene Pool
Porter, Tom
American Biology Teacher, 58 (2) 114–17 Feb 1996

Corpus Morphus: The Human Anatomy Board Game.
McIntire, Cecil L
American Biology Teacher, 57 (8) 538–43 Nov–Dec 1995

BUSINESS STUDIES

Formal Planning and the Performance of Business Simulation Team
Hornaday, Robert W; Curran, Kent E
Simulation & Gaming, 27 (2) 206–22 Jun 1996

Teams: The Name of the School and Business Game
O'Leary, Pat Wilson
Business Education Forum, 50 (4) 11–14 Apr 1996

Learning and Learning-to-learn by Doing: Simulating Corporate Practice in Law
School
Okamoto, Karl S
Journal of Legal Education, 45 (4) 498–512 Dec 1995

Simulating Design in the World of Industry and Commerce: Observations from a
Series of Case Studies in the United Kingdom
Denton, Howard G
Journal of Technology Education, 6 (1) Fall 1994

Using Computer Simulations for Group Projects in Business School Education
Tompson, George H
Journal of Education for Business, 71 (2) 97–101 Nov–Dec 1995

Japanese for Business Purposes: A Simulation Approach
Urabe, Sadako
Paper presented at the Annual Easter Michigan University Conference on
Languages and Communication for World Business and the Professions, 13th,
Ypsilanti, MI, April 6–8 1995, 19pp

HEALTH STUDIES

Teaching Pairs of Preschoolers with Disabilities to Seek Adult Assistance in
Response to Simulated Injuries: Acquisition and Promotion of Observational
Learning
Christensen, Ann Marie *et al.*
Education and Treatment of Children, 19 (1) 3–18 Feb 1996

Connectionist Modeling as the Basis for Multimedia Clinical Patient Simulations
with Diagnostic Capabilities
Bergeron, Bryan P *et al.*
Journal of Educational Multimedia and Hypermedia, 4 (2–3) 257–70 1995

Experiential Learning about the Elderly: The Geriatric Medication Game
Oliver, Carol H *et al.*
American Journal of Pharmaceutical Education, 59 (2) 155–8 Sum 1995

Evaluation of a Computer Simulation in a Therapeutics Case Discussion
Kinkade, Raenel E *et al.*
American Journal of Pharmaceutical Education, 59 (2) 147–50 Sum 1995

Microcomputer-based Programs for Pharmacokinetic Simulations
Li, Ronald C *et al.*
American Journal of Pharmaceutical Education, 59 (2) 143–7 Sum 1995

HUMANITIES

The Use of Language Functions in Mathematical Group Games. Teacher Insights
Black, Carolyn; Huerta, Maria G
Bilingual Research Journal, 18 (3–4) 161–7 Sum–Fall 1994

The Intercultural Communication Negotiation Simulation: An Instructional Model
for Teaching/Training Intercultural Communication Skills
Samp, Jennifer A
Version of a paper presented at the Annual Meeting of the International
Communication Association, 45th, Albuquerque, NM, May 25–9, 1995, 39pp

Simulating the Lausanne Peace Negotiations, 1992–1993: Power Asymmetries in
Bargaining
Beriker, Nimet; Druckman, Daniel
Simulation & Gaming, 27 (2) 162–83 Jun 1996

A Pioneer Simulation for Writing and for the Study of Literature
McCann, Thomas M
English Journal, 85 (3) 62–7 Mar 1996

Conflict in the Balkans: A Classroom Simulation
Major, Marc; Nelson, Kari
Social Studies 86 (5) 205–13 Sep–Oct 1995

Using Role Playing in Argument Papers to Deconstruct Stereotypes
Moore, Vincent
Teaching English in the Two-Year College, 22 (3) 190–96 Oct 1995

JUGAME: Game Style ICAI system for Kanji Idiom Learning
Hayashi, Toshihiro; Yano, Yoneo
In: *Educational Multimedia and Hypermedia*, 1994, Proceedings of ED-MEDIA
94 – World Conference on Educationa Multimedia and Hypermedia, Vancouver,
BC, Canada, June 25–30 1994, 7pp

Exploring America in Computer Simulation Games
Miller-Lachmann, Lyn *et al.*
MultiCultural Review, 4 (3) 44–6, 48–52 Sep 1995

Indian Reservation Gaming: Much at Stake
Firkus, Angela; Parman, Donald L
OAH Magazine of History, 9 (4) 22–7 Sum 1995

Marking GCSE Role Play
Hurman, John
Language Learning Journal, (13) 19–21 Mar 1996

MANAGEMENT STUDIES

The Evaluation of a Management Simulation as a Method of Learning
Engeholm Gerard M; Bigel, Kenneth S
Business Education Forum, 50 (4) 21–4 Apr 1996

Personality, Organizational Culture, and Cooperation: Evidence from a Business
Simulation.
Chatman, Jennifer A; Barsade, Sigal G
Administrative Science Quarterly, 40 (3) 423–43 Nov 1995

Events Management Education through CD-ROM Simulation at Victoria
University of Technology
Perry, Marcia *et al.*
In: *Learning Technologies: Prospects and Pathways*, Selected papers from
EdTech '96 Biennial Conference of the Australian Society for Educational
Technology, Melbourne, Australia, July 7–10 1996; see IR 017 931; 4pp

SCIENCE AND TECHNOLOGY

CPU SIM: A Computer Simulator for Use in an Introductory Computer Organization-Architecture Class
Skrein, Dale
Journal of Computing in Higher Education, 6 (1) 3–13 Fall 1994

Simulation of a Forensic Chemistry Problem: A Multidisciplinary Project for Secondary School Chemistry Students
Long, G A
Journal of Chemical Education 72 (9) 803–4 Sep 1995

Issues in Project-based Science Activities: Children's Constructions of Ocean Software Games
Yarnall, Louise; Kafai, Yasmin
Paper presented at the Annual Meeting of the American Educational Research Association, New York, April, 1996, 29pp

STEPS: A Simulated, Tutorable Physics Student
Ur, Sigalit; VanLehn, Kurt
Journal of Artificial Intelligence in Education, 6 (4) 405–37 1995

Pipe Flow Simulation Software: A Team Approach to Solve an Engineering Education Problem
Engel, Renata S *et al.*
Journal of Computing in Higher Education, 7 (2) 65–77 Spr 1996

An African Chemistry Connection: Simulating Early Iron Smelting
Murfin, Brian
Science Teacher, 63 (2) 36–9 Feb 1996

Using a Microcomputer in the Teaching of Gas-Phase Equilibria: A Numerical Simulation
Hayward, Roger
Australian Science Teachers Journal, 41 (4) 52–6 Dec 1995

Impact of Simulator-Based Instruction on Diagramming in Geometrical Optics by Introductory Physics Students
Reiner, Miriam *et al.*
Journal of Science Education and Technology, 4 (3) 199–226 Sep 1995

Simulated Space Shuttle Mission
Gurnon, Roy K
Science Scope, 18 (2) 13–16 Oct 1994

Rock and Mineral Board Game
Grambo, Gregory
Science Activities, 32 (2) 21–7 Sum 1995

Diagnosing and Altering Three Aristotelian Alternative Conceptions in Dynamics:
Microcomputer Simulations of Scientific Models
Weller, Herman G
Journal of Research in Science Teaching, 32 (3) 271–90 Mar 1995

COMPANION: An interactive Learning Environment Based on the Cognitive
Apprenticeship Paradigm for Design Engineers Using Numerical Simulations
Hilem, Y; Futtersack, M
In: *Educational Multimedia and Hypermedia*, 1994, Proceedings of ED-MEDIA
94 – World Conference on Educational Multimedia and Hypermedia, Vancouver,
BC, Canada, June 25–30 1994 7pp

INDUCT: A Game of Scientific Induction
Thiagarajan, Raja; Thiagarajan, Silvasailam
Simulation & Gaming, 26 (4) 511–17 Dec 1995

Game-display Board Activities for Science Teaching
Chung, C M *et al.*
Journal of Science Education and Technology, 5 (2) 141–54 Jun 1996

Computer Simulations as Tools for Teaching and Learning: Using a Simulation
Environment in Optics
Eylon, Bat-Sheva *et al.*
Journal of Science Education and Technology, 5 (2) 93–110 June 1996

A Simulation Problem with Many Solutions
Kung, George; Mitchell, Richard
Mathematics and Computer Education, 30 (2) 130–38 Spr 1996

SOCIAL SCIENCES

Total Enterprise Simulation Performance as a Function of Myers-Briggs
Personality Type
Gosenpud, Jerry; Washbush, John
Simulation & Gaming, 27 (2) 184–205 June 1996

Race and Sex Differences in Reactions to a Simulated Selection Decision
Involving Race-based Affirmative Action
Doverspike, Dennis; Arthur, Winfred Jr
Journal of Black Psychology, 21 (2) 181–200 May 1995

Stimulating Statistical Thinking through Situated Simulations.
Derry, Sharon *et al.*
Teaching of Psychology, 22 (1) 51–7 Feb 1995

Using Riddles and Interactive Computer Games to Teach Problem-solving Skills
Doolittle, John H
Teaching of Psychology 22 (1) 33–6 Feb 1995

The Numbers Game: Gender and Attention to Numerical Information
Jackson, Linda A *et al.*
Sex Roles: A Journal of Research 33 (7–8) 559–68 Oct 1995

Best Use: A Cash Game to Explore Persuasion
Thiagarajan, Sivasailam
Performance and Instruction, 35 (1) 10–13 Jan 1996

Using Simulations to Teach Leadership Roles
Pickert, Sarah M
Teaching Education 5 (1) 37–42 Fall–Win 1992

Planning with Computers – A Social Studies Simulation.
Teague, Maryanne; Teague, Gerald
Learning and Leading with Technology, 23 (1) 20, 22 Sep 1995

Broken Squares: A Simulation Exploring Cooperation and Conflict
Stanford University, CA, Stanford Program on International and Cross Cultural
Education, 1994, 17pp

Simulated Conversations: The McGill Negotiation Simulator
Roston, John
In: *Educational Multimedia and Hypermedia*, 1994, Proceedings of ED-MEDIA
94 – World Conference on Educational Multimedia and Hypermedia, Vancouver,
BC, Canada, June 25–30 1994, 7pp

Chapter 24

Publishers of games and simulations in the UK, the USA, Europe and Australia

Ray Land, Napier University, Edinburgh

UK SIMULATIONS PUBLISHERS

Aberdeen University Press
c/o James Thin Ltd, 53–59 South Bridge,
Edinburgh, EH1 1YS
Tel: (0131) 556 6743
Fax: (0131) 557 8149

Edward Arnold Ltd
338 Euston Road, London, NW1 3BH
Tel: (0171) 873 6000
Fax: (0171) 873 6024

Avebury
Ashgate Publishing Group,
Gower House, Croft Road,
Aldershot, Hants, GU11 3HR
Tel: (01252) 331 551
Fax: (01252) 344 405

AVP, Publishers of Educational
Resources
School Hill Centre,
Chepstow, Monmouthshire, NP6 5PH
Tel: (01291) 625 439
Fax: (01291) 629 671

B T Batsford Ltd
4 Fitzhardinge Street,
London, W1H 0AH
Tel: (0171) 486 8484
Fax: (0171) 487 4296

Blackwell Publishers
108 Cowley Road,
Oxford, OX4 1JF
Tel: (01865) 791 100
Fax: (01865) 791 347

Cambridge University Press
The Edinburgh Building,
Shaftesbury Road,
Cambridge, CB2 2RU
Tel: (01223) 312 393
Fax: (01223) 315 052

Careers and Occupational Information
Centre
Dept of Employment, Room E415,
Moorfoot, Sheffield, S1 4PQ
Tel: (0114) 259 4564
Fax: (0114) 275 2035

Cassell plc
Wellington House, 125 Strand,
London, WC2R 0BB
Tel: (0171) 420 5555
Fax: (0171) 240 7261

Centre for Innovation in Mathematics
Teaching
School of Education, University of Exeter,
St Luke's, Exeter, EX1 2LU
Tel: (01392) 217 113
Fax: (01392) 499 398

Chartwell-Bratt (Publishing & Training) Ltd
Old Orchard,
Bickely Road, Bromley, BR1 2NE
Tel: (0181) 467 1956
Fax: (0181) 467 1754

Commercial Devices
5 Farm Buildings,
Palmers Moor, Thornborough,
Bucks, MK18 2DJ
Tel: (01280) 824 100
Fax: (01280) 824 200

Computational Mechanics Publications Ltd
Ashurst Lodge,
Ashurst, Southampton, S04 7AA
Tel: (01703) 293 223
Fax: (01703) 292 853

Computers in Teaching Initiative, Centre for History with Archaeology & Art History
University of Glasgow,
1 University Gardens,
Glasgow, G12 8QQ
Tel: (0141) 330 6336
Fax: (0141) 330 5518

Construction Industry Research & Information Association
6 Storey's Gate, London, SW1P 3AU
Tel: (0171) 222 8891
Fax: (0171) 222 1708

Development Education in Dorset
East Dorset Professional Education Centre,
Kingsleigh Secondary School,
Hadow Road, Bournemouth, BH10 5HS
Tel: (01202) 532 484
Fax: (01202) 396 932

Economics and Business Education Association
1A Keymer Road,
Hassocks, West Sussex, BN6 8AD
Tel: (01273) 846 033

Edward Elgar Publishing Ltd
8 Lansdown Place,
Cheltenham, Glos, GL50 2HU
Tel: (01242) 226 934
Fax: (01242) 262 111

Elm Publications
Seaton House, Kings Ripton,
Huntingdon, Cambs, PE17 2NJ
Tel: (0148 73) 238/254
Fax: (0148 73) 359

Energy Consultancy
24 Elm Close, Bedford, MK41 8BZ
Tel: (01234) 262 677

Framework Press
Parkfield, Greaves Road,
Lancaster, LA1 4TZ
Tel: (01524) 396 02
Fax: (01524) 841 520

Gordon & Breach Publishers Ltd
PO Box 90, Reading, RG1 8JL
Tel: (01734) 560 080
Fax: (01734) 568 211

Gower Publishing Co
Gower House, Croft Road,
Aldershot, Hants, GU11 3HR
Tel: (01252) 331 551
Fax: (01252) 344 405

Hall Marketing
Studio 11, Colman's Wharf,
45 Morris Road, London, E14 6PA
Tel: (0171) 537 2982

Harvard University Press
Fitzroy House, 11 Chenies Street,
London, WC1E 7ET
Tel: (0171) 306 0603
Fax: (0171) 306 0604

Hobsons Publishing plc
Bateman Street,
Cambridge, CB2 1LZ
Tel: (01223) 354 551
Fax: (01223) 323 154

Hodder & Stoughton Ltd
338 Euston Road,
London, NW1 3BH
Tel: (0171) 873 6000
Fax: (0171) 873 6024

Holt, Rinehart & Winston
24–28 Oval Road, London, NW1 7DX
Tel: (0171) 267 4466
Fax: (0171) 482 2293

Horwood Ellis Ltd, Publisher
Campus 400, Marylands Avenue,
Hemel Hempstead, Herts, HP2 7EZ
Tel: (01442) 881 900
Fax: (01442) 882 099

Interscience Publishers
Division of John Wiley Ltd,
Baffins Lane, Chichester,
West Sussex, PO19 1UD
Tel: (01243) 779 777
Fax: (01243) 775 878

**Keele Mathematical Education
  Publications**
c/o Dept of Education,
University of Keele,
Keele, Staffs, ST5 5BG
Tel: (01782) 621 111
Fax: (01782) 714 113

Kogan Page Ltd
120 Pentonville Road,
London, N1 9JN
Tel: (0171) 278 0433
Fax: (0171) 837 6348

Addison-Wesley Longman Ltd
Finchamstead Road,
Wokingham, Berkshire RG11 2NZ
Tel: (01279) 623 623
Fax: (01279) 431 059

McGraw-Hill Book Co Europe
Shoppenhangers Road, Maidenhead,
Berks, SL6 2QL
Tel: (01628) 234 32
Fax: (01628) 35895 & 770224

Mechanical Engineering Publications Ltd
Northgate Avenue,
Bury St Edmunds, Suffolk, IP32 6BW
Tel: (01284) 763 277
Fax: (01284) 704 006

Mercat Press
c/o James Thin, 53–59 South Bridge,
Edinburgh, EH1 1YS
Tel: (0131) 556 6743
Fax: (0131) 557 8149

MIT Press Ltd
Fitzroy House, 11 Chenies Street,
London, WC1E 7ET
Tel: (0171) 306 0603
Fax: (0171) 306 0604

Multilingual Matters Ltd
Frankfurt Lodge,
Clevedon Hall, Victoria Road,
Clevedon, North Somerset, BS21 7SJ
Tel: (01275) 876 519
Fax: (01275) 343 096

Network Exhibitions & Conferences Ltd
Ceased trading 1992, titles acquired by:
Bee Vee Promotions Ltd,
Fleece Yard, Market Hill,
Buckingham, MK18 1JX
Tel: (01280) 815 226
Fax: (01280) 815 919

Nottingham Trent University
Dryden Street Library,
Dryden St, Nottingham NG1 4FZ
Tel: (0115) 948 6435
Fax: (1015) 941 5380)

Open University Press
Celtic Court, 22 Ballmoor,
Buckingham, MK18 1XW
Tel: (01280) 823 388
Fax: (01280) 823 233

Oxford University Press
Walton Street, Oxford, OX2 6DP
Tel: (01865) 567 67
Fax: (01865) 566 46

Peter Peregrinus Ltd
Michael Faraday House,
Six Hills Way, Stevenage, Herts, SG1 2AY
Tel: (01438) 313 311
Fax: (01438) 313 465

Pergamon Press Ltd
(an imprint of Elsevier Science Publishers)
The Boulevard, Langford Lane,
Kidlington, OX5 1GB
Tel: (01865) 843 000
Fax: (01865) 843 010

Pineridge Press Ltd
54 Newton Road,
Mumbles, Swansea, SA3 4BQ
Tel: (01792) 361 557
Fax: (01792) 361 557

Pitman Publishing
128 Long Acre, London, WC2E 9AN
Tel: (0171) 379 7383
Fax: (0171) 240 5771

Plenum Publishing Co Ltd
88/90 Middlesex Street, London, E1 7E2
Tel: (0171) 377 0686
Fax: (0171) 247 0555

Prentice-Hall
Campus 400, Maryland Avenue,
Hemel Hempstead, Herts, HP2 7EZ
Tel: (01442) 881 900
Fax: (01442) 882 099

Research Studies Press Ltd
24 Belvedere Road,
Taunton, Somerset, TA1 1HD
Tel: (01823) 336 197
Fax: (01823) 253 252

Royal Aeronautical Society
4 Hamilton Place, London, W1V 0BQ
Tel: (0171) 499 3515
Fax: (0171) 499 6230

Sage Publications Ltd
6 Bonhill Street, London, EC2A 4PU
Tel: (0171) 374 0645
Fax: (0171) 374 8741

SAUS Publications
School for Advanced Urban Studies,
University of Bristol,
Rodney Lodge,
Grange Road,
Bristol, BS8 4EA
Tel: (0117) 974 1117
Fax: (0117) 973 7308

Scholastic Publications Ltd
Villiers House,
Clarendon Avenue,
Leamington Spa, Warwickshire,
CV32 5PR
Tel: (01926) 887 799
Fax: (01926) 883 331

Stable Ltd
Glebe House,
Church Street, Crediton,
Devon, EX17 2AF
Tel: (01363) 777 575
Fax: (01363) 776 007

E & F N Spon
(an imprint of Chapman & Hall)
2–6 Boundary Row,
London, SE1 8HN
Tel: (0171) 865 0066
Fax: (0171) 865 9623

Sydney University Press
Distributed by:
Oxford University Press,
Walton Street, Oxford, OX2 6DP
Tel: (01865) 567 67
Fax: (01865) 566 46

Taylor and Francis Ltd
1 Gunpowder Square,
London,
EC4 3DE
Tel: (0171) 583 0490
Fax: (orders & trade dept) (01256) 479 438

University of Manchester
Department of Agricultural Economics,
Oxford Road, Manchester, M13 9PL
Tel: (0161) 273 5539
Fax: (0161) 274 3346

John Wiley & Sons Ltd
Baffins Lane, Chichester,
West Sussex, PO19 1UD
Tel: (01243) 779 777
Fax: (01243) 775 878

Winslow Press
463 Ashley Road, Parkstone,
Poole, Dorset BII14 0AX
Tel: (01202) 715 349
Fax: (01202) 736 191

WRW (Water Research Centre) plc
Henley Road,
Medmenham, Marlow, Bucks, SL7 2HD
Tel: (01491) 571 531
Fax: (01491) 411 059

Wye College
School of Rural Economics & Related
    Studies,
Department of Agricultural Economics,
Ashford, Kent, TN25 5AH
Tel: (01233) 812 401
Fax: (01233) 813 320

UK GAMES PUBLISHERS

Nexus Special Interests Ltd
Nexus House, Boundary Way,
Hemel Hempstead, Herts, HP2 7ST
Tel: (01442) 665 51
Fax: (01442) 669 98

Academic Press Inc (London) Ltd
24–28 Oval Road, London, NW1 7DX
Tel: (0171) 267 4466
Fax: (0171) 482 2293/(0171) 485 4752

Butterworth & Co Ltd
Halsbury House, 35 Chancery Lane,
London, WC2A 1EL
Tel: (0171) 400 2500
Fax: (0171) 400 2842

Chapman & Hall Ltd
2–6 Boundary Row,
London, SE1 8HN
Tel: (0171) 865 0066
Fax: (0171) 522 0101

David & Charles plc
Brunel House, Newton Abbot,
Devon, TQ12 4PU
Tel: (01626) 611 21
Fax: (01626) 644 63

Elsevier Science Publishers Ltd
The Boulevard, Langford Lane,
Kiddlington, OX5 1GB
Tel: (01865) 843 000
Fax: (01865) 843 010

Tolley Publishing Co Ltd
Tolley House, 2 Addiscombe Rd,
Croydon, CR9 5AF
Tel: (0181) 686 9141
Fax: (0181) 681 3155

Hobsons Publishing plc
Bateman Street, Cambridge, CB2 1LZ
Tel: (01223) 354 551
Fax: (01223) 323 154

KeyNote Publications Ltd
Field House, 72 Oldfield Road,
Hampton, Middlesex, TW12 2HQ
Tel: (0181) 783 0755
Fax: (0181) 783 1940

Kogan Page Ltd
120 Pentonville Road, London, N1 9JN
Tel: (0171) 278 0433
Fax: (0171) 837 6348

Partizan Press
818 London Road,
Leigh-on-Sea, Essex, SS9 3NH
Tel: (01702) 739 86
Fax: (01702) 739 86

Shaw & Sons Ltd
Shaway House,
21 Bourne Park, Bourne Road,
Crayford, Dartford, DA1 4BZ
Tel: (01322) 550 676
Fax: (01322) 550 553

Shelter Publications
88 Old Street, London, EC1V 9HU
Tel: (0171) 253 0202
Fax: (0171) 490 8918

Stanley Thornes (Publishers) Ltd
Ellenborough House, Wellington Street,
Cheltenham, Glos, GL50 1YW
Tel: (01242) 584 429
Fax: (01242) 221 914

US SIMULATIONS PUBLISHERS

Addison-Wesley
Rte 128, Reading, MA 01867
Tel: 617-944-3700/800-447-2226
Fax: 617-944-9338

American Mathematical Society
Box 6248, Providence, RI 02940
Tel: 401-455-4000/800-321-4267
Fax: 401-331-3842

Ann Arbor Science Publishers Inc
Drawer 1425,
Ann Arbor, MI 48106, USA
Tel: 313-761-5010

Brookings Institution
1775 Massachusetts Ave NW,
Washington, DC 20036-2188
Tel: 202-797-6000/800-275-1447
Fax: 202-797-6004

Brooks-Cole Publishing Co
Division of Wadsworth Inc,
555 Abrego St,
Monterey, CA 93940
Tel: 408-373-0728/800-354-9706
Fax: 408-375-6414
*(UK distributor: International Publishing
Services)*

Butterworth-Heinemann
313, Washington St, Newton, MA 02158
Tel: +1 800 366 2665
Fax: 617-279-4851

CRC Press Inc
2000 Corporate Blvd NW,
Boca Raton, FL 33431
Tel: +1 800 272 7737
Fax: 407-994-3625
*(UK distributor: Mosby-Year Book Europe
Ltd)*

Delmar Publishers Inc
Box 15-015, Two Computer Drive W,
Albany, NY 12212
Tel: 518-459-1150/800-347-7707
Fax: 518-459-3553
(UK distributor: International Thomson)

Elsevier Science Publishing Co
655 Avenue of the Americas,
New York, NY 10010
Tel: +1 383 5800
Fax: 212-633-3880

Free Press
Front & Brown StS
Riverside, NJ 08075
Tel: 212-702-2000
Fax: 212-605-9364

Harvard University Press
79 Garden Street, Cambridge, MA 02138
Tel: 617-495-8562/800-448-2242
Fax: 800-962-4983

Houghton Mifflin Co
222 Berkley St, Boston, MA 02116
Tel: +1 800-225-3362
Fax: 617-227-5409

IEEE Press
*Division of Institute of Electrical &
    Electronics Engineers Inc,*
PO Box 1331, 455 Hoes Lane,
Piscataway, NJ 08855-1331
Tel: +1 800 678 4333
Fax: 908-981-1855
(UK distributor: Electronica Books Ltd)

IEEE Computer Society Press
10662 Los Vaqueros Circle, PO Box 3014,
Los Alminos, CA 90720
Tel: 714-821-8380/800-272-6657
Fax: 714-821-4010
(UK distributor: Electronica Books Ltd)

Richard D Irwin Inc
Subsidiary of The Times Mirror Co,
1333 Burr Ridge P, Burr Ridge, IL 60521
Tel: +1 800-634-3966
Fax: 708-798-6296
(UK distributor: Addison-Wesley)

Kluwer Academic Publishers
Subsidiary of Wolters-Kluwer,
101 Philip Drive, Norwell, MA 02061
Tel: 617-871-6600/6300
Fax: 617-871-6528
*(European distributor: Kluwer Academic
    Publishers, The Netherlands)*

Johns Hopkins University Press
2715 North Charles St,
Baltimore, MD 21218-4319
Tel: 410/5166930
Fax: 410/5166998

McGraw-Hill, Inc
1221 Avenue of the Americas,
New York, NY 10020
Tel: 212/512-4471
Fax: 212/512-2186

Charles E Merrill Publishing Co
1300 Alum Creek Drive,
Columbus, OH 43216
Tel: 614-258-8441

MIT Press
55 Hayward Street,
Cambridge, MA 02142
Tel: 617-625-8481
Fax: 617-258-6779

National Academy Press
2101 Constitution Avenue NW,
Washington DC, 20418
Tel: 202/3343-037
Fax: 202/3342-793

Praeger Publishers Inc
One Madison Avenue, New York, NY 10010
Tel: 212-685-5300
Fax: 212-685-0285
(UK distributor: Distropa Ltd)

Prentice-Hall
440 Sylvan Avenue,
Englewood Cliffs, NJ 07632
Tel: 201-592-2000/800-223-1360

PWS-Kent Publ Co
Division of Wadsworth Inc,
20 Park Plaza, Boston, MA 02116
Tel: 800-842-3636
Fax: 617-338-6134
*(UK distributor: International Thomson
    Publishing Services Ltd)*

Sage Publications Inc
2455 Teller Road,
Newbury Park, CA 91320
Tel: 805-499-0721
Fax: 805-499-0871

South-Western Publishing Co
Subsidiary of The Thomson Corporation,
5101 Madison Road, Cincinnati, OH 45227
Tel: 513-271-8811/800-842-3636

Springer-Verlag New York Inc
175 Fifth Avenue, New York, NY 10010
Tel: 800-777-4643
Fax: 212-473-6272

St Mary's Press
St Mary's College
702 Terrace Heights,
Winona, MN 55987-1320
Tel: 507-457-7900/800-533-8095
Fax: 507-457-7990

TAB Books Inc
Division of McGraw-Hill,
11311 Monterey & Pinola Ave,
Blue Ridge Summit, PA 17294-0850
Tel: 717-794-2191/800-233-1128
Fax: 717-794-5344/2080
*(UK distributor: McGraw-Hill Book Co
    Europe)*

University of Chicago Press
5801 South Ellis Avenue,
Chicago, IL 60637
Tel: 312-702-7706
Fax: 312-702-9756
also
5720 S Woodlawn Ave,
Chicago, IL 60637
Tel: 312-702-7600
Fax: 312-702-0172

University Press of America
4720 Boston Way,
Lanham, MD 20706
Tel: 301-459-3366/800-462-6420
Fax: 301-459-2118

Van Nostrand Reinhold
Division of The Thomson Corporation,
115 Fifth Avenue,
New York, NY 10003
Tel: 212-254-3232/800-555-1212
Fax: 212-254-9499/212-475-2548

West Publishing Co
620 Oppermon Drive, PO Box 64833,
St Paul, MN 55164-1803
Tel: 800-328-2209

Westview Press
Subsidiary of SCS Communications Inc
5541 Central Ave,
Boulder, CO 80301
Tel: 303-444-3541
Fax: 303-449-3356

John Wiley & Sons Inc
605 Third Ave,
New York, NY 10158-0012
Tel: 212-850-8832/6000
Fax: 212-850-8888/6088

Year Book Medical Publishers Inc
(now Mosby-Year Book Inc)
11830 Westline Industrial Drive,
St Louis, MO 63146
Tel: 314-872-8370
Fax: 314-432-1380
(UK distributor: Mosby-Year Book Europe)

EUROPEAN SIMULATIONS PUBLISHERS

Akademie Verlag Gmbh
Leipziger Strasse 3–4,
Postfach 1233, 0-1806, Berlin, Germany
Tel: + 37 (02) 223 60
Fax: + 37 (02) 223 6357

Akademiai Kiado Es Nyomda
PB 245, 1519 Budapest, Hungary
Tel: + 36 (01) 181 2131
Fax: + 36 (01) 166 6466

Birkhauser Verlag AG
Klosterberg 23, Postfach 133
CH-4010 Basel, Switzerland
Tel: + 41 (061) 205 0707 736
Fax: +41 (061) 205 0792
Dekker (Marcel) AG
Hutgasse 4, Postfach 812,
CH-4001 Basel, Switzerland
Tel: 010 41 61 261 8482
Fax: 010 41 61 261 8896

Elsevier Science Publishers
PO Box 211, 1000 AE Amsterdam,
The Netherlands
Tel: (20) 48 53 911
Fax: (10) 48 53 809

Gordon & Breach Science Publishers, SA
Switzerland
*(UK distributor: Scientific & Technical
Book Service Ltd, Reading)*

Adam Hilger
(now IOP Publishing Ltd)
Techno House, Radcliffe Way,
Bristol, BS1 6NX
Tel: (0117) 929 7481
Fax: (0117) 929 4318

Industriens Utredningsinstitut
(Institute for Economic & Social Research)
POB 5501, 114 85 Stockholm, Sweden
Tel: (08) 783-80-00
Fax: (08) 661-79-69

Kluwer Academic Publishers Group
7–11 Kamerlingh Onnesweg, PO Box 322,
3300 AH Dordrecht, The Netherlands
Tel: 010 31 78 524 400
Fax: 010 31 78 183 273

Martinus Nijhoff Publishers
7–11 Kamerlingh Onnesweg, PO Box 322,
3300 AH Dordrecht, The Netherlands
Tel: 010 31 78 524 400
Fax: 010 31 78 183 273

Rotterdam University Press
(Universitaire Pers Rotterdam NV)
Heemraadssingel 112, POB 1474,
Rotterdam, The Netherlands

Sijthoff Pers BV
Koopmanstraat 9, Rijswijk PO Box 16050
2500 AA The Hague, The Netherlands
Tel: (70) 319 09 11
Fax; (70) 390 64 47

Springer-Verlag Gmbh & Co KG
Heidelberger Platz 3,
Postfach W-1000 Berlin 33, Germany
Tel: + 49 (030) 820 7464
Fax: + 49 (030) 820 7473

VCH Verlagsgesellschaft GmbH
PO Box 10 11 61,
D-69451 Weinheim, Germany
Tel: (6201) 606 402
Fax: (6201) 606 184

**Verlag der Fachvereine an der
  ETH-Zurich**
Universitatsstr 19,
CH-8006 Zurich, Switzerland

Vieweg Publishing
Friedrich Vieweg & Sohn Verlag
Postfach 1546
D-65005, Wiesbeden, Germany
Tel: +49 611 160225
Fax: +49 611 160225

AUSTRALASIAN SIMULATIONS PUBLISHERS

Butterworth & Co (Asia) Pte Ltd
(UK distributor: Butterworth & Co Ltd,)
Holsbury House, 35 Chancery Lane,
London WC2A 1EL
Tel: 0171 400 2500
Fax: 0171 400 2842

Sydney University Press
c/o University of Sidney,
Press Building,
Sydney NSW 2006, Australia
Tel: +61 2 692 2886

World Scientific Publishing Co
Singapore
(*UK distributor: World Scientific
  Publishing Co Pte Ltd*)
73 Lynton Mead,
Totteridge,
London N20 8DH
Tel: 0181-446-2461
Fax: 0181-446-3356
in Singapore:
1022 Hougang Avenue,
1 # 05-35 20
Tai Seng Industrial Estate
Singapore 1953
Tel: +65 382 5663
Fax: +65 382 5919

Chapter 25

Useful contact organizations for networking

Ray Land, Napier University, Edinburgh

AETT – Association for Educational Training and Technology
c/o Roy Winterburn, AETT Administrator,
Higher Millbrook, Beavor Lane,
Axminster, Devon, EX13 5EQ

British Gas Education Service
PO Box 70, Wetherby,
West Yorkshire, LS23 7EA

Centre for British Teachers
EFL Publications,
Headgate House, Head Street,
Colchester, Essex, CO1 NS

Centre for World Development Education
Regent's College, Inner Circle,
Regent's Park, London, NW1 4NS

Christian Aid
PO Box 100,
London, SE1 7RT

COIC
Room W 1108,
Moorfoot, Sheffield, S1 4PQ

Commercial Devices
5 Farm Buildings,
Palmers Moor, Thornborough,
Bucks, MK18 2DJ

CVS Advisory Service
237 Pentonville Road,
London, N1 9NJ

Daedal Training Ltd
Peak House,
66/68 Croydon Road,
Beckenham, Kent, BR3 4AA

GBS Management Games
Guardian Business Services,
21 John Street, London, WC1

Housing Support Team
64–66 Newington Causeway,
London, SE1 6DF

ISAGA – International Simulation and Gaming Association
c/o Jan Klabbers,
Secretary, ISAGA,
Oostervelden 59,
6681 WR Bemmel, The Netherlands

Maxim Training Systems Ltd
57 Ship Street, Brighton,
East Sussex, BN1 1AF

Neighbourhood Initiatives Foundation
Suite 23/25, Horsehay House,
Horsehay, Telford,
Shropshire, TF4 3PY

New Games Ltd
PO Box 542,
London, NW2 3PQ

New Grapevine Ltd
416 St Johns Street,
London, EC1V 4NJ

Oxfam Education
274 Banbury Road,
Oxford, OX2 7DZ

Practical Games Ltd
40A Bluecoat Chambers, School Lane,
Liverpool, L1 3BX

**SAGSET – The Society for Active
    Learning**
c/o Jill Brookes, SAGSET,
Administrator, Gala House,
3 Raglan Road, Edgbaston,
Birmingham, B5 7RA

**SEDA – Staff and Educational
    Development Association**
c/o Jill Brookes, SEDA Administrator,
Gala House, 3 Raglan Road, Edgbaston,
Birmingham, B5 7RA

Skillsline
Lemna House, 15 Lemna Road,
Leytonstone, London, E11 1HX

**The New International Management
    Game**
ICL-Cranfield Business Games Ltd,
Cranfield, Bedford, MK43 0AL

Training Business Products
141 Great Charles Street,
Birmingham, B3 3JR

Training Tomorrow's Managers
Management Games Ltd,
Methwold House, Northwold Road,
Methwold, Thetford, Norfolk, IP26 4PF

Youth Clubs UK
Keswick House, 30 Peacock Lane,
Leicester, LE1 5NY

Notes for the contributors to the 1998 *Yearbook*

Please submit your article on paper *and* disk, stating the word-processing package used (this should always be IBM-compatible or Macintosh).

The title of the paper or article should be in bold, with an initial capital for the first word of the title only, and for proper nouns. Your name(s) should then follow on the next line, in italics. Try to use size 12 type for the entire manuscript, including headings. Your manuscript should be double-line spaced – this helps us to make changes without having to bother you for a 'clean copy'.

New paragraphs should be separated by an extra line spacing. You can also:

- use bullet points
- with the main items listed
- in a simple and appealing form.

In the above example, there is an extra line space above and below the list.

Feel free to use headings but keep them short. Keep a double-line space between the end of the last paragraph and the next heading.

This is a secondary heading

Distinguish headings in the text by all capitals for primary headings (see References heading on next page) and bold, initial capitals only for secondary headings (as above). Do not leave a line space between the heading and the start of the next piece of text.

Sometimes our authors give references which could contain surnames and a date (Jones and Davies, 1984), although if three or more authors are involved it should be Jones *et al.* (1984). The full reference goes at the end of the article. Also, you might want to include a quote:

'all quotes longer than four lines should be indented so that they clearly stand apart from the main body of your narrative.' (Bevan *et al.*, 1992)

Please ensure that all quotes are properly referenced, and all works cited have a full reference at the end of your paper, including authors and initials, date of publication, name of publication, name of publisher and place of publication for books. For journal articles, the name of the article, journal, volume and issue number is needed. See the References section at the end of this article for layout.

Any tables, figures or diagrams should be on separate sheets with an indication in the text of roughly where you would like them placed. For example insert the instruction:

[table 1 about here]

At the end of your paper, add the heading 'About the author'. Under this, please say a few things about yourself and include an address for correspondence with interested readers. We do not want long autobiographies – just a couple of sentences!

REFERENCES

Bevan, B, Thomas, L, Reed, H and Evans, C (1992) *This is the title of a book,* Kogan Page, London.
Jones, I and Davies, D (1984) This is the title of an article, *Journal of Something or Other,* 16 (2), 234–6.

Authors should send their papers and articles to: Danny Saunders, Simulation and Gaming Yearbook Editor, University of Glamorgan, Pontypridd, Mid-Glamorgan CF37 1DL, UK.